Executive Support Systems

The Emergence of Top Management Computer Use

by

John F. Rockart

and

David W. De Long

Dow Jones-Irwin
Homewood, Illinois 60430

JFR: For Elise

DWD: For my sister Betsy

Excerpts from THE INFORMATION EDGE by N.
Dean Meyer and Mary E. Boone. Published by Holt,
Rinehart and Winston of Canada, Limited. Copyright
©1987. Reprinted by permission of Gage Educational
Publishing Company, Agincourt, Ontario. Published in
the United States and internationally (except Canada) by
McGraw-Hill Book Company, New York, N.Y.

Dow Jones-Irwin is a trademark of Dow Jones & Company, Inc.

©J. F. Rockart and D. W. De Long, 1988

This publication is designed to provide accurate and
authoritative information in regard to the subject matter
covered. It is sold with the understanding that neither the publisher nor
the copyright holder is engaged in rendering legal, accounting, or
other professional service. If legal advice or other expert
assistance is required, the services of a competent
professional person should be sought.

*From a Declaration of Principles jointly adopted by a Committee
of the American Bar Association and a Committee of Publishers.*

Production manager: Carma W. Fazio
Designer: Sam Concialdi
Compositor: Carlisle Communications, Ltd.
Typeface: 11/13 Caledonia
Printer: Arcata Graphics/Kingsport

ISBN   0-87094-955-1

Library of Congress Catalog Card No. 87–72026

Printed in the United States of America

890K5432109

ACKNOWLEDGMENTS

This book is an attempt to describe and interpret a concept that has been rapidly taking shape in recent years. The idea of computer use by senior managers was still a Buck Rogers fantasy in 1976 when Ben Heineman, chief executive at Northwest Industries, began using a terminal to monitor and plan the growth of his nine operating units. Indeed, it was the vision and persistance of Heineman, and a handful of other senior executives, who first saw the potential information technology held for senior management, that was responsible for giving birth to the concept of executive support systems, as we now recognize it.

Today, about 10 percent of large U.S. companies have senior managers with direct access to computer workstations. We expect that this number will grow substantially in the future. We have spent many hours in the last few years talking with these pioneering ESS users, as well as information systems people concerning the challenging task of designing and implementing systems that would, in fact, define the emerging field in which they were working

This book would not have been possible without the cooperation and encouragement of dozens of forward thinking executives and innovative systems people who shared their experiences and ideas with us. It is not possible to name all the people who graciously gave of their time to reflect on what they had learned in developing and using ESS. Many are identified in chapters of the book, as we quote their ideas on various aspects of ESS. Suffice it to say, we are grateful for their vision, and for that of those left unnamed, in applying the technology and their willingness to share what they have learned (sometimes painfully), so others might benefit.

Several people, however, have contributed an inordinate amount to our understanding of ESS. John Kogan of Arthur Andersen & Company and Gary Gulden of The Index Group have done their own ground breaking work in the ESS field. They have freely shared their ideas and findings with us, greatly influencing our thinking and adding to our database of "real world" cases. John took part in some of our field work and, for this, we owe him special thanks.

In addition, Professor Michael Treacy and Eliot Levinson contributed substantially to the early concepts of executive support developed at the Sloan School of Management's Center for Information Systems Research (CISR), our academic home. Over the years, a number of Sloan School Master's students have added substantially to our ESS case study research through their thesis work. We would like to thank them all for their contribution to this effort. Most especially we are grateful to Jeff Turner, Peg Dickerman, and Hans Bunaes whose work we have quoted.

Judith Quillard, CISR's associate director, and Elise Rockart patiently read the entire manuscript and diplomatically kept bringing us back on course, both challenging and supporting us throughout the sometimes arduous writing process. Their enthusiasm made it much easier to stay focused on our goal. Nancy Forster was a cheerful, but tough, editor who plowed through our frequently overblown prose to produce a tighter, more readable manuscript.

Finally, creating this book would have been a considerably less enjoyable task without the good-humored support of Jacqui Taylor and Grace Brennan. Jacqui combined creative word processing skills and her artful administrative abilities to make the emerging manuscript understandable. As always, Grace was there when we needed her to provide additional administrative and secretarial support. In the end, it is Jacqui and Grace who have allowed us to share our ideas with others. To them, and to all who helped make this book a reality, we offer our heartfelt thanks.

John F. Rockart
David W. De Long

CONTENTS

*Assumptions about the Business. Off-Hours Data
Access.* Conclusion.

CHAPTER 1

INTRODUCING EXECUTIVE SUPPORT SYSTEMS

Computer use by senior managers is, at best, controversial. Many commentators on the management scene have, with varying degrees of emotion, pointed out the folly of tying the executive to a computer terminal. The fundamental argument made by these nay-sayers is straightforward and logical. Senior executives contend with multiple, often strategic, issues in an unstructured, complex, and changing environment. To deal with this environment, they need up-to-date, externally oriented, mostly "soft" information. This type of information can best be obtained from subordinates and others either in person or by telephone. Computers, in addition to being hard to use initially, have traditionally provided only "hard," historical, internally oriented data. Thus, they seem an unlikely substitute for the executive's human information sources.

Nevertheless, personal computers and terminals *are* making inroads into the executive suite. Something new is happening in executive offices throughout the world.

At Lockheed-Georgia, a subsidiary of Lockheed Corporation and a major producer of cargo aircraft, executives have been using an executive support system (ESS) for the past eight years. The system, which combines off-the-shelf hardware with software developed in-house, is used largely to monitor the status of operations. Among the benefits identified by top management are better information, improved communications, an evolving understanding of information requirements, and cost reductions.[1]

1

At ConAgra, a diversified food and agricultural products company, Chairman and CEO Mike Harper communicates often with his senior managers by electronic mail. Harper introduced an ESS to the company's top 75 executives in 1982 to help manage ConAgra's phenomenal growth from $1 billion in 1980 to more than $6 billion in 1986. Today, he uses the system to monitor the weekly performance of the corporation's diversified holdings, as well as to access external data about competitors and financial and commodities markets.

Executive support systems also are appearing in unlikely places, such as the office of the top executive of the state of New Hampshire. *Time* magazine reports:

> John Sununu, 46, is not just another well-heeled computer buff. He is the governor of New Hampshire, and the data he pores over so diligently represent the state's $1 billion in annual expenditures. Using the computer and modem in his office in Concord, he can punch in his name and secret password, log on to the state's IBM 4361 mainframe computer, and get a quick reading, in glowing green digits, of the state's financial health: room-and-meal tax returns ($30.3 million as of last November), business-profits taxes ($28.4 million), out-of-town travel expenses for the leaders of the legislature ($300). "It is my conviction that one needs to go down to the lowest source to get intimate, unbiased data," says Sununu, glancing at the screen of his desktop machine.
>
> The Republican governor's prowess with computers has become legendary in New Hampshire. When a party worker complained that he was having trouble with a mass-mailing program, Sununu spent a few minutes at his keyboard and solved the problem. Reviewing an environmental group's study of the impact of a new dam, Sununu zeroed in on a questionable variable in the calculations and set the record straight.[2]

In spite of the burgeoning interest in ESS, many of those knowledgeable about management have been far from convinced. These individuals, writing from 1982 to 1985 in prestigious journals, present a common theme that the computer offers little, if anything, to a senior executive.

> *The Wall Street Journal:* Sure computers are useful. In some cases they are indispensable tools. But the key word is tool—that is, something a laborer uses to produce results. . . . If you are a manager, keep your hands off those keys and printouts.[3]

Interfaces: It is the exceptional CEO who will take the time to learn and become competent in even the easiest to use of the planning languages. If the CEO is the principal target of the DSS movement, it is probably barking up the wrong tree.[4]

Sloan Management Review: The job of the top manager has not been affected significantly by the computer. Most important management problems have not been solved by automation.[5]

Harvard Business Review: Efforts to convince executives to move into the electronic office have met flat resistance. And vendors' claims for the accomplishments of so-called decision support systems have attracted little executive attention—with a few rule-proving exceptions.[6]

Fortune: The most important factor keeping the computer out of many executive offices is the realization, sometimes barely conscious, on the part of managers that this technological wonder has, as yet, little to offer them. The nature of their work—in a word, unstructured—is such that it's not particularly susceptible to computerization.[7]

Each of the authors of the above statements is a respected observer of the management world. Together, they perceive the senior executive as someone whose interests are too focused, who does not have time to learn a new technology, and who has too little to gain to be enticed into meaningful ESS usage. Despite these and other nay-sayers who disparage executive use of information technology (IT), the number of computer-based systems utilized by executives in large organizations continues to increase. Indeed, many managers still have no interest in applying computers in their jobs, but a growing number are using computers—some to great advantage—to aid in managing their organizations.

GROWING USE OF ESS

Much has changed in the few years since the phenomenon of executive computer use was first identified by Rockart and Treacy in the *Harvard Business Review.*[8] At the time only a handful of top managers were making use of information technology. But, in late 1984, a telephone survey of 45 *Fortune* 500 companies revealed that two-thirds of them had at least one executive, and usually several, with a computer terminal or personal computer on his or her desk.[9] While telephone surveys are far from totally reliable, the evidence of increasingly widespread use of computer workstations by executives is growing. In a study carried out in late 1985 and 1986 by Jeffrey Moore of Stanford University, 94 out of 1,000 firms contacted had at least one executive who was a hands-on computer user. Even though he identified slightly less than 10 percent of the firms in his sample as having executive computer users, Moore comments, "Given the high resistance to change in work patterns by senior executives, as found by Mintzberg and others, this penetration by computers into the domain of executive management is quite impressive in so short a period of time."[10]

Like any new application of information technology, ESS is fraught with pitfalls. There are issues of computer illiteracy, inadequate data availability, and organizational resistance, all of which make the installation of executive support systems difficult. Not surprisingly, the percentage of ESS failures is high. Nevertheless, more and more executives are overcoming these hurdles to establish effective computer support systems. A few additional examples:

- At Gillette North America, Executive Vice President Derwyn Phillips uses his ESS to get quick status updates on businesses he oversees. After being out of the office for a few days, Phillips can turn on his system and note changes in market position and daily sales activity in his three divisions. He also can get updated competitive information, such as new product announcements.

- When the CEO of Lincoln National Life, a large insurance company, returns from a trip, he uses his terminal at home to check the electronic mail messages that have accumulated during his absence. In the next hour or two he will "clean off his desk," responding to computer-generated reports, queries, and requests for action from his subordinates. The CEO's use of his firm's extensive electronic mail system greatly eases the communications bottleneck inherent in top management positions, and allows him to be more proactive in dealing with the information that comes to him.

- The former president of Banco Internacional, a Colombian subsidiary of Citibank, began each day at his computer terminal to get an overview of the bank's business. With access to extensive operational data, the president used the system to identify business trends and look at customer information. When he saw something unusual (e.g., excessive overdrafts), he called the branch manager or account officer responsible. The president used this computer system to implement his marketing strategy for the bank by encouraging subordinates to focus on the same information he did.[11]

- The chairman of a large manufacturing company utilizes a series of computer-based models that allow him to question not only the numbers, but also the assumptions that go into his firm's sales forecasts. Using a terminal both at the office and at home, he looks at a series of alternative scenarios to get as many perspectives as possible on the company's future sales. Unlike the three prior systems above, which are used widely in their organizations, only the chairman and the CFO make use of this system.

- At a major bank, the president's administrative staff uses word processors to produce a daily summary of the chief executive's incoming correspondence, which averages 150–200 pieces a day. The system saves the president considerable time in processing his mail. The chief executive's staff also uses the system to track correspondence forwarded to other departments for action. The computer automatically sends follow-up notices to the departments, and has helped reduce response time for mail processing from an average of 15 to 5 days.

The cases above represent varied applications and impacts that can result when top managers begin to use information technology. But the question remains: Are these executive computer users just the few rule proving exceptions? Or, are they representative of a significant trend in the way in which organizations will be managed at the top in the years to come? Are there significant benefits from these systems for a senior executive? Here is what some of the users have to say:

Finn Caspersen, chairman of Beneficial Corporation:

I have the terminal in my office, one at home, and a portable terminal to carry when I'm traveling. . . .We're operating in real-time decision making at Beneficial. I believe that this is not an accepted way of doing business [in other organizations]. Yet, it's an absolutely great method for doubling your productivity. I'd say mine has increased 50 to 100 per cent. I know that my counterparts in competitive organizations are not using the computer as I am, and that gives me an advantage over them.[12]

Ronald Compton, president of American Re–Insurance Company:

In every element of this business, I'm somehow assisted by the computer. In my world the computer takes the place of pencils, paper, and hand calculator. I write messages on it. I do financial modeling, and I use it to inform others.[13]

William Glavin, vice chairman of Xerox Corporation:

A key to the success of the Executive Support System has been its usefulness. The last thing in the world that I need in my office is a piece of hardware that does not help me manage more effectively. Technology for the sake of technology is both unneeded and unwanted. The Executive Support System is neither. It provides me with easy access to the corporate management data base.

The system is embedded in the business process of our senior management and is an integral part of our business planning process and our operations reviews. Frankly, the Executive Support System is so ingrained in the way we manage the business that it's difficult to imagine life without it.[14]

Reasons for Growth in ESS

Despite these comments, there is no evidence, in 1987, that automation is turning the executive suite upside down, nor is it significantly altering the nature of top-management work for very many executives. Yet we believe the spread of executive support systems is a trend that is gaining momentum. There are several reasons for this.

First, despite what some critics say, the use of information technology to support executives makes good managerial sense.

We will make this argument in Chapter 3 when we examine what it is that executives actually do. Despite the complex, unstructured, and unpredictable nature of their work, there are many logical applications of IT which can effectively support executive tasks.

Second, the technology, both hardware and software, is rapidly improving. Faster hardware with expanded capabilities is now being joined with easier-to-use software designed expressly for executive use. Applications for managers that were technically impractical and too costly only a few years ago have now become significantly easier to implement.

A third reason computer-based executive support will continue to spread is that more and more top managers are becoming computer literate. For some, this is happening as the result of a personal desire to learn and use the technology; for others, because of a felt need to understand how subordinates are using it; or, for a few, because of a sense of IT's strategic importance to the firm. Familiarity often increases interest in using information technology to better manage the organization. In addition, many middle managers who have come to rely heavily on computers in their jobs are now being promoted to the executive ranks.

Reasons Against

Despite these forces that argue for the growth of executive support systems, it is important to listen to those who question the value of computer-based support for top management. Lost sometimes in the emotional rhetoric that inevitably accompanies any technological change are at least four important points raised by those who challenge the concept of executive support systems.

The first point is that ESS does not fit the management styles or needs of today's executives. It would be foolish to argue that computers can comfortably support the workstyles of all executives. They cannot. *Executive support systems are not, in the near future, appropriate for every senior manager.* The differences between individual executives are well documented. Managers differ in cognitive style, orientation to detail, and work habits, as well as many other dimensions. As of late

1987, it is far from clear that computer use by executives can significantly improve their bottom lines. A decision to leave computer use to others is a perfectly logical and defensible one for many executives—most especially for those who have long tenure, understand their industries well, and are richly supported by staff personnel.

The second point is that ESS cannot provide the type of information executives need most. At least 15 years ago, Henry Mintzberg identified this problem. He said:

> The central problem in MIS design is the verbal nature of the manager's information. As long as much of his information is non-documented and remains largely unknown and inaccessible to specialist and computer alike, it is folly to believe that the information specialist can design an effective MIS for the manager.[15]

Mintzberg's message is still valid today. Most of the information necessary to effectively carry out a senior executive's job is still stored only in the minds of subordinates and other executive contacts. Although the situation is changing as increasing amounts of text, data, and images are becoming available on-line, the computer is not, and will not be for the foreseeable future, the primary source of executive information. (Yet there is another implication of Mintzberg's statement. If "much" of the information needed is non-documented and inaccessible, then *some* is or can be accessible through electronic media. Mintzberg suggested that executives fill many roles. Some of these roles, it would seem, should be supportable through computer-based text and data.)

Another point raised by ESS critics is the plethora of potentially negative impacts of the technology. Concerning one of these, William King writes:

> There is a mesmerizing quality about the PC and its spreadsheets and other analytic programs. It is very easy to become engrossed in the ability to manipulate numbers and to instantly see the ramifications of change through a complex set of financial displays.
>
> In fact, it is so easy to do that it is also easy to lose sight of reality—to begin to believe that the computer model's numerical forecasts are real and that they describe future outcomes that

will, in fact, come to pass. . . . The computer model's forecasts are based solely on those predictions about the future that we are able to quantify. Those things that are not readily quantifiable are usually omitted, and in being omitted there is a danger that they may be ignored.[16]

King raises a significant issue. Executive support systems do not provide added value just because they exist. In fact, they can be counterproductive. An ESS can enable a manager to communicate, plan, and control the business more effectively, but whether or not this happens depends on the person using the system. As with any technology, especially a new one, there is a very real potential for misuse. It is, we expect, possible to be lulled into believing that a computer-projected scenario is, in fact, reality. Perhaps an even more dangerous misuse of the system arises when executives pay too little attention to unintended and unwanted organizational side-effects of these systems—a point we will explore in some depth in Chapter 10.

Finally, critics of ESS do not have to look far to find many failed attempts at implementing such systems for executives. The reality of the early days of executive support is that the failures most probably still outnumber the successes. Wayne Burkan offers a common scenario. He says:

Why do I feel that [ESS] . . . is dangerous? . . . The executives get access to it and since it doesn't smoke, explode, and sparks don't fly when they press a button, they start using it and say it is great. But . . . that maxes out. Reality begins to set in and they say this is really a kind of a toy and is not doing the things they wanted it to do. So use begins to diminish precipitously. . . . In many cases, at this point, it is thrown out of the office or, if it remains, it is of very little use.[17]

Burkan's scenario is not a figment of his imagination. It is one we have seen numerous times. The resulting message can be read in one of two ways—either executive support systems are totally useless, or ill-conceived and poorly implemented systems are useless. Taking a positive viewpoint, the warning for the implementation process is only too clear.

Critics of executive use of computers must face the fact that, today, dozens of such systems are in use, many executives are satisfied with the results they are obtaining, and the use of ESS is growing in corporate offices. Yet, the preceding four issues are very real. The technology is still not effective for *all* managers today. The computer is far from a panacea for *all* of the information needs of even those senior executives who decide to use it. There are many individual and organizational side-effects of the use of these systems. And last but certainly not least, inadequate conception and implementation, as in all systems, computer-based or otherwise, can lead to failure.

The issues noted above, in our minds, boil down to two central questions. First, for those executives intrigued by the potential of these systems, which executive tasks are most appropriate to be supported by computer-based systems? Second, how does one effectively go about the implementation process while ensuring a minimum number of unintended side effects? It is to these two major issues that this book is devoted.

Following Chapter 2, which describes what ESS is (and is not), as we view it, Chapters 3–6 examine the nature of managerial work and detail the ways in which the systems we observed fit the tasks of senior executives. Chapters 7–11 then deal with the very significant and somewhat hazardous implementation process. In the final two chapters, we note some interesting impacts of ESS on organizations and draw a few final conclusions.

The remainder of this book should be read with tempered expectations. There are things for which the computer is useful and things for which it is not. It is, today, far from the dominant weapon in the executive's arsenal. The computer is, for most, a minor weapon. Yet, executive support systems have intriguing possibilities that must be assessed, and there are complex issues that must be dealt with for successful implementation.

Research Basis for the Book

This book is the result of several years of research at the Center for Information Systems Research (CISR) at MIT's Sloan School of Management. In 1985 and 1986 we travelled throughout the U.S., Canada, and Great Britain to 30 companies interviewing about five ESS developers and executive users in each firm.

Time spent in each company ranged from a half-day to several days. An interview outline guided discussions with technical and staff people involved with the systems, as well as executive users. The interview outline was used to gather a core of well-defined, hard data concerning key features of each system—features which had appeared to be important in earlier 1980–84 studies on ESS conducted at CISR. The interviews, however, were also used as an evocative device aimed at having the subject describe his or her impressions of the system. Emphasis was placed on the reasons for and value of the systems, as well as their design elements and implementation characteristics.

Additional data for the book have come from discussions with more than one hundred other people at seminars on executive support, or on the telephone. Our findings are the result of the willingness of many executives and systems designers to share their experiences and the insights they gained while designing, installing, and using executive support systems. Our research philosophy and methodology are best described by Henry Mintzberg as "direct research." He says:

> While systematic data create the foundation for our theories, it is the anecdotal data that enable us to do the building. Theory building seems to require rich description, the richness that comes from anecdote. We uncover all kinds of relationships in our "hard" data, but it is only through the use of this "soft" data that we are able to explain them, and explanation is, of course, the purpose of research.[18]

In researching and writing this book, we have attempted to reflect Mintzberg's approach. We present many hard facts. But the real feel for the subject is best captured in the words of those interviewed—words which we will often quote. An increasing amount of empirical data concerning executive support systems is becoming available as we write. Most is in the form of individual case studies or brief interviews with a panel of senior executives now using computer workstations. To this scant but growing body of knowledge, we hope to add further clarity as to which executive tasks can best be supported by computer-based systems, and ways to approach the difficult task of implementation of these systems.

NOTES

1. George Houdeshel and Hugh J. Watson, "The Management Information and Decision Support (MIDS) System at Lockheed-Georgia," *MIS Quarterly*, March 1987, pp. 127–140.
2. "The Granite State of the Art," *Time*, January 27, 1986, p. 70. Copyright 1986 Time, Inc. All rights reserved. Reprinted by permission from TIME.
3. Jack Falvey, "Real Managers Don't Use Computer Terminals," *Wall Street Journal*, February 7, 1983, p. 22.
4. C. J. Naylor, "Decision Support Systems or Whatever Happened to M.I.S.?", *Interfaces*, vol. 12, no. 4 (August 1982), p. 94.
5. John Dearden, "SMR Forum: Will the Computer Change the Job of Top Management?", *Sloan Management Review*, vol. 25, no. 1 (Fall 1983), p. 59.
6. Copyright 1985 by the President and Fellows of Harvard College; all rights reserved. Reprinted by permission of *Harvard Business Review*. "What Happened to the Computer Revolution?" by Lynn M. Salerno, (November-December 1985), vol. 63, no. 6, p. 130.
7. Walter Kiechel III, "Why Executives Don't Compute," *Fortune*, November 14, 1983, p. 244.
8. John F. Rockart and Michael E. Treacy, "The CEO Goes On-Line," *Harvard Business Review*, January-February, 1982.
9. David W. De Long and John F. Rockart, "A Survey of Current Trends in the Use of Executive Support Systems," *Working Paper No. 121*, Center for Information Systems Research, Sloan School of Management, MIT, Cambridge, Mass., November 1984.
10. Jeffrey H. Moore, "Senior Executive Computer Use" (Unpublished working paper, Stanford Graduate School of Business, Palo Alto, Calif., 1986), p. 10.
11. Peter G.W. Keen, "The On-Line CEO: How One Executive Uses MIS" (Unpublished working paper, Micro Mainframe, Inc., 1983).
12. N. Dean Meyer and Mary E. Boone, *The Information Edge*, Agincourt, Ontario: Gage Educational Publishing, 1987), p. 213.
13. Ibid., p. 216.
14. William F. Glavin, Speech to the Society for Information Management, Miami, Florida, March 27, 1987.
15. Henry Mintzberg, "The Myths of MIS," © 1982 by the Regents of the University of California. Reprinted from the *California Management Review*, vol. 15, no. 1 (Fall 1972), p. 96. By permission of The Regents.

16. William R. King, "Editor's Comment," *MIS Quarterly,* October 1985, pp. xi–xii.
17. Wayne Burkan, "Decision Support Systems In the End-User Environment." (Text of presentation at POSP General Meeting, New Orleans, January 1986), p. 18.
18. Henry Mintzberg, "An Emerging Strategy of 'Direct' Research," *Administrative Science Quarterly,* December 1979, p. 587.

CHAPTER 2

THE NATURE OF ESS

Confusion hovering around many aspects of executive support systems poses problems for those grappling with the subject. The attributes of these systems and the applications they provide are very much open to debate. What one manager defines as "executive support," another discounts as "electronic mail" or "just a personal computer." Even the name of the field is uncertain. *Executive information systems* and *executive decision support* are two other terms which are commonly used to describe computer systems used by top management.

The purpose of this chapter is to review the literature on ESS and to differentiate the concept from an older one—decision support systems (DSS). In the process, we offer our own definition of executive support systems and summarize the three major types of applications we found in our research. Finally, we provide a sample of the 30 companies we studied, as well as our own criteria for what determines a successful ESS.

That uncertainty should exist around the concept of ESS is not surprising. It is typical of a new field. And executive support has only begun to emerge in the 1980s. Like many other evolving concepts, ESS was initially confused with its predecessor—decision support systems (DSS). The earliest writings in the ESS field, much of it the work of MIT authors, pointed out some of the differences between ESS and DSS. But these articles also reflected their DSS heritage. As such, they emphasized the data-analysis aspects of ESS, either overlooking or underreporting communications and office-support applications, such as electronic mail and word processing.

Rockart and Treacy popularized the term "executive information support (or 'EIS') systems" in 1981 in several working papers and a *Harvard Business Review* article.[1] In their first paper, they analyzed the activities of 20 executives and made distinctions between DSS and EIS based on the different management tasks supported by each type of system. Executive activities tended to be less structured, more ad hoc, and wider-ranging than those of middle management DSS users.

Rockart and Treacy, however, saw EIS as intensely data-oriented systems designed to provide information for executive use to improve managerial planning, monitoring, and analysis.[2] Such systems require a vastly broader base of data than a typical DSS. An "information support data base," drawing data from the firm's transaction-processing systems as well as from external sources was, in fact, the most significant common feature of the systems Rockart and Treacy studied. Access to this data was achieved primarily through the use of fourth-generation user-oriented languages and menus.

By 1983 the infant concept of EIS had been renamed ESS, and Scott Morton made further distinctions between executive and decision support systems. He argued that ESS provide capabilities to meet the "various and variable" information needs of executives, while DSS are generally focused on a single recurring and somewhat structured decision area. In addition, Scott Morton contended that the models so typical of DSS cannot provide the flexibility needed by executive decision-makers. ESS, therefore, are data-retrieval rather than model oriented.

Keen continued this focus on hard, numerical data.[3] He saw ESS as a management concept with two basic capabilities—data retrieval and analysis. Contending that these systems reflect the executive's management style, as well as his or her concept of the business, Keen noted that there is no typical ESS. In the end, however, he blurred the distinction between DSS and ESS by recombining them: "One useful way of viewing an ESS, or any similar Decision Support System, is as a computerized staff assistant."[4]

Eliot Levinson broadened the concept in his study of five ESS installations. Defining ESS as "terminal-based systems designed to aid senior executives in the management of the firm,"[5] he was the first to document ESS beyond the context of data retrieval and analysis. Levinson distinguished between "executive office automation," which focuses on user efficiency, and emphasizes personal support and communications tools; and "business-oriented" systems, which utilize DSS tools and focus on increasing user effectiveness. Levinson noted a text and communication orientation in some ESS systems, but he dismissed these office automation systems he found, saying that this class of system quickly fell into disuse.

Later in 1984, the De Long and Rockart study of 45 randomly-selected *Fortune* 500 companies also broadly defined ESS as

> the routine use of a computer terminal for *any* business function. The users are either the CEO or a member of the senior management team reporting directly to him or her. Executive support systems can be implemented at the corporate and/or divisional level. (emphasis added)[6]

Today this definition requires one significant modification. Use of ESS does not require hands-on access to the technology by the executive. In fact, a number of systems that clearly support senior executives are accessed primarily by the senior manager's staff. We consider these to be executive support systems if they have been designed expressly for the senior manager, and have had a major impact on the executive's work. Thus, for purposes of this book, we will define ESS as

> the routine use of a computer-based system, most often through direct access to a terminal or personal computer, for any business function. The users are either the CEO or a member of the senior management team reporting directly to him or her. Executive support systems can be implemented at the corporate or divisional level.

(In many large organizations, senior executives with major responsibilities exist in the third tier of management. Although almost all of the systems we saw were used by the top two levels of management, very few examples in this book are drawn from the third tier, and the exact boundaries of these systems are yet to be determined).

DSS versus ESS—Some Major Differences

As noted, there was a clear bias in the early ESS literature. In their work, Rockart, Treacy, Scott Morton, Levinson, and Keen all saw ESS as an extension of a data-driven DSS concept. Despite attempts to distinguish executive support systems from DSS, the few successful systems they observed bore remarkable similarities to DSS. The emphasis was on data and analysis. Little attention was given to the use of text or communications capabilities. Although the literature is somewhat vague on the definition of DSS, it appears that the major distinguishing features of these systems are:

- Orientation to a single decision maker, or class of decision makers, dealing with a specific "semi-structured" decision.
- Decision is repetitive, justifying large development costs.
- System is model-oriented and data-intensive.[7]

Confusion between DSS and ESS concepts is common, even among executives users. Comments from managers in one high technology firm that we studied illustrate the point:

Chairman: The key difference is that an ESS must be easy for a very infrequent user to use. DSS are more suited to lower-level specialists, although the underlying information may be the same as in an ESS. An executive, by definition, is interrupt-driven, and he's all over the place geographically, and has special logistical problems in that sense. Also, executives work in teams and in a meeting environment, so there are special problems with presenting information for use.

President: I never have understood the difference between DSS and ESS.

CFO: A DSS is a specific set of task-oriented applications, while an ESS is utilized to try to change the productivity of executives by changing the capital-to-labor input ratio.

Personnel VP: A DSS is a system that will present a manager with an integrated view of a set of facts and trends that will aid a decision-making process. ESS provide the tools he needs to do his broader job. I'd be hard pressed to separate the two concepts clearly, however, because the differences are subtle.

R&D VP: ESS are designed to support top management both as a collective group and as individual heads of functions. I have great difficulty making a distinction between ESS and DSS. It depends on the user, the output, and the nature of use, even though the two systems may be technically the same.

Confusion between executive support and decision support systems is significant because a narrow or hazy view of ESS will limit the potential of ESS for top management. The view of ESS as an extension of decision support technology limits creativity in selecting applications that might be developed. Moreover, it creates significant problems for implementation. In the case above, problems arose because managers within the same company did not share a common understanding of ESS design and installation.

To understand what an ESS is, one must differentiate it from the older DSS concept. It is true that executive support systems serve a different master—one whose broader, more diffuse roles require systems quite different than those which serve subordinates. It is also true that they are data-retrieval rather than model oriented, with broader capabilities than the usual DSS. In recent years, however, a deeper understanding of the *roles* of senior executives, together with increased empirical evidence of the use of ESS, has underscored the fact that the original data-driven, analysis-oriented perspective of ESS is far from sufficient. Much more is involved.

For years, management theorists have recognized that communication underlies many tasks of senior management. By mid–1983, Treacy argued that early conceptions of ESS, including his own, were flawed because they overlooked the communications component.[8]

Several other researchers have worked to broaden the scope of executive tasks which can be served by effective ESS. Following the lead of Daft and Weick,[9] Zmud states that it is the executive's role "to be aware of things, to make sense of things, and to translate these interpretations of the firm's internal and external environments into meaning; e.g., mission, strategy, and action for organizational participants."[10] To support this role, Zmud notes the need for strategic "scanning" capabilities in an executive support system, as well as what he terms "executive thought support," rather than decision support.

Zmud also highlights the need for communication capabilities in ESS. Focusing on the equivocal nature of information received by senior executives, he stresses the need for "soft" and "rich" textual data which can enable improved comprehension of complex issues. He says:

> Managers, in general, process information to reduce uncertainty and to reduce equivocality (Daft/Lengel 1984). . . . Equivocality refers not to a lack of information but to an ambiguity with information; i.e., multiple and conflicting interpretations about some organizational situation.
>
> When equivocality is high . . . increased emphasis is placed on the role of informal, typically face-to-face, information systems and on the use of soft, rather than hard, information (Brookes 1985). Soft information refers to that which arises in oral communications and which requires little reflective activity: gossip, ideas, opinions, predictions, appraisals, and explanations.
>
> An information system able to transport soft information is quite different from that which only transports hard information. Daft and Lengel (1984) refer to such a capability as the "information richness" of a communications channel, with high richness characterized by the opportunity for immediate feedback, for many types of cues, for the personalization of messages, and for language variety.
>
> Given the importance of rich communications channels, such as meetings, conferences, and similar person-to-person contacts, office automation applications would seem to be a critical component of a successful EIS. Electronic mail, voice-store-and-forward, computer conferencing, and bulletin boards, for example, provide the potential, at least, for rich communication.[11]

In recent years Jeffery Moore of Stanford University has conducted two studies on executive computer use. In interpreting the results of these studies, he has gone to great pains to indicate that executive use does not follow the DSS paradigm. In the first study, conducted with Brian S. Mittman, he asserts:

> The decision-making model implicit in DSS work assumes the existence and knowledge of goals and preferences, assumptions about the future, and the operation of cause-effect relationships.

All of these inputs are necessary for the proper identification and evaluation of alternatives, and eventual selection of a single course of action. The number of decision situations for which these inputs exist may be quite limited, however. Many decision situations, in particular those found at senior management levels, are characterized by ambiguities in preferences (March, 1978), non-existence of assumptions, or complete uncertainty concerning the future, and incomplete knowledge of cause-effect relationships.[12]

In analyzing the results of 19 executive interviews, Mittman and Moore cast further doubt on DSS usage at senior levels:

> Prescribed analytical uses of DSS—"what if" analysis testing assumptions about uncertain values, the application of quantitative techniques in support of judgment, and the ability to analyze decision problems quickly—characterize few of the executives' computer uses. True DSS use . . . occurred very rarely, even among the executives who had significant amounts of computing experience, access to large amounts of internal and external data, and who used spreadsheet packages regularly for control and communication purposes. In spite of recent changes which have led to increases in managerial computer use (e.g., improvements in hardware and software and increasing managerial exposure to computers and modeling), DSS use by these managers is a relatively insignificant fraction of their general computer use.[13]

In a second study based on 94 executive interviews, Moore divided executive computer usage into three segments: planning and decision support (DSS), management control (MIS), and office automation (OA). DSS tasks included forecasting, modelling, and sensitivity analysis. MIS tasks were characterized by summary reporting of such information as sales, order status, production, and inventory. OA tasks were categorized as word processing, electronic mail, calendaring, and personal scheduling. In Moore's words:

> DSS refers to using a computer to analyze the effects of future actions in order to establish a decision, policy, or rule of behavior, and almost always involves an explicit predictive model. MIS refers, in general, to using a computer to analyze current status, given a decision rule or policy, to determine the degree of compliance with some given standard of performance. Under MIS,

performance models are almost always implicit, in contrast to those of DSS. OA refers to using a computer to effect office-oriented transactions, often related only indirectly to decision making for planning (DSS) or control (MIS).[14]

Moore found a far greater occurrence among senior executives of MIS tasks than those traditionally associated with DSS. Moreover, he says, "Status information appears to be of more importance to more senior managers than the 'what if' analysis that precedes policy setting. In contrast, decision support dominates the use of computers by the more functionally oriented and lower-ranked vice president positions, at least for the most important tasks."[15]

Moore's explanation for the status reporting orientation of senior executives and the DSS orientation of their subordinates is perceptive and deserves to be quoted in full:

> Upper-middle (VP level) and functional managers are closer organizationally to the environments they manage and, hence, rely less on media, like MIS, to communicate status or feedback information. On the other hand, these managers are at a level in which the structure of budgetary, performance, and planning information is both tactical and hard (quantitative), leading to shorter time horizons in planning, rapid feedback cycles, and more concrete measures of performance. This provides an almost ideal environment for the tactical, quantitative, short time horizon, highly structured models characteristic of spreadsheet-oriented DSS applications, the modal DSS application of the sample. It is not an accident that such a large percentage of functional areas in the sample is represented by accounting and financial managers.
>
> Conversely, top-most managers are the most remote from the firm's operations and crave status information, opting to use the new medium of the computer for status reports. For them, planning, analysis, and other decision-support tools are less valuable because the nature of their planning task is strategic with less structure, vague or conflicting measures of performance, and longer time horizons. Their information needs for decision support are soft (qualitative) and often require external data (competitor behavior, regulatory and political actions, and social factors) not readily available from within the firm. As a result, their planning-oriented tasks are not a good fit for most common applications of a budget-focused spreadsheet model. Hence, top

executives use the new medium more frequently for the structured applications of MIS.[16]

In sum, most researchers today agree that executive support systems are a different breed than traditional decision support systems. Nevertheless, there is a nagging question as to whether the roles of senior managers are different enough from their subordinates to justify a separate class of systems.

What makes ESS a meaningful term? Why is it necessary to have a concept of executive computer use that is different from, but still includes, some traditional office automation and decision support applications? Keen would suggest that classifying a system as an ESS "must lead to some actions, by the designers or users, that would not have occurred otherwise; the actions should contribute to the effective development of the system or its effective use."[17] In this context, we shall discuss the four major ways that executive support differs from lower-level decision support or office automation systems. These are the application set which constitutes an ESS, the software utilized, the implementation process, and the organizational impacts of the system.

The Application Set

The major thing that differentiates the concept of executive support from more traditional decision support and office automation concepts is the broader range of applications included in ESS. The concept of executive support systems embraces many of the standard DSS and OA applications. But, the executive's environment and role are so complex and multi-faceted that additional applications are needed to serve each manager's particular needs.

The executive's remoteness from day-to-day operations of the company creates a need for effective systems to monitor performance in many critical business areas. Also, coping with a complex, changing environment justifies increasing access to external data on the industry, competitors, and customers. The executive's desire to understand the subtleties of internal and external environments suggests a need for the richness of textual information. In addition, to lead an organization effectively, the executive requires "outgoing" communication capability. Any of these applications may be used by managers and professionals further down in the organization, but only at the executive level are they combined conceptually into one management support system.

The Software Utilized

With few exceptions, ESS has not been differentiated in the past from lower-level office automation or decision support systems in terms of its hardware and software requirements. Off-the-shelf terminals and personal computers are typical of the hardware utilized, and the software also includes familiar components, the same components which are used for a secretary's electronic mail system or to provide a middle manager's on-line sales reports.

Recently, however, this software homogenization has begun to change with the advent of products designed specifically for executive use, such as Pilot's COMMAND CENTER and Comshare's COMMANDER EIS. Each of the ESS software products now coming to market has a different design philosophy reflecting different conceptions of the executive's job. But most of these products are designed to effectively support the major tasks at the heart of the executive function today—tasks such as internal and external monitoring, communications, and limited analysis. This type of software, tailored to the needs of senior executives, will continue to evolve over the next several years.

New Implementation Issues

Yet another factor that differentiates executive support systems from other managerial support systems is the myriad of additional complications that arise during the implementation process. Because the hardware and software have, in the past, been similar to that used in lower-level systems, it has been easy to assume that the implementation process is also the same. Given the user's position in the organizational hierarchy and special needs for support, however, ESS installation presents a set of unique and difficult problems.

The range of ESS implementation issues will be explored in depth in the second half of this book. A few of the problems which complicate ESS development and installation are:

- The need for adequate time for the executive to define the system's requirements. Only the executive users can assure that the system will meet their highly personalized support needs, but time is a precious commodity for senior managers and is often hard to obtain for projects like this.
- The unique, often absolutely necessary role of the "operational sponsor" (see Chapter 7).
- The difficulty in creating a system for executives that is flexible enough to address their often rapidly changing business needs.
- The problem of getting access to multiple sources of data which may not be readily available for technical, managerial, or political reasons.
- The need for individualized training and intensive support for executive users.
- The perceived, or actual, organizational impacts of providing people at the top with electronic access to the firm's information.

These are just a few of the implementation issues to consider when installing an ESS. Although individual problems similar to these certainly occur when developing other types of systems, these hurdles are more concentrated when implementing systems for top management.

Organizational Impacts

The actions of a top executive significantly affect the behavior of the organization below. Nowhere is this more evident than in the executive's use of computer-based systems. For example, the president of Banco Internacional forced his entire organization to be more marketing oriented by constantly monitoring customer information and holding his employees accountable for being informed about customer activity. At Beneficial Corporation, chairman Finn Caspersen spearheaded a drive to automate his management team from the top down by installing and actively using an office automation system that today includes 1,200 terminals.

Traditional decision support and office automation systems can have significant individual and departmental impacts, but rarely do these systems affect the organization as a whole. Executive support systems, on the other hand, can affect the operations and priorities of the business right down to the clerical level. At Banco Internacional, account managers began monitoring the numbers they knew the president was checking. If an executive relies on electronic mail, then his subordinates usually will be forced to do the same. In the end, an ESS has more far-reaching impacts on the organization than other types of computer systems have had in the past.

ESS—is "Hands-On" Necessary?

Throughout this book we focus on executives making hands-on use of the technology. While this is the dominant model of well-designed executive systems today, it is not necessarily a criterion for defining ESS. In our research, we found a few examples of managers whose workstyles or ways of thinking have been influenced by ESS, yet they only access the system through staff assistants. For example, the president of a diversified electronics company rarely sits at his terminal to view operating results. Instead, he relies on his financial analysts to access the system (which was developed at his request) to produce fast, sophisticated analysis of divisional performance. Just knowing the system's analytic capabilities, and the data available to him, the president asks more knowledgeable "what if" questions of his staff. Moreover, he has achieved his objective to upgrade the planning, control, and analytic capabilities of the corporate office.

In a similar case, the CEO of a large food distribution company was not getting the financial information he needed. Not wanting to use the computer himself, he turned to a systems analyst with his request for a greater range of more detailed information. His new reports, formatted with text and graphics, are produced on a Hewlett-Packard Laserjet printer. They provide complete operations updates in a consistent, personalized format that fits his managerial approach to the monitoring process.

These are two examples of executives who chose a hands-off approach in using computers. Indeed, we have been impressed by these and other systems where direct terminal use by senior management is either minimal or non-existent. Nevertheless, we would argue that these systems are executive support applications because they were initiated by the chief executive to address his own information needs.

The key to the effectiveness of these systems is not the time spent at the computer workstation. Rather, for the executive, it is the time spent thinking through and accomplishing the tasks illustrated in the first two steps in Figure 2–1. The first of these is the identification of the areas of the business which are most important for the organization—the organization's "critical success factors" (see Chapter 9). Second is the identification of the information (both numerical and text) the executive needs to plan or track progress in each of these areas. It is of far less importance whether this information is accessed (step three) directly by the executive or indirectly through staff members who format it and produce reports for the senior manager. There are benefits to direct access. But hands-on access is not as important as the need to discern what information should be available to top management, through which medium (e.g., paper reports or electronic mail), in what formats, and with what frequency.

TYPES OF ESS APPLICATIONS

Until now, we have talked generally about executive support applications. But in the dozens of companies where we found senior managers using computers, specific application patterns appear which can be viewed along two dimensions. One dimension is the *function* the manager performs, such as communication, performance monitoring, or analysis. The second dimension is the *managerial purpose* for which the executive uses the system. Common purposes are office support, management control, and enhancing the executive's "mental model."

Figure 2–1
Three Key Steps

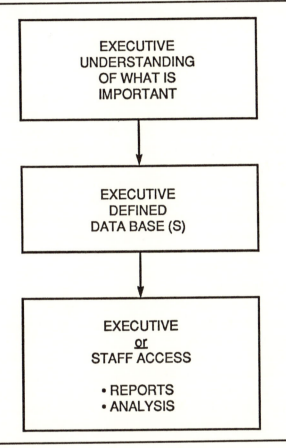

Although not all applications fall neatly into these categories, they capture the sense of what we have seen.

Along the first dimension—function—we see executives using three types of ESS capabilities:

Communication
This function is supported by terminal-based access to applications such as electronic mail and computer conferencing. The executive's terminal is usually networked to others in the company, although, in a few early cases, we found managers using

stand-alone personal computers for text or data analysis that was then awkwardly transferred to a communication network. Although unreported in early research on ESS, the use of terminals for communication purposes, particularly electronic mail, has emerged as a major factor in computer-based executive support.

Status Access
Another set of applications provides the manager with access to a predetermined and preformatted set of reports through a terminal. The data used to generate status reports may be updated hourly, daily, weekly, monthly, or quarterly depending on the particular system, but the report formats and number of reports available are fixed. A hierarchy of menus often allows movement from report to report, but there is limited, if any, ability to see data in other than pre-stored report formats. Used to monitor the organization's progress, status access applications play a major role in most ESS.

Query and Analysis
These applications allow the executive to perform random and unstructured analysis of data, or modeling, and can be created using fourth-generation tools such as SAS, FOCUS, NOMAD, and EXPRESS to access corporate or divisional databases. Additional software support comes from spreadsheet packages, such as Lotus 1–2–3, which are available on personal computers and may or may not be linked to corporate data bases.

The use of computer systems for ad hoc querying of corporate data bases is still relatively rare at the senior management level. There are many reasons for this. They include time pressures which force executives to delegate analysis to staff; a disinclination to take time to learn the software needed to analyze data; and a sense that such analysis is not part of the executive role. The pioneers in ESS, such as Ben Heineman at Northwest Industries, were very analytical. A smaller segment of early adopters moving in behind them also were interested in doing their own analysis. Today, however, analysis is a poor third, trailing communication and status reporting, in ESS applications used by senior management.

A second way to categorize the applications we have seen is in terms of the managerial purpose for which a particular capability of ESS is used. We believe this is the key dimension, and it includes three categories which will be noted briefly here. The rationale underlying this structuring will be described in Chapter 3, and the applications to be found in each category will be dealt with in detail in Chapters 4–6.

The three managerial purposes which, we believe, underlie the use of ESS are:

1. The support of particular office functions in an attempt to improve the executive's effectiveness and efficiency.
2. Improved support of the organization's planning and control processes. The objectives of this type of ESS can range from merely enhancing an existing control system, to changing fundamental aspects of the way the organization is managed by redesigning the entire planning and control process.
3. The clarification or enhancement of the individual manager's mental model of the firm's business environment.

INDIVIDUAL VS. ORGANIZATIONAL SYSTEMS

One important trend in ESS design is the increased number of executive applications that are part of a system used throughout the organization. In many cases, an ESS is designed explicitly to change an existing organizational process. In contrast, the early ESS identified by Rockart and Treacy were designed for individual executives.[18] Most of these systems depended upon a specific individual's workstyle and were structured primarily for that executive's use. Examples of these highly individual systems included:

- At Northwest Industries, president and chief executive Ben Heineman worked at his terminal almost every day analyzing performance reports from his nine operating companies. Heineman's system became his most important tool for monitoring and planning, yet virtually none of Northwest's other senior executives used it.

- Gerald Viste, president and COO of Wausau Insurance Companies, accessed industry information to analyze his company's competitive position. Before his retirement, others began to use Viste's approach, yet the system was primarily his.

- The president of Thermo Electron, George Hatsopoulos, developed models of his company, industry, and the economy to help him formulate the company's strategic direction.[19]

While early ESS focused on what the technology available at the time could do for an individual, newer systems tend to be broader in scope, being designed for use throughout the executive's organization. For example:

- At Phillips Petroleum Company, the top 10 executives in the Petroleum Products and Chemicals Group have on-line access to varying levels of daily sales and refinery data, as well as international news summaries updated three times a day. They also communicate regularly by electronic mail. The spread of this system to his entire top management team was driven by Executive Vice President Robert Wallace, who saw use of the information technology as essential to managing his recently restructured organization in an increasingly competitive environment.

- At Xerox Corporation, Chairman David Kearns and President Paul Allaire implemented an ESS that is used by almost all senior managers for communication and review of performance data. The system has also resulted in a restructuring of the company's strategic planning process that now requires all business units to submit their plans over an electronic network.

- At Hercules, a large chemical manufacturer, 80 senior managers have on-line access to data about their unit's performance. The spread of this ESS was driven by former Chairman and CEO Alexander Giacco, although he rarely used the system himself. He was primarily interested in encouraging more active analysis of available information by his management team. Giacco said, "The purpose of the sales inquiry system is to draw management's attention to the pieces of information that are important to the organization."[20]

- The president of a large electronics corporation pushed for a streamlined reporting system that changed the way the entire organization handled performance data.

These four systems have much broader impacts in their organizations than the early ESS implemented by Heineman, Viste, and Hatsopoulos. Such organizational systems also are much more apt to continue in use after the executive moves on. As the concept of ESS matures, there is a clear trend away from individual systems towards organizational systems, linking executives to their subordinates and to their peers. This trend will enhance the long-term impact of ESS.

Let us now look at a sample of the firms using ESS from which our findings are drawn.

COMPANIES SURVEYED

Here is a sample of the 30 companies we have studied in detail. The 16 described here mostly represent success stories and will be used as illustrations throughout the book. We will also draw lessons from other successful firms, as well as a few which had systems that failed. The names of some of the companies have been changed—they are indicated by an asterisk (*). In most cases, this was done at the company's request to protect their confidentiality.

*Auto Electronics, Inc.** is a $2 billion division of a major car manufacturer. At the general manager's direction, terminals were installed in both the offices and homes of all 14 members of the senior management team. The system was implemented rapidly. The most frequently used applications have been electronic mail, status access, spreadsheets, and company news.

Banco Internacional de Columbia, a Citicorp subsidiary, installed an ESS under the direction of President Mike Jensen to effect managerial change. To help implement his new marketing strategy, Jensen used the system to monitor and analyze the bank's performance, including profitability trends, expenses, daily balance sheets, and the status of all customer accounts.

Beneficial Corporation, under the direction of CEO Finn Caspersen, installed a 1,200-terminal, organization-wide office support system. All top executives have terminals on their desks. The major application is electronic mail, and data retrieval capabilities are being added.

The Boeing Company.   Three separate ESS have been developed in this aerospace company, one at corporate headquarters, and two in divisions. The one in the Boeing Aerospace Company is used by almost all the vice presidents to access performance and activity reports, company news, and electronic mail.

*Diversified Electronics Corporation.**   The CFO encouraged development of an ESS to automate financial reporting and to meet specific requirements of the new president. Although only used occasionally by the CEO, the ESS enhanced the analytic capabilities of his financial staff, thus providing the chief executive with vastly improved reports. With faster and better reporting, he was able to spend more time on planning and strategic issues and less time on monitoring operations.

Firestone.   Faced with large financial losses, this Ohio-based tire company's new CEO developed an ESS to help identify areas where he could better control costs. In the process, the company undertook a huge renovation of its basic accounting systems. Subsequently, the ESS became the foundation for attempts at developing an organization-wide budgeting model.

Gillette Company.   Derwyn Phillips, executive vice president of Gillette North America (GNA), implemented an ESS that not only transformed the way he processes information personally, but also improves management reporting by executives in the three divisions which report to him. Phillips and his managers primarily use the system for performance monitoring and competitive analysis.

International Computers Ltd.(ICL).   At least eight senior managers in this British computer company have independently developed ESS within their divisions or functions. Directors of sales, personnel, and various product and marketing groups all use terminals regularly to monitor performance, do analysis, and communicate by electronic mail.

Lincoln National Corporation is a large insurance holding company based in Fort Wayne, Indiana. CEO Ian Rolland sponsored the implementation of an office system which has spread throughout the organization to all levels of management. The primary applications at the executive level are electronic mail, performance monitoring, and word processing.

*Michigan Motors Company** is a division of a major car manufacturer. The general manager requested an ESS for his executive team because he felt they needed better information to make decisions. The system is used primarily for performance monitoring and electronic mail.

*Northern Bank's** chairman sought to improve his efficiency by automating many of the tasks performed by his administrative support staff. Among the most heavily used applications of this system are correspondence tracking, electronic mail, and an automated Rolodex.

Phillips Petroleum Company.   Robert Wallace, executive vice president of the firm's Petroleum Products and Chemicals Group, installed an ESS to improve the quality and timeliness of the information he needed to manage his recently restructured "downstream" operations. Wallace and his nine senior managers use the system daily to monitor economic and political news relevant to the business, as well as internal supply and marketing data critical to pricing decisions. Electronic mail is also a heavily-used feature of the system.

Raytheon Corporation.   The general manager of the Missile Systems Division installed an ESS to help him monitor the status of the division's major programs. The initial system has since spread down into the organization where it spawned a wide range of new applications.

Stowe Computers, Inc.*   The CEO of this large computer manufacturer ordered the development of an ESS to improve executive productivity and to help shift the company's technology-driven culture to a more marketing oriented one. Two attempts were made to install terminals in the offices of the senior executives and, in both cases, the systems went largely unused. Executives not only found it very difficult to access corporate data bases, but they also found the information not timely enough to be useful.

United Retailing, Inc.*   Faced with major revenue losses and an antiquated performance tracking system, the vice president of operations developed an ESS that streamlined the reporting process for key operating numbers from the firm's 1,000 department stores. The new control system allowed more timely and detailed analysis, which supported top management in redirecting the business.

Xerox Corporation.   President Paul Allaire sponsored the implementation of an ESS to enhance the company's management processes, with a particular focus on improving the effectiveness of the corporate staff. The system is used by most senior managers for corporate planning, electronic mail, and monthly performance reporting.

A word of caution. In most cases, the ongoing use and impact of an executive support system are largely dependent on the individual manager for whom the system was originally developed. Our research has taken place over several years and, in that time, a number of the executives we studied have moved on to other positions or retired. As a result, their systems have either taken on a new look under their successor, or they have fallen into disuse. We have used the present tense throughout the book where, to the best of our knowledge, the systems are still being actively used. It is inevitable, however, given executive turnover, that some of the systems reported on here are no longer in use.

The Effect of Company Size

One consideration in discussing executive support systems is the size of the company, operating unit, or function involved. A senior executive in a $10 billion company has a broader set of concerns and a more complex organization than an executive in a $10 million company. Our research focused on medium to large corporations in which executives are traditionally removed from day-to-day operations and are supported by staff personnel. The same is not true in small businesses. John Dearden of Harvard Business School, while criticizing ESS, has, nonetheless, addressed the special needs of small business:

> In my opinion, the greatest impact of the personal computer will be on managers of small businesses. These managers make many line decisions and can use a computer in such applications as inventory control and other logistic operations. Further, small businesses tend to be limited in both the quality and quantity of their staff because of financial constraints. Managers of these small businesses may be able to use the computer for analysis as well as retrieval of information.[21]

The focus of this book is on computer use by managers in large organizations. While much of the book is relevant to executives in smaller firms, the examples used are more germaine to senior managers in major corporations.

WHAT IS A SUCCESSFUL ESS?

One of the most difficult questions concerning executive support systems is "How do we know if a system is effective or successful?" This question goes beyond the issue of cost justification, which will be addressed in Chapter 9. Keen showed that defining and quantifying the benefits of a decision support system is very difficult.[22] ESS prove to be no less challenging because their benefits can be even more intangible and transient. Crowston and Treacy emphasize, however, that the issue of assessing economic impacts has haunted all forms of information technology investments throughout the computer age. Current systems are perhaps the most difficult to justify since they are designed to do much more than automate single functions at decreased costs. In addition, many systems today are just one input of many in rapidly changing organizations. Attempts to separate an individual application's effect are, therefore, often nearly impossible. Crowston and Treacy comment:

> Currently, systems are often used to enhance performance without any necessary reduction in organizational costs. With some systems, the benefits are better decision making, improved communications, or other semi-tangible instrumental changes. With systems that try to affect the competitive position of the firm in its marketplace, the benefits are usually even less tangible.
>
> The lack of measures of enterprise performance impacts is a serious practical and theoretical problem. In practice, we assume that our systems will deliver bottom-line value, but we can neither predict that value for the investment decision, nor measure it once the system is in place.[23]

Economic justification, however, represents only part of a system's value. Our research shows at least six criteria for judging ESS. Most often the judgements on these criteria are implicit. In fact, it is *very* rare for the benefits of an ESS to be explicitly assessed, either before or after the system is installed.

1. *How much time does the executive spend using the system?* This superficial criterion is often used by ESS developers to judge the success of a system. ("If the boss uses it, it must be successful.") Of course, if the manager never uses the computer, it is hard to argue that the system is contributing to organizational effectiveness, unless hands-on use has been delegated. But use alone does not mean increased effectiveness because there is no direct relationship between time at the terminal and executive performance.

2. *Does the system save the executive time and allow more work to get done?* This is a question of increased efficiency or logistical support. To some, this is what executive support is all about. For others, a system that focuses only on increasing top management efficiency is selling short the technology's potential.

3. *Does the ESS change how the executive thinks about using and managing information technology?* Educating top management about computer technology and its expanding capabilities to provide competitive advantage is an objective of some ESS advocates. Although part of this educational objective may be realized, the ESS will languish when its applications are not focused on a significant business need. Education is a measurable but secondary criterion for success, often a by-product of an effective ESS.

4. *Does it change the way the organization utilizes technology?* This is a result of the change in mind-set just described. Seldom a criterion to justify ESS, increased technology utilization by the organization is often a major benefit of a system installed for top management. Once educated, executives are more likely, for better or worse, to accelerate the use of information technologies in the organization.

5. *Does the system improve the executive's understanding of and control over the business?* This intangible benefit is an explicit or implicit criterion for success in the minds of several executives interviewed. These executives are striving to reduce the uncertainty they feel about their environment or to make sense of equivocal information. An effective ESS will enhance their mental model of the business and competitive environment by creating a better understanding of cause and effect relationships.

6. *Does the system improve the organization's planning and control process?* This is one of the most tangible measures of ESS effectiveness. Providing more timely and better quality information to top management can have a major impact on an organization's management processes. But it can also generate the most resistance from other parts of the firm during the implementation process. Changing information flows within an organization alters the power structure, and this can be extremely upsetting to subordinate line managers and staff alike.

There is no right way to assess the effectiveness of an ESS because every manager will have different criteria for judging success. Equally important, these criteria will change over time as the system evolves or the executive's perceived support needs change. Organizations also have very different needs. One may need a tighter control process or improved planning system, while another may not.

The final judgement concerning the quality of a particular ESS, however, will be determined largely by the executives' expectations and their perception of the system's ability to meet their particular support needs. Viewed from this perspective, a system that is a raving success for one executive might be a dismal failure for another. This highlights the need for early clarification of the system's purpose, as discussed in Chapter 9.

In our view, however, there is a hierarchy to keep in mind when evaluating an ESS, from both individual and organizational perspectives. The criteria for a successful ESS, from most to least valuable, are:

1. It changes or enhances the way the executive thinks about the business—in other words, it improves the manager's mental model of the firm.

2. It provides the executive with better planning and control capabilities.

3. It leverages the manager's time, allowing the company to take better advantage of the executive's experience, expertise, and perspective.

4. It educates the executive about the use and potential of information technologies.

NOTES

1. John F. Rockart and Michael E. Treacy, "Executive Information Support Systems," *Working Paper No. 65*, Center for Information Systems Research, Sloan School of Management, MIT, Cambridge, Mass., November 1980; John F. Rockart and Michael E. Treacy, "The CEO Goes On-Line," *Working Paper No.67*, Center for Information Systems Research, Sloan School of Management,

MIT, Cambridge, Mass., April 1981; John F. Rockart and Michael E. Treacy, "The CEO Goes On-Line," *Harvard Business Review,* January-February 1982.

2. John F. Rockart and Michael E. Treacy, "Executive Information Support Systems," *Working Paper No. 65,* Center for Information Systems Research, Sloan School of Management, MIT, Cambridge, Mass., November 1980.

3. Peter G.W. Keen, "The On-Line CEO: How One Executive Uses MIS." Unpublished working paper, Micro Mainframe, Inc., 1983.

4. Ibid., p. 27.

5. Eliot Levinson, "The Implementation of Executive Support Systems," *Working Paper No. 119,* Center for Information Systems Research, Sloan School of Management, MIT, Cambridge, Mass., October 1984.

6. David W. De Long and John F. Rockart, "A Survey of Current Trends in the Use of Executive Support Systems," *Working Paper No.121,* Center for Information Systems Research, Sloan School of Management, MIT, Cambridge, Mass., November 1984, p. 3.

7. See Peter G.W. Keen and Michael S. Scott Morton, *Decision Support Systems: An Organizational Perspective.* (Reading, Mass.: Addison-Wesley, 1978); Ralph H. Sprague, Jr., and Eric D. Carlson, *Building Effective Decision Support Systems* (Englewood Cliffs, N.J.: Prentice-Hall, 1982); Michael S. Scott Morton, "The State of the Art of Research in Management Support Systems," reprinted in *The Rise of Managerial Computing,* John F. Rockart and Christine V. Bullen, eds. (Homewood, Ill.: Dow Jones-Irwin, 1986).

8. Michael E. Treacy, "Executive Support Systems," Speech to Center for Information Systems Research Summer Session, Cambridge, Mass., June 16, 1983.

9. R.L. Daft and E.K. Weick, "Toward a Model of Organizations as Interpretation Systems," *Academy of Management Review,* vol.9 (1984), pp. 284–295.

10. Robert W. Zmud, "Supporting Senior Executives Through Decision Support Technologies: A Review and Directions for Future Research," *Decision Support Systems: A Decade in Perspective,* E.R. McLean and H.G. Sol, eds. (Amsterdam: Elsevier Science Publishers, 1986), p. 90.

11. Ibid., p. 92.

12 Brian S. Mittman and Jeffrey H. Moore, "Senior Management Computer Use: Implications for DSS Designs and Goals," *Proceedings of DSS-84 Conference,* Institute for Decision Support Systems, April 1984, p. 48.

13. Ibid., p. 47.
14. Jeffrey H. Moore, "Senior Executive Computer Use." Unpublished working paper, Stanford Graduate School of Business, Palo Alto, Calif., 1986, p. 6.
15. Ibid., p. 8.
16. Ibid., p. 9.
17. Peter G.W. Keen, "Decision Support Systems: A Research Perspective," *Working Paper No. 54*, Center for Information Systems Research, Sloan School of Management, MIT, Cambridge, Mass., March 1980, p. 3.
18. John F. Rockart and Michael E. Treacy, "The CEO Goes On-Line," *Harvard Business Review*, January-February 1982.
19. Ibid.
20. David Roman, "A Top Down MIS Mandate," *Computer Decisions*, November 18, 1986, p. 30.
21. John Dearden, "SMR Forum: Will the Computer Change the Job of Top Management?", *Sloan Management Review*, vol. 25, no.1 (Fall 1983), p. 60.
22. Peter G.W. Keen, "Value Analysis: Justifying Decision Support Systems," *MIS Quarterly*, vol. 5, no.1 (1981).
23. Kevin Crowston and Michael E. Treacy, "Assessing the Impact of Information Technology on Enterprise Level Performance," *Working Paper No.143*, Center for Information Systems Research, Sloan School of Management, MIT, Cambridge, Mass., October 1986, p. 1.

CHAPTER 3

ESS AND THE NATURE OF EXECUTIVE WORK

According to Keen and Hackathorn, "A central theme in decision support is that one cannot improve something one does not understand. The act of 'supporting' a manager implies a meshing of analytic tools into his or her existing activities".[1] The development of a computer-based executive support system requires a similar understanding of what it is that executives do. Unfortunately, there is no position in the organizational hierarchy that is less understood than that of the senior executive. Virtually all existing studies of senior executives at work have been comprised either of small samples or have covered very limited periods of time, or both. What top managers actually do remains somewhat of a mystery.

The purpose of this chapter is to review the existing research on executive work and to note areas of agreement between the literature and the practice which we have observed in the area of executive support systems. As noted in the previous chapter, our studies of companies with an ESS in place suggest that there are three central managerial purposes being served by these systems. Although it is a rough categorization, executives appear to be developing systems to:

1. Gain benefits of applications generally associated with office support, including systems such as electronic mail and word processing.
2. Improve systems which support the organization's planning and control processes.

3. Develop, clarify, or enhance the individual manager's mental model of the firm's business environment.

Research which seeks to develop categorizations like these is difficult at best. The literature on executives suggests a need for many different types of executive support systems, as well as for none at all. As researchers we must take into account Weick's warning against seeing only those facts which support our own implicit models.[2] Nevertheless, evidence from the field does point toward the three major uses of ESS noted above, and the literature provides a solid case for them.

To illustrate that case, we will review the writing of those theorists who provide insights into the work of senior executives. In particular, we will focus on three researchers—Mintzberg, Kotter and Isenberg—who aim specifically at understanding the role of the senior line executive. We have also drawn heavily on the work of two other researchers—Anthony and Jaques—whose findings provide useful insights into the role of ESS in top management work.

Each of these researchers provides a different perspective. Mintzberg's model of management roles is probably the best known characterization of the activities of senior executives. Anthony's planning and control framework offers a functional view, while Kotter's studies of top management work provide a useful behavioral framework for studying ESS. All three conceptions, however, merely describe what can be perceived of executive work by an external observer. They lack a cognitive perspective. Therefore, we will also draw heavily on work by Jaques and Isenberg, who focus on cognition as a major aspect of the management function. Other contributions to the relatively sparse academic literature on senior executives will also be cited where appropriate.

Mintzberg's Activities View

Mintzberg is best known for his role theory, based on his study of five chief executives, which categorizes executive activities into ten distinct roles.[3] Mintzberg's research on the work of top management represents a sharp departure from the classical way of describing managerial work. This traditional approach, introduced by Henri Fayol in 1916, characterized executive work as a set of composite functions—planning, organizing, coordinating, commanding, and controlling. Mintzberg effectively argued, however, that this classical conception of managerial work did not describe what executives actually did, but rather described "vague objectives of managerial work."[4] Mintzberg's studies are rooted in an approach to managerial research that believes in systematic analysis of the characteristics and content of managers' work activities. The father of this school is Sune Carlson, whose study of nine Swedish executives is considered the first significant empirical study of managerial work.[5] Carlson used a diary method to gather data on the *characteristics* of executive work, and his major findings centered around the communication patterns of chief executives, as well as their long days and fragmented work schedules. Because of the inherent limitations of the diary method in accurately assessing work activities, however, Carlson was able to offer little insight as to the content of executive work.[6]

Mintzberg overcame this problem by relying on the structured observation of five executives to develop a description of what managers actually do. He divided executive activities into ten distinct roles, a categorization that remains the most influential framework defining the work of senior executives. Mintzberg's ten roles are divided into three groups: interpersonal, informational, and decisional. The roles, and the fundamental activities carried out by the executive in each, are:

INTERPERSONAL ROLES

Figurehead. Carries out a symbolic role as head of the organization, performing routine duties of a legal or social nature.

Leader. In the most widely recognized managerial duty, is responsible for motivation and "activation" of subordinates, as well as staffing, training, promoting.

Liaison. Develops and maintains a personal network of external contacts who provide information and favors.

INFORMATIONAL ROLES

Monitor.   Seeks and receives a wide variety of special information to develop a thorough understanding of the organization and the environment. In this role, the executive serves as the nerve center of internal and external information about the organization.

Disseminator.   Transmits information received from outsiders or from subordinates to other members of the organization. Information ranges from factual information to value statements designed to guide subordinates in decision making.

Spokesman.   Communicates information to outsiders on the organization's plans, policies, actions, results, etc.

DECISIONAL ROLES

Entrepreneur.   Searches the organization and environment for opportunities and initiates "improvement projects" to bring about change; supervises design of certain projects as well.

Disturbance Handler.   Responsible for corrective action when the organization faces important, unexpected disturbances.

Resource Allocator.   Allocates organizational resources of all kinds.

Negotiator.   Represents the organization in major negotiations.[7]

Working in the decade prior to the rise of end-user computing, Mintzberg, of course, saw no direct use of computers by the executives he studied. He focused on the observable characteristics of executive work. He reported brevity of attention to any activity, fragmentation of effort, and an emphasis on verbal communication. Observing very little use of hard, quantifiable data in his research, he wrote:

> I was struck during my study by the fact that the executives I was observing—all very competent by any standard—are fundamentally indistinguishable from their counterparts of a hundred

years ago (or a thousand years ago, for that matter). The information they need differs, but they seek it in the same way—by word of mouth. Their decisions concern modern technology, but the procedures they use to make them are the same as the procedures of the 19th–century manager. Even the computer, so important for the specialized work of the organization, has apparently had no influence on the work procedures of general managers.[8]

Mintzberg's findings are often used to argue against automation in the executive suite. When looked at more carefully, however, Mintzberg's model actually does disclose reasons why information technology could be used to support many executive roles. This is because of the pervasive impact of information on virtually all of the roles. The monitoring and disturbance handling roles, for example, both represent activities where access to hard, structured information is extremely useful and readily available today in organizations of any size. In carrying out both of these roles, the presence of monthly and sometimes weekly printed reports is common.

Further, Mintzberg says that executives use the information they collect in four ways: (1) to disseminate it to others; (2) to develop value positions for the firm; (3) to identify business problems and opportunities; and (4) "to develop mental images—'models' of how his organization and its environment function . . ."[9]

Mintzberg contends that mental models help the executive deal with the complexity inherent in his job. He says, "In effect, the manager absorbs information that continually bombards him and forms it into a series of mental models—of the internal workings of his organization, the behavior of subordinates, the trends in the organization's environment, the habits of associates, and so on. When choices must be made, these models can be used to test alternatives." And he concludes that "the effectiveness of the manager's decisions is largely dependent on the quality of his models."[10]

Mintzberg not only recognizes the importance of mental models, but also acknowledges the potential for computer support in enriching these models. He states, "One way to improve the manager's models is to expose him systematically to the best available conceptual understanding of the situations he faces. A key role of the management scientist could be to put good models into the manager's head. . . . The manager will develop models of these things anyway; by explicit focus on them, the management scientist can help ensure that the models are the best ones possible."[11]

Anthony's Planning and Control Framework

An expanded view of the executive's monitoring role suggested by Mintzberg is evident in Anthony's model of planning and control.[12] His framework consists of three categories:

> *Strategic planning.* The process of deciding on objectives of the organization, on changes in these objectives, on the resources used to attain these objectives, and on the policies that are to govern the acquisition, use, and disposition of these resources.
>
> *Management control.* The process by which managers assure that resources are obtained and used effectively and efficiently in the accomplishment of the organization's objectives.
>
> *Operational control.* The process of assuring that specific tasks are carried out effectively and efficiently.[13]

Anthony notes that both planning and control are included in each of the activities. He concedes that the lines between his three categories are blurred. He does point out, however, that the activities listed under strategic planning are heavily oriented toward planning; that those labelled management control are a mixture of both planning and control; and that operational control activities are almost exclusively concerned with control.

Examples of activities that fall under the three major framework headings are shown in Table 3–1.

For ESS purposes, Anthony's concept of "management control" is most significant. He contends that the several activities it includes are carried out, in part, by senior management. In

Table 3–1
Examples From Anthony's Planning and Control Framework

Strategic Planning	Management Control	Operational Control
Planning the organization	Planning and monitoring staff levels	Controlling hiring
Setting financial policies	Working capital planning and control	Controlling credit extension
Acquiring a new division	Measuring, appraising, and improving management performance	Measuring, appraising, and improving workers' efficiency

Source: ©1965 by the President and Fellows of Harvard College; all rights reserved. Adapted with permission from *Planning and Control Systems: A Framework for Analysis* by Robert N. Anthony (Boston, Mass.: Division of Research, Graduate School of Business Administration, Harvard University, 1965), p. 19.

practice, management control is observable in budgeting, sales quotas, personnel policies, and other widely-used management systems.

Anthony's approach is drawn from the broader school of cybernetic theory developed by Weiner[14] and Beer.[15] It is really a cybernetic model representing a feedback loop.

The basic steps in the feedback loop are shown in Figure 3–1. The reasons for each step are fairly obvious. Control without knowledge of desirable results is meaningless,[16] so managers need a plan. But a plan without follow-up is also of little value. Thus, planning and control are intimately joined in both a cybernetic model and in the world of management practice.

This framework of planning and control is, of course, not a complete model of management. It offers only a limited perspective on the work of top managers because it focuses primarily on just two of the several roles—monitoring and resource allocation—that Mintzberg identifies in executive work. But they are clearly critical roles, and roles in which information plays a vital part. More recently, others have worked to provide more specific alternative views of the control process (in which plan-

Figure 3–1
Basic Feedback Loop

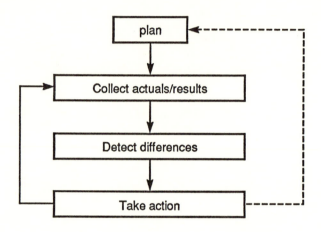

ning in all cases is either explicit or implicit). Best known among these are Merchant,[17] who expands on diverse measures for results, actions, and personnel controls; Ouchi[18] who builds on the work of Thompson[19] and approaches the control process from an organizational perspective; and Williamson,[20] who takes an economic approach. Although their various theoretical and/ or pragmatic approaches differ, all, like Anthony, acknowledge the need for information to facilitate the control function.

Kotter's Process View

While Mintzberg has an activities view of executive work, and Anthony offers a model of a particular managerial function, Kotter presents a process model.[21] Using data gathered from in-depth interviews and structured observation of 15 general managers, Kotter concludes that executives' efforts center around two key processes: agenda setting and network building.

Agendas are loosely connected goals and plans, addressing a wide range of financial, product/market, and organizational issues. According to Kotter, they cover short, medium, and long-term responsibilities.[22] Drawing from his research on 15 general managers (GMs), Kotter draws a clear distinction between formal plans and managerial agendas. He notes that:

> The GMs' agendas always included goals, priorities, strategies, and plans that were not in the written documents. This is not to say that the formal plans and the GMs' agendas were incompatible; generally, they were rather consistent. They were just different in at least three important ways. First, the formal plans tended to be written mostly in terms of detailed financial numbers; the GMs' agendas tended to be less detailed in financial objectives and more detailed in strategies and plans for the business or the organization. Second, formal plans usually focused entirely on the short and moderate run (three months to five years); GM agendas tended to focus a bit more on a broader time frame, including the immediate future (1-30 days) and the longer run (5-20 years). Finally, formal plans tended to be more explicit, rigorous, and logical, especially regarding how various financial items fit together; GM agendas often contained lists of goals or plans that were not as explicitly connected.[23]

Kotter's second management function, network building, means developing cooperative relationships with all those people who may play a role in providing information for development and implementation of the executive's emerging agenda. The network consists not only of direct subordinates and superiors, but also of many other people at all levels in the manager's organization. Included are external suppliers, customers, politicians, bankers, and others, whose support can be helpful in defining and implementing the executive's agenda. The executive's network often includes hundreds of people with various types and intensities of relationships.

Kotter's concept of network building provides a strong indication of the importance of communication to executives. To Kotter, communication, either formal or informal, is half the game.

Jaques' Cognitive View

Mintzberg, Anthony, and Kotter all have useful conceptions of top management work, but they leave out one important element—cognition. How do executives think about what they do? This is critical because many believe that the primary difference between top executives and middle managers is in their cognitive approaches to work.

Jaques presents one cognitive view of management.[24] His stratified-systems theory of organizations identifies seven levels common to bureaucratic hierarchies, with the boundaries between each level, or stratum, representing qualitative shifts in the nature of work at each level. The seven strata are defined by relative shifts in the "time span of discretion." Jaques says that time span of discretion is established by measuring the task with the longest target completion time in the role.[25] His seven levels of work in organizations are shown in Table 3–2. Also described in the table are the primary activities of each level in the organization from shop floor to chairman. The activities represent the primary tasks at each level that differentiate it from the level below.

Paralleling the different time horizons for individuals' work, according to Jaques, are different levels of abstraction, as represented in the last column of the table. Jaques postulates that "how any two people perceive the same problem or activity will be different according to the differences in their level of abstraction".[26]

The difference in the "quality of abstraction" is particularly noticeable between levels three and four, the latter being the first level of general management. The first three levels of abstraction represent work that involves relatively concrete types of thinking. "Perceptual-motor concrete" is a mode of work that involves direct perceptual contact with the physical output, such as a stockroom clerk filling an order, or a secretary typing a memo. The second level, "imaginal concrete," requires the use of imagination in constructing a project, but deals with projects for which the final output can be visualized in concrete terms. A foreman at this level, for example, would plan and implement a training program for workers who will operate new machines

Table 3-2
Jaques' Seven Levels of Work

Time Span		Stratum	Organizational Level	Main Activity	Level of Abstraction
20 Years		VII	Corporation	Providing overall strategic direction	?
		VI	Corporate group of subsidiaries	Creating strategy and translating it into business direction	Institution-Creating
10 Years		V	Corporate subsidiary and top specialists	Redefining goals and determining field operations	Intuitive Theory
5 Years		IV	General Management and chief specialists	Creating methods of operation	Conceptual Modeling
2 Years					
		III	Departmental managers and chief specialists	Organizing programs into systems of work	Imaginal Scanning
1 Year		II	Front-line managerial, professional, and technical	Generating programs of work	Imaginal Concrete
3 months		I	Office and shop floor	Doing concrete tasks	Perceptual-Motor Concrete
1 day					

Abstract, Indirect or General Command

Concrete Direct Command

Source: Elliott Jaques, A *General Theory of Bureaucracy*, p. 153. Copyright ©Gower Publishing Company, Ltd., Hampshire, England. Adapted with permission of the author.

being installed. The third level of abstraction is "imaginal scanning" which involves a position such as sales manager, in which it is impossible to comprehend an entire area of responsibility at once, although the whole can still be mentally scanned, one piece at a time.

Jaques emphasizes that between levels three and four there is a "profound change in the quality of abstraction used in carrying out tasks: it is a change from the concrete to the abstract mode of thought and work."[27] He says, "The qualitative jump from level three [departmental manager] to level four [general management] is that at level four neither the output nor the project can be forseen in concrete terms, even by imaginal scanning. The project cannot be completely constructed. It remains a combination of a conscious subjective picture, incomplete in itself, whose specific total form and content are unconsciously intuitively sensed but cannot quite be consciously grasped."[28]

The fifth level of abstraction is called the level of "intuitive theory" because it is based on the intuitive theories an individual has developed out of his experience. Jaques says executives at this level are preoccupied with shaping the future and they tend to delegate current operations based on plans and policies already specified. We concede that above level five insufficient empirical work has been done to characterize the qualitative differences in the modes of work at levels six and seven.

While Jaques' conception of the organization in terms of "time span of discretion" remains controversial, his recognition that individuals work with different levels of abstraction is intuitively valid, and is useful for thinking about differences between the work of middle managers and executives.

Isenberg's Cognitive Overview

In a forthcoming work, *Managerial Thinking: An Inquiry Into How Senior Managers Think,* Isenberg argues that "managerial cognition" is a critical variable for understanding the management process. Unfortunately, he points out, virtually all the major studies of executive work have treated cognitive capabilities as a background issue. One reason for this lack of attention is that there is no one well-accepted cognitive view of management. Acknowledging this, Isenberg provides multiple perspectives on executive cognition. Three of these are particularly informative.

One cognitive perspective identified by Isenberg is "Manager as Decision Maker." This has been a popular concept of management, particularly among those seeking to support executives with traditional decision support systems technology (DSS). Isenberg, however, finds this conception flawed. He contends that rarely can the actual moment of decision be observed. Executives do not usually make major decisions by choosing from a set of predetermined alternatives. In fact, able executives make few decisions and virtually all of these have been extensively worked upon over a period of time by staff and subordinate line managers.

Isenberg's view finds support in the work of a wide range of researchers including Simon,[29] Keen,[30] and Moore.[31] Keen notes that decision support systems are designed to support decision makers in semi-structured tasks. Most executive decisions, however, involve problems that are unstructured, complex, and influenced by many people. Isenberg leads one away from thinking of the "executive as decision maker" as a fundamental design strategy for senior management systems.

A second cognitive perspective identified by Isenberg which is useful in comprehending the role of executive support systems is "Manager as Sensemaker." This conception focuses on how managers impose cognitive structures on their environments. Using this cognitive model, Brief and Downey drew on case studies to argue that Henry Ford and Alfred Sloan's differing mental models resulted in very different business strategies and organizational structures at Ford and General Motors.[32] In similar fashion, Donaldson and Lorsch studied the goal formulation and strategic decision-making processes in a dozen *Fortune* 500 companies.[33] They found that "strategic decisions are not the product of simple economic logic alone. Because these decisions often depend on forecasts of future events, they involve considerable uncertainty and ambiguity. To analyze these complexities, top managers draw upon their experience and judgement—judgement that has been shaped by the shared beliefs passed on to them by their predecessors."[34] This concordance of shared beliefs, experience, and judgement suggests a "world view" which strongly affects the management of an organization.

Weick has also been very influential in developing this "Manager as Sensemaker" school.[35] His concept of "enactment" holds that organizational members impose a cognitive structure on an ill-defined stream of organizational events, then act as if this mental model were the true organizational reality.

The concept of mental models, to which Mintzberg refers, was first developed in the 1940s and its use has been largely restricted to the psychology literature. In his book *Mental Models,* Johnson-Laird makes the following observations as a way of defining this elusive concept:

> All our knowledge of the world depends on our ability to construct models of it.
>
> Mental models play a central and unifying role in representing objects, states of affairs, sequences of events, the way the world is, and the social and psychological actions in daily life. They enable individuals to make inferences and predictions, to understand phenomena, to decide what action to take and to control its execution, and above all to experience events by proxy.
>
> Since mental models can take many forms and serve many purposes, their contents are very varied. They can contain nothing but tokens that represent individuals and identities between them, as in the sort of models that are required for syllogistic reasoning. They can represent spatial relations between entities, and the temporal or caused relations between events. . . . Models have a content and form that fits them to their purpose, whether it be to explain, to predict, or to control. Their structure corresponds to the perceived or conceived structure of the world.[36]

Management scientists have traditionally worked to develop explicit formal models. Implicit mental models share some of the same characteristics (simplification of reality, emphasis on relationships, etc.). But their significance and uses are different. Treacy describes the differences this way:

> Senior executives use models for planning and control. Their models are intuitive and implicit. They are mental representations of real-

ity—abstractions of complex decision contexts—that executives use to simplify the decision process, to identify important variables, and to generate and evaluate alternatives. They are not usually put down on paper, built into a computer program, analyzed quantitatively, or even viewed as models. . . But, they are arguably the most important models for planning and control, because they are powerful and they get used.

Does the executive really need an explicit or formal model to understand his or her operations? Explicit models are easily shared and they can be analyzed using a range of techniques. Some would argue that even a manager who understood the firm's operations very well could benefit by formal modeling of those operations. Others might argue that what the executive needs is not formal models, but support for his or her implicit modeling, so that the weaknesses of this abstract mental modeling can be reduced.

The answer depends upon the type of decision contexts faced by the executive.[37]

Isenberg does not explicitly use the term "Manager as Organizational Process Designer," but this third cognitive perspective is implicit in some of his earlier work. In a study of 12 division managers, he found that executives tend to think about problems of two kinds: (1) how to create effective organizational processes, and (2) how to deal with one or two critical issues or general goals. Isenberg contends that these two modes of thought underlie Kotter's critical networking and agenda-building activities.[38] Isenberg contends, as many previous studies have shown, that the executive mind is "imperfectly rational." But, he says, the problem with abandoning our rational ideal of management ignores the fact that even if executives do not think systematically and logically, organizations still must try to act rationally in pursuit of the firm's goals. As part of this focus on creating effective organizational processes, Isenberg concludes:

One alternative to the vain task of trying to rationalize managers is to increase the rationality of organizational systems and processes. Although organizational behavior is never completely rational, managers can design and program processes and systems that will approach rationality in resource allocation and employment.[39]

Isenberg argues that it is important for top management to rationalize certain organizational functions because "rational systems free senior executives to tackle the ambiguous, ill-defined tasks that the human mind is uniquely capable of addressing."[40] This seems to make a strong case for the types of computer-based office-support and monitoring applications that executives are employing to save time for more unstructured activities. These ESS applications, which are attempts to rationalize certain organizational and personal systems, will be reported on in detail in the next two chapters.

Isenberg's research builds a strong case for the importance of managerial cognition when studying executive work. Thinking about the senior manager as a decision maker, sense-maker, or organizational-process designer not only shows the wide range of cognitive perspectives on executive work, but it also provides new insights into why and how ESS really can be useful.

Let us examine the three major purposes of ESS in the context of the different conceptions of executive work described above.

Support for Mental Models

Mintzberg, Kotter, Jaques, and Isenberg, among others, all provide insights into the concept of executives' mental models. Mintzberg acknowledges the existence and importance of mental models but, because his focus is executive *activities,* he does not try to relate the significance of mental models to executive work.

Kotter does not explicitly recognize the concept of mental models, but his process view of executive work implicitly depends on the existence of such a concept. From one perspective, agenda building is seen as the determination and prioritization of the problems and opportunities facing executives—a process which is heavily dependent on the implicit or explicit models available to them.[41] Agendas grow more robust as executives come to understand their new roles, as their cognitive maps become stronger, and as the maps are tested and refined by new feedback collected through the executive's network. Kotter says:

> Executives begin the process of developing these agendas immediately after starting their jobs, if not before. They use their knowledge of the businesses and organizations involved along with new information received each day to quickly develop a rough agenda—typically, this contains a very loosely connected and incomplete set of objectives, along with a few specific strategies and plans. Then over time, as more and more information is gathered, they incrementally (one step at a time) make the agendas more complete and more tightly connected.[42]

Isenberg links agendas and mental models when he develops the case for managerial cognition as a critical element in executive work. He points out that "Kotter's notion of the manager's agenda is by definition a *cognitive* structure for organizing the manager's many tasks . . ."[43]

Isenberg also observes:

> Managers have an organized mental map of all the problems and issues facing them. The map is neither static nor permanent; rather, managers continually test, correct, and revise it. In the words of one CEO, "the executive takes advantage of the best cartography at his command, but knows that that is not enough. He knows that along the way he will find things that change his maps or alter his perceptions of the terrain. He trains himself the best he can in the detective skills. He is endlessly sending out patrols to learn greater detail, overflying targets to get some sense of the general battlefield."[44]

Jaques indirectly focuses on the importance of mental models. He points out that the key cognitive difference between level three departmental managers and level four general managers is the *need* for modeling at the fourth level. Identifying the need for conceptual modeling at levels four and above helps explain why some executives would, consciously or unconsciously, try to apply information technology to their model-building processes. Jaques' insights into the cognitive differences between levels of management also suggest that differences should exist between executive support systems and systems designed for lower-level managers.

Reviewing the literature on executive work we learn several things about mental models relevant to our understanding of ESS. There seems to be agreement among researchers that the concept of mental models is critical to understanding executive work. Kotter's concept of agenda-building appears to be based on it. And, in fact, Jaques seems to argue that the work of general managers *requires* mental modeling. Finally, it is somewhat ironic that Mintzberg, whose research on one level seems to argue against executive computer use, was the first of the authors quoted here to suggest that computer support could enrich top-management models of the business. Mintzberg's idea was that the technology would be used by management scientists on the staff to help make the executives' models more explicit, testable, and, thus, easier to communicate. What he did not foresee was that executives would actually be using the technology directly to help them think about their businesses.

We know enough about mental models to talk about them as a critical factor in executive work, and thus, ESS. Cognitive modeling remains enough of a mystery, however, that consciously designing an ESS to help enrich an executive's mental model is still very difficult. To date, systems that support the executive in improving his or her comprehension of reality have almost always been designed with other more concrete goals in mind. Yet, in interviews, many executives return time after time to points which indicate significant ESS use to support, test, or communicate their cognitive maps.

Improving Organizational Planning and Control Systems

Anthony, Mintzberg, Kotter, and Isenberg all contribute to our understanding of how ESS improves organizational systems. Early research in executive support by Rockart and Treacy reported on the use of computer support by individual executives.[45] The first ESS were designed to support top managers alone, with little regard for the system's impact on the organization. Our recent research, however, indicates that this has changed. Indeed, many of the systems perceived to be most successful today are those that have affected changes in the organization's planning and control processes.

Several of the roles identified by Mintzberg—specifically, entrepreneur, monitor, leader, disturbance handler, and resource allocator—all clearly show a need for structured "hard" data. However, standard reporting systems, usually covering from one month to a year, are often inadequate for top management. As Jaques and Kotter point out, top managers have a broader time horizon than that covered by the average formal planning and control system. Executives are interested in information that covers periods ranging from very short term (1–30 days) to 20 years. Working with the newly available information technology, many are striving to change both the information they receive personally and that which is disseminated through the organization. In this way, they are changing their planning and control systems.

Improving organizational planning and control systems is an objective of ESS for two reasons. First, executives need more timely and better-quality data to fulfill today's increasingly demanding roles of monitor and resource allocator. Speeding up the handling of information closes the feedback loop identified by Anthony, and thus increases control in these roles. Increased control can serve to reduce uncertainty, an objective long ago identified by Cyert and March as fundamental.[46] Nowhere is uncertainty more a factor than in top management functions.

The second reason is that developing more rational organizational systems enables top management to focus on other more undefined and uncertain strategic issues. Isenberg says:

> Rational systems free senior executives to tackle the ambiguous, ill-defined tasks that the human mind is uniquely capable of addressing.
>
> In fact, it may seem paradoxical that managers need to create rational systems in order to creatively and incrementally tackle the nonrecurrent problems that defy systematic approaches.[47]

In one sense, the development of executive support systems can be perceived as an attempt by management to rationalize, with the help of automation, as many of their tasks as possible. This allows more time for the highly uncertain and nonsystematic functions, which rightfully should take up most of their time. There are some tasks, which top managers must repeat periodically, such as determining executive compensation, or reviewing monthly sales figures. So systems are set up to support these tasks. Their primary benefits are time saved, and better information available for decision making.

This reasoning has received support from other researchers. Huber, for example, offers this related observation:

> We recognize, of course, that a good deal of the information relevant to top management will not be available through computers. Certainly a good deal of politically or socially sensitive information will not. What C² (computers and communications) technology will do, however, is reduce the amount of time needed to scan less sensitive environments and thus produce more time for chats and gossip sessions that provide the soft and sensitive information that the manager needs to complete his or her mental model.[48]

Organizational systems are linked to mental models. It is evident in our research that executives are using ESS to communicate their own mental models of the business to the rest of the organization. Usually, they do this by changing the planning and control systems. These enhanced systems, in turn, help enrich the executive's mental model. Thus, it is an interactive process. Developing an ESS to improve planning and control processes will often enhance the top manager's way of thinking about the business, which, in turn, will lead to the development of better systems that further enhance the mental model.

Office Applications

Compared to the literature on mental models and planning and control systems, management theorists have written little about enhancing the efficiency or effectiveness of senior management through improved office systems.

There are, however, some "glancing blows" from the literature which point out the value of improved office systems for senior management. The applications which fall into the domain of office automation usually do one of two things for the users: improve communications, or improve access to information. What is known about executive work supports the need for these systems. Virtually all of Mintzberg's roles argue for communications support. Communications also pervades Anthony's framework for planning and control. And Kotter's concept of developing a network implies a need to improve communications capabilities. Given these needs for better communication, it should not be surprising that electronic mail is one of the most common ESS applications.

With regard to the need to provide improved systems for information access, Isenberg contends that executives try to rationalize their organization's systems to simplify the task of running the organization. This particular tendency would logically extend to their own information-access systems. Tickler files, automated Rolodexes, and calendaring are all evidence of this drive to simplify as many personal systems as possible.

CONCLUSION

The views we hold of executive work greatly influence how we think about executive support systems.[49] Reviewing the literature on top management work serves two purposes. First, it can point to areas in which computer-based systems can logically aid managers. Second, reviewing the literature can help ESS researchers, developers, and users become more conscious of the implicit models they have of the executive function. Only by making these beliefs explicit can we begin to reflect on their influence on ESS design.

It is evident that the applications of computer-based systems at senior management levels are diverse. Each is targeted at fulfilling specific needs of a particular executive. Yet the bulk of the applications which are viewed as successful by the executives we interviewed do appear to fall within one of the three categories mentioned at the outset. The applications themselves will be reviewed in Chapters 4–6.

NOTES

1. Peter G.W. Keen and Richard D. Hackathorn, "Decision Support Systems and Personal Computing," *Working Paper No.47*, Center for Information Systems Research, Sloan School of Management, MIT, Cambridge, Mass., October 1979, p. 4.

2. Karl E. Weick, "Theoretical Assumptions and Research Methodology Selection," in *The Information Systems Research Challenge,* edited by F. Warren McFarlan (Boston, Mass.: Harvard Business School Press, 1984).
3. Henry Mintzberg, *The Nature of Managerial Work* (New York: Harper & Row, 1973).
4. Ibid., p. 10.
5. Sune Carlson, *Executive Behavior: A Study of the Work Load and the Working Methods of Managing Directors* (Stockholm: Strombergs, 1951).
6. Henry Mintzberg, *The Nature of Managerial Work* (New York: Harper & Row, 1973), p. 203–4.
7. Ibid., chapter 4.
8. Copyright © 1975 by the President and Fellows of Harvard College; all rights reserved. Reprinted by permission of *Harvard Business Review.* "Manager's Job: Folklore and Fact," by Henry Mintzberg (July-August 1975), p. 54.
9. Henry Mintzberg, *The Nature of Managerial Work* (New York: Harper & Row, 1973), p. 70.
10. Ibid., p. 89–90.
11. Ibid., p. 157.
12. Robert N. Anthony, *Planning and Control Systems: A Framework for Analysis* (Boston, Mass.: Division of Research, Harvard Business School, 1965).
13. Ibid., pp. 16–18.
14. Norbert Weiner, *Cybernetics: or Control and Communication in the Animal and Machine* (Cambridge, Mass.: MIT Press, 1948).
15. Stafford Beer, *Cybernetics and Management* (New York: Wiley & Sons, 1959).
16. Kenneth A. Merchant, *Control in Business Organizations* (Marshfield, Mass.: Pitman, 1985).
17. Ibid.
18. William Ouchi, "A Conceptual Framework for the Design of Organization Control Mechanisms," *Management Science,* vol. 25, (September 1979).
19. J. D. Thompson, *Organizations in Action* (New York: McGraw-Hill, 1967).
20. Oliver E. Williamson, *Markets and Hierarchies* (New York: Free Press, 1975).
21. John P. Kotter, *The General Managers* (New York: The Free Press, a Division of Macmillan, Inc., 1982).

22. John P. Kotter, "What Effective General Managers Really Do," *Harvard Business Review,* vol. 60, no. 6 (November-December 1982), p. 160.
23. From THE GENERAL MANAGERS by John P. Kotter. Copyright © 1982 by The Free Press, a Division of MacMillan, Inc. Reprinted by permission of the publisher, p. 61.
24. Elliott Jaques, *A General Theory of Bureaucracy* (Hampshire, England: Gower Publishing Co., 1976).
25. Ibid., p. 109.
26. Ibid., p. 139.
27. Ibid., p. 147.
28. Ibid., p. 149.
29. Herbert A. Simon, *Administrative Behavior* (New York: Macmillan Company, 1957).
30. Peter G.W. Keen, " 'Interactive' Computer Systems for Managers: A Modest Proposal," *Sloan Management Review,* Fall 1976.
31. Jeffrey H. Moore, "Senior Executive Computer Use." Unpublished paper, Stanford Graduate School of Business, Palo Alto, Calif., (1986).
32. Arthur P. Brief and H. Kirk Downey, "Cognitive and Organizational Structures: A Conceptual Analysis of Implicit Organizing Theories," *Human Relations,* vol. 36, no. 12 (1983).
33. Gordon Donaldson and Jay W. Lorsch, *Decision Making at the Top* (New York: Basic Books, 1983).
34. Ibid., p. 9.
35. Karl E. Weick, *The Social Psychology of Organizing* (Reading, Mass.: Addison-Wesley, 1979).
36. P.N. Johnson-Laird, *Mental Models* (Cambridge, Mass.: Harvard University Press, 1973), p. 397, 402, 410. Reprinted by permission.
37. Michael E. Treacy, "Supporting Senior Executives' Models for Planning and Control," in *The Rise of Managerial Computing,* John F. Rockart and Christine V. Bullen, eds. (Homewood, Ill: Dow Jones-Irwin, 1986), pp. 172–174.
38. Daniel J. Isenberg, "How Senior Managers Think," *Harvard Business Review,* November-December, 1984, p. 82.
39. Copyright © 1975 by the President and Fellows of Harvard College; all rights reserved. Reprinted by permission of *Harvard Business Review.* "How Managers Think," by Daniel J. Isenberg, November-December 1984, p. 88.
40. Ibid., p. 89.
41. William F. Pounds, "The Process of Problem Finding," *Sloan Management Review,* Fall 1969, pp. 1–19.

42. Copyright © 1975 by the President and Fellows of Harvard College; all rights reserved. Reprinted by permission of *Harvard Business Review.* "What Effective General Managers Really Do," by John P. Kotter, vol. 60, no. 6, (November-December 1982b), p. 161.
43. Daniel J. Isenberg, *Managerial Thinking: An Inquiry Into How Senior Managers Think.* Forthcoming book, p. 12.
44. Copyright © 1975 by the President and Fellows of Harvard College; all rights reserved. Reprinted by permission of *Harvard Business Review.* "How Senior Managers Think," by Daniel J. Isenberg, November-December 1984, p. 87
45. John F. Rockart and Michael E. Treacy, "The CEO Goes On-Line," *Harvard Business Review,* January-February 1982.
46. Richard M. Cyert and James G. March, *A Behavioral Theory of the Firm* (Englewood Cliffs, New Jersey: Prentice-Hall, 1963).
47. Copyright © 1975 by the President and Fellows of Harvard College; all rights reserved. Reprinted by permission of *Harvard Business Review.* "How Senior Managers Think," by Daniel J. Isenberg, November-December 1984, p. 89.
48. George P. Huber, "The Nature and Design of Post-Industrial Organizations," *Management Science,* vol. 30, no. 8 (August 1984), p. 947.
49. Michael E. Treacy and David W. De Long, "Executive Support Systems Technology and Design." Unpublished paper, October 1985.

CHAPTER 4

THE USE OF ESS FOR OFFICE SUPPORT APPLICATIONS

Virtually all executives believe there is much more to do than time allows. This, at least implicitly, leads to a concern for being more efficient. Business psychologists Greiff and Munter write:

> Time is the prime source of pressure for executives. *Time.* "I'm always trying to be such a good guy, being a boss, father and husband. I just never have any bloody time for myself." Executives worry about schedules, deadlines, quarterly and annual reviews and "getting there first." But they also worry about time to play, time to educate themselves in fields of special interest, time to grow personally, time for family, time that isn't programmed, time to do nothing.[1]

In *The Effective Executive,* Drucker offers a related perspective:

> The executive's time tends to belong to everybody else. If one attempted to define an "executive" operationally (that is, through his activities) one would have to define him as a captive of the organization. Everybody can move in on his time, and everybody does. There seems to be very little any one executive can do about it. He cannot, as a rule, like the physician, stick his head out the door and say to the nurse, "I won't see anybody for the next half hour." Just at this moment, the executive's telephone rings, and he has to speak to the company's best customer or to a high official in the city administration or to his boss—and the next half hour is already gone.[2]

Drucker goes on to predict, in his 1967 book, that the time shortage for executives will only get worse in the future. He concludes:

> One important reason for this is that a high standard of living presupposes an economy of innovation and change. But innovation and change make inordinate time demands on the executive.[3]

Twenty years later, innovation and change are more pertinent than ever. And the time pressures on senior management certainly have not diminished. In response to these pressures, many senior executives are seeking information-technology assistance to increase their efficiency in many day-to-day tasks. For help in this area, they are utilizing office support functions of ESS. Although *office automation* is the term commonly used for many of the functions described in this chapter, it is a catchall whose boundaries are not clear. To an increasing number of information systems (IS) researchers there are huge differences between office *automation,* which suggests the mechanization of office tasks, and *support,* which implies aiding the person in the accomplishment of a task. For the balance of this book, therefore, we use the term *office support* for those applications which provide efficiency gains in day-to-day office tasks.

Top management's ever-present sense of a time shortage is one of two driving forces behind executive use of office support (OS)systems. The other is the aggressive marketing of computer-based office systems by major vendors. Let us briefly highlight these two forces (a market pull and a supplier push) behind OS-based ESS, and then discuss the applications they generate.

The Market Pull

"Just get me a system that will save me time," was the plaintive cry of one computer company vice president, who echoes the words of many executives. Virtually all senior managers experience great time pressures, and their need for help in reducing time constraints is painfully obvious to those around them.

Mintzberg sums up the problem this way:

> My own study of chief executives found no break in the pace of activity during office hours. The mail . . . telephone calls . . . and

meetings . . . accounted for almost every minute from the moment these men entered their offices in the morning until they departed in the evenings. A true break seldom occurred. Coffee was taken during meetings, and lunch time was almost always devoted to formal or informal meetings. When free time appeared, ever-present subordinates quickly usurped it.[4]

The executive assistant to the chairman of Northern Bank studied his boss's work habits and found that the chairman spent an average of nine minutes on each issue that came before him in the course of a day. "We realized that every nine minutes we could save the chairman by applying the technology would enable him to deal with one more topic that day," said the assistant.

Consultant Bruce Henderson, on the other hand, highlights the time drain of ceremonial functions and "fire fighting," saying:

> Ordinarily, the day-to-day demands on top executive time require a large amount of effort to perform the ceremonial functions. For example, anyone who reads the daily reports on the activities of the chief executive of the United States cannot help wondering when he has any time left for business. Equally pressing are the demands for controlling the organization. Some call this "fire-fighting"—solving the ever present problems of operation.
>
> Only after the needs of operating and controlling the organization have been satisfied is there any time available for planning the future. Yet it is precisely in the growth planning area that there is no substitute or delegate who can replace the chief executive.[5]

The Supplier Push

The other major force promoting office support systems for top management is the ready availability of this type of software for ESS designers, and the relative ease of installation of OS packages. Products like IBM's PROFS, DEC's ALL-IN-ONE, and Data General's CEO are being marketed aggressively.

This is a classic case of "technology-push." The office has become an important battlefield for vendors. Often OS systems enter the organization at lower levels, and the cost of spreading them to the top levels of the firm seems relatively small.

This perception of low cost and easy implementation, however, can be an unfortunate lure and trap for ESS designers. In far too many cases, we have seen these "easy" OS systems dropped onto executive desks without sufficient thought about how they will be used.

An OS smorgasbord is a passive and technology-driven approach to supporting executives with its cafeteria-style selection of electronic mail, word processing, spreadsheets, graphics, and calendaring. In a situation where the executive has given little thought to the kind of support *needed* to perform the job better, he or she is often loath to commit the time necessary for learning to operate the system. A considerable number of systems have languished or failed because of this.[6]

Nonetheless, the number of office-support-oriented ESS is growing. And, where the application fits a well-defined and well-understood management need, these systems can be extremely useful. We have identified seven types of OS applications being used by executives today. They fall into three categories:

1. Communications-based applications: electronic mail, news, and word processing.
2. Data analysis tools: spreadsheets.
3. Organizing tools: electronic calendars, automated Rolodexes, tickler files, etc.

The communications-based applications seem to be the most significant, yet some executives do find the other OS capabilities useful. We will look at each of these in turn.

COMMUNICATIONS-BASED APPLICATIONS

Electronic Mail

In 1972, Mintzberg wrote:

> One can perhaps visualize the organization of the future with teletype terminals in the offices of each senior executive. Then, true to the managers' information needs, the transmission of instant communication would be automated. The transmitter of information would simply choose which managers were to receive a current bit of news. He would then key in the code to

open the proper channels, and would enter the message which would appear simultaneously in the appropriate offices.[7]

Mintzberg's vision is coming true, albeit in a somewhat different form. The teletype has turned into a PC, but the "transmission of instant communication" is becoming a reality. By far, the most significant OS application for executives is electronic mail (EM). Electronic mail provides terminal-to-terminal (one-to-one or one-to-many) communication of what is usually a text-based message, memo, or report. The capability also exists to "mail" graphics, as well as tabular material, such as spreadsheets.

EM—Getting Started
Electronic mail springs from different roots and follows different development patterns from organization to organization. In a few cases, EM has developed to the point where virtually every manager and employee in the firm has access to a terminal with one or several mail systems. The 3,000 terminals in Lincoln National's home office provide communication capabilities for the firm's top managers. At the Beneficial Corporation 600 terminals were installed in a single year, starting in the offices of the top 40 executives.

The presidents of these two companies are avid hands-on users of their EM systems. Beneficial's chairman Finn Caspersen receives 30–40 messages a day. Lincoln's chief executive Ian Rolland insists that the system has increased his own productivity 10–15 percent because he can communicate with his subordinates so much faster.

Interestingly, these two companies achieved their heavy penetration of electronic mail very differently. Lincoln installed terminals in the offices of their executives in 1980. The system's designers took a "tool–box" approach, providing any user who wished it with an assortment of office support applications. Electronic mail was not viewed as a critical application at the outset. In fact, CEO Ian Rolland used the system primarily for management control. Over time, however, electronic mail has become the feature that has had the greatest impact on the organization.

At Beneficial, CEO Finn Caspersen recognized the potential benefits of providing communication capabilities for his management team, and pushed to have an office support system installed throughout the organization from the top down in 1984. Electronic mail immediately became the primary application, with Caspersen one of its leading proponents.

At ConAgra, a major food and agricultural products firm, CEO and Chairman Mike Harper has taken a somewhat different and more exclusive tack for the electronic mail system he initiated. At first, the ESS was directed towards only about 75 senior managers, but, like many successful systems, it has since expanded and is today providing worldwide communications capabilities for about 180 managers. Its use is expected to expand even further. The electronic mail capability was developed because Harper wanted to have real-time, as well as asynchronous, communication with his executives. The system includes filing, "blind copy" capability, and tickler file functions.

Harper did not force electronic-mail use, but made clear to his subordinates that the fastest way to get messages to him was via E-mail. He regularly uses the terminal for one and a half hours in the morning, arriving at the office at 6:30 A.M. and working at it until 8:00 A.M. Continual use is made of the system during the day. When talking on the phone, Harper may put his headset on and pull up items from the electronic mail files. Often, he checks on an individual's file to ensure that he covers appropriate issues. He also uses the electronic mail system to file information about other people and projects.

In some high-tech organizations, electronic mail use spreads very rapidly and widely. GenRad is a large manufacturer of automated test equipment, and Donald Sundue, corporate director of MIS, says, "The demand for electronic mail was far greater than expected, resulting in rapid implementation throughout all levels of the company. Executives, many of whom were reluctant users at first, found the system indispensable in meeting their communication requirements and eliminating telephone tag."[8]

In contrast to these cases, however, the penetration of electronic mail is frequently more uneven. In most companies, EM is not so pervasive or integrated that the CEO in New York City can communicate with the sales manager in Boise, Idaho. Usually, EM spreads irregularly through an organization when initiated by top management. It may be used heavily by a few vice presidents or division general managers and, hence, by their subordinates; but only occasionally by other vice presidents, and rarely by the chief executive. At Owens Corning Fiberglas, when an ESS was installed, the six senior executives involved each used the system for different purposes. Initially, only one used electronic mail extensively and required that his subordinates use it as well.

Executives use EM in two ways. There are those who make hands-on use of this technology, sending and receiving messages on their terminals. And there are a significant number of executives who delegate EM use to their secretaries.

Even among managers who type and read messages on their ESS, there is a range of usage. First, there are executives, like Rolland and Caspersen, for whom electronic mail often becomes the primary form of communication within the organization, supplanting some face-to-face meetings and considerable telephone use. These heavy users spend a significant amount of time at the terminal reading mail and typing messages.

A second type of electronic-mail user simply takes advantage of EM as a coordination tool. Instead of typing lengthy messages, many managers send short "two-liners," such as, "Call me tomorrow at 4 P.M. and be prepared to talk about. . . ." The chairman of a large manufacturing company notes that he saves a tremendous amount of time using EM in this way, particularly when dealing with managers at distant plants.

In contrast to the "hands-on" approach, often an intermediary, such as the executive's secretary, is used. Many senior managers either do not feel comfortable with or do not feel the need to use the terminal directly for electronic mail. At Northern Bank, the chairman's secretary sorts his messages three times a day and presents him with a hard-copy document containing the important ones. The chairman finds this use of EM valuable because he can still exchange ideas and information with subordinates around the world several times a day in a way that eliminates "telephone tag" and overcomes time-zone differences.

A vice president of sales in a high technology company also uses EM with the help of his secretary. He dictates replies for her to input, but resists typing the messages himself. "It's much easier and more appropriate to let my secretary do it," he says. "She has to manage me and that's not an easy job. If I tried to use electronic mail myself, she'd lose control over me."

What Influences EM Use?

McKenney identifies four variables that influence the use of electronic mail.[9] Although his research was conducted mostly at middle levels of the organization, our data from senior levels parallels his findings. McKenney concludes, "In organizations where there is a wide set of relationships from intensive to occasional EM use, growth in use is heavily dependent upon role models, individual preference, the demands of specific tasks, and the adaptability of the system."[10]

Role models.   As in our research, McKenney found that senior executives who used electronic mail heavily were influential role models. He wrote, "The two most effective champions were senior executives, one the CEO of the insurance company and the other an executive vice president. Both used EM for the majority of their communication. In those organizations most people used EM, which led to another conjecture: . . . EM use by a superior influences managers to use EM, while lack of use by top managers discourages use."[11]

Our data supports this hypothesis, although there were some notable exceptions. Beneficial, Lincoln National, Auto Electronics, Michigan Motors, ConAgra, and Xerox all have executive sponsors who are heavy electronic-mail users, and this is reflected in a high degree of use throughout each organization. In a few unusual cases, however, heavy use by the senior executive is not enough to bring subordinates to the terminal. When the general manager of an auto parts manufacturer tried to force his direct reports to use EM on a PROFS system, the long-time director of engineering told his boss, "If you want to talk with me, pick up the phone and call because I'm not hitting any keys." Years of close friendship allowed the director of engineering to express a view held covertly by others.

Personal style.   McKenney, finding evidence of EM "holdouts" in his research, points to the most significant factor influencing executive EM use—personal style. He described one resistant subordinate as:

> an imposing, eloquent chap who never used EM, but depended on the phone and [face-to-face meetings]. He agreed that he spent more hours in a car going to meetings than needed, but he felt that the meetings were a necessary part of his job and his effectiveness. His job was to define final product specifications of a product with the marketing and engineering people, a negotiating role for which he felt EM was inappropriate. This suggests that EM may not be a universal solution. Jobs that require high social skills may attract individuals with a style that does not include EM use.[12]

McKenney's comment is even more pertinent at the executive level. While many senior managers gladly take up electronic mail, others still find it too impersonal or awkward to use. These executives usually feel strongly about the importance of face-to-face communication, or at least the need to capture nuances from the tone of the other person's voice on the telephone.

Other executives find that electronic mail simply does not fit their work style. A division director at ICL says, "I do about 18 hours of reading per week, most of it outside of working hours. For most of the paperwork I go through I attach a note with the action to be taken. Electronic mail would not work for this." He referred, of course, to his particular system. The "attach a note" feature is widely available on EM systems today.

Nature of the task. McKenney's third variable influencing electronic-mail use is the nature of the specific tasks being performed. He says:

> EM use is more time efficient than other forms of communication and offers useful characteristics for certain tasks, especially tasks that require ongoing communication with several individuals about precise actions. A consistent theme voiced by all EM users was the improved accuracy of messages via EM versus the phone or [face-to-face] meetings, probably due to its written form.[13]

We found that electronic mail use by executives centered on a few types of communication tasks.

1. Coordination: "The time of tomorrow's management committee meeting has been changed to . . ."
2. Monitoring: "What have you done lately on project X?"
3. Passing information: "At lunch today, our supplier told me to expect . . ."
4. Document review: "Let me suggest one change in the draft of that report you sent me . . ."

In each case, EM is used to communicate brief, timely information or queries, as well as to respond to others' requests, while minimizing intrusion on ongoing work.

EM is especially helpful in tasks that involve coordination across time zones. One well-pleased user at Auto Electronics is the director of manufacturing services whose managers are scattered around the world. "Electronic mail has improved the quality of my worklife," he says, "because now I don't have to call Singapore from home late at night. And outlying forces feel more a part of the organization because they are getting information at the same time we are."

Also grappling with time zone problems, the director of European operations for another organization sums up his experience this way:

> One issue I've had to face as a European executive . . . is that it would be easy for me to get out of touch with what's going on in the divisions, at corporate [headquarters], and in the subsidiaries. I need to keep at least weekly contact with people in the U.S. divisions, and I often need daily communication with them. I'm in contact with corporate [headquarters] approximately 25 times a week. If I tried to do all this by phone, I'd be on the phone all day. . . . the time-zone problem is alleviated by electronic mail. We have a branch of the company in Japan that is the counterpart to this organization. Japan is now on electronic mail and it's like we found them again! We simply couldn't call them on the phone because of the time zone problem.[14]

In a 1986 speech, C.J. Murphy, senior vice president of Kodak, sounded the same note, saying, "Another benefit of our communications network is the ability to inquire about data—anywhere in the world, any time of the day. Thus, even though there is a 14-hour time difference between my office and my plant manager's in Australia, I can touch base with him through a query on my electronic communications system. And he can respond in the same way. I remember when I'd have to sit up half the night to place a direct call on an urgent matter."[15]

At ICL, the director of Group Information Services for the British computer manufacturer has nine managers covering 16 sites in the U.K. He says, "Because everyone is traveling so much, we can spend days trying to reach people." He insists that his staff use EM.

The general manager of Michigan Motors believes, however, that electronic mail should *not* be used for certain tasks. "For example," he says, "when sales forecasts are being changed or updated, I want people to talk with me. I want to be able to respond to my managers whether their data is good or bad. It's okay to use electronic mail as a reference—information after the fact. But the human nuances—the way people look, their attitudes, feelings—that go with information being delivered in person are missing from the system, and that bothers me."

System capability. Another variable identified by McKenney as influencing electronic mail usage is the adaptability and user friendliness of a specific system:

> The company A system was very simple to use, with electronic mail as its primary purpose. The result was that users in company A all felt comfortable with the system and could use it on a sporadic basis, as needed. With only five commands to learn in a simple protocol, a novice at company A could become a competent mail user after 15 minutes of instruction.
>
> Company B's system was an elegant workstation system that included electronic mail. In company B, users required about eight hours of training. ... The complexity of company B's system made it difficult to use casually. One became an experienced user or tended not to use it or to hand it over to a secretary.[16]

Executives are notoriously inconsistent in their use of computers because of heavy travel schedules and the demands of current business problems. The executive may use his terminal five days in a row and then not turn it on for three weeks. Thus a mail system whose commands are difficult to remember is likely to be discarded, or, at the least, to get used much less than a simpler system.

The Advantages of Electronic Mail

Now that we have examined the major variables influencing the use of electronic mail, let us examine the benefits—and drawbacks—of EM use for executives.

First, it can provide logistical support, helping executives communicate more efficiently with more people. In his research, McKenney found that users could send four to five electronic-mail messages in the time it took for every phone call. A vice president for strategic planning at Lincoln National recalls that in order to inform subordinates before electronic mail, he would send a memo through the central word processing department and then wait several days for it to be delivered by inter-office mail. But now, using word processing and EM, he can communicate technical planning data throughout his organization in a couple of minutes. In addition, a "certified mail" feature lets him know who has received and read the message.

Electronic mail reduces the "information float" in an organization because subordinates can no longer claim, rightly or wrongly, that the boss's memo was delayed in the inter-office mail. One company president saw the response to his routine queries drop from an average of ten days to three days when he began communicating with subordinates by electronic mail.

Beneficial's chairman Finn Caspersen enjoys a similar quick response time:

> For me, the computer is a communication device, and the primary function of the chairman is to communicate. . . . I use it both to send and receive all my internal mail. I generate 90 to 95 percent of my electronic mail by typing it myself, despite the fact that I'm a very poor typist! It allows me to operate in a whole different time frame. Instead of having a memo wind its way through the system for five to seven days, I can get a response in half an hour.[17]

This phenomenon, however, is not universally appreciated. One middle manager put it this way:

I hated electronic mail at first because you had to respond quicker than in the past. There was no buffer anymore. I couldn't use the interoffice mail system as an excuse or claim that it was stuck in somebody else's in-basket. I was doing twice the work I had been doing before the system came in. But after six months I got used to it, and I started sending memos over the system myself, instead of going to the word processing center. Over time, I realized it was to my advantage to use electronic mail—when I wanted a response fast or wanted to cover myself by having the correspondence on file.

EM also makes communications more efficient by reducing telephone tag. A study of electronic-mail users at Manufacturers Hanover Trust showed that senior managers estimated EM use saved them an average of 23 minutes per day.[18] Reporting on findings in two banks, McKenney says:

The shift from phone to EM systems reduced by 6–7 percent the time managers spent communicating. . . . Internal phone use was negligible for the groups that relied on EM. All users seemed satisfied that EM helped them communicate more quickly and reliably, eliminating telephone tag.[19]

Not only does electronic mail have the potential of making the executive a more efficient and effective communicator, it can also increase his or her visibility into the organization. Executives using electronic mail experience an extended reach, presence, and sense of control. Because they can communicate more often, executives find it easier to delegate. One senior vice president explained it this way:

It's very hard to teach managers when to yell for help. Either they yell too early, in which case you're doing their job, or they yell too late when they're already in trouble. But electronic mail gives me a way to nudge someone. It gives me a delicate touch and allows me a wider span of control. Electronic mail is a very non-threatening form of management.

Data on how electronic mail will impact the span of control for middle and upper management is still sparse, but an increasing number of executives are predicting EM will make a difference. Raymond Le Boeuf, purchasing vice president at

PPG Industries, a glass, paint, and chemicals manufacturer, suggests that management structures will flatten out once senior managers begin using electronic mail. He says, "You're going to have fewer top managers and more people reporting to them."[20]

Caspersen at Beneficial also foresees fewer layers of management: "The span of control is so much better. . . . I can communicate with or yank figures from any manager anywhere. We can make a decision now in a quarter to half the time it took before."[21]

There are also benefits derived from using a terminal at home to access the firm's electronic-mail system. Lincoln National's chief executive travels often and regularly accesses his terminal at home. He says, "This means that I can access the system at night and expedite the notes and memos that have accumulated while I was gone, so I don't spend hours the next morning going through paper that has accumulated on my desk. It helps me manage my time." Not only does EM enable him to handle this "paperwork" without secretarial support, but it also eases the bottleneck his travel creates for subordinates trying to communicate with him.

EM access at home also allows more spontaneous communication of ideas. The chairman of a large manufacturing company says, "Having a personal computer at home helps me sleep better. When I used to wake up in the middle of the night with a problem on my mind, the more I tried to forget it the less I was able to fall back asleep. Now if that happens, I go to my computer and make a notation. Or, I send a message to someone else so they can worry about it."[22] Lest this sound strange, think how often executives jot notes to themselves using pencil and paper.

Of the 10 companies we studied where electronic mail was the predominent ESS application, six equipped their executives with terminals at home. Other research bears out this finding of 50–60 percent home terminal usage among executives.[23]

And the Disadvantages.

There is potentially a negative side to accessing electronic mail at home. When Auto Electronics installed DEC Pro 350 terminals in the homes of its 14 senior executives, the general manager became an active user of electronic mail on nights and weekends. Wives soon found their husbands regularly sneaking off to check their terminals for messages from the boss. The potential of the technology to allow work to intrude even more than it already does on an executive's personal life has not gone unnoticed in companies where a workaholic chief executive inadvertently uses electronic mail to impose his or her workstyle on others. One planning director characterized the problem this way:

> The technology tempts you to work even longer hours because the difference between your home and office environment and, for that matter, between your car and office (thanks to cellular phones), is shrunk significantly. Now, in a sense that's an advantage because it helps you organize your life better. But it also places the temptation for becoming a workaholic rather strongly in front of you.

Another potentially negative side effect of linking to a company-wide EM system is the proliferation of junk mail. Subordinates may begin sending copies of irrelevant messages to top management and it can become necessary to find a way to filter out these unwanted communications. This problem may grow in the future as electronic mail becomes more common. One executive vice president already experiencing the problem says, "There is a danger in electronic messaging because the system commands no priority, and I'm getting a proliferation of garbage. My adrenelin goes up when I log onto the system and see 'mail waiting.' I expect that it's important. This happened the other day and what I got was some innocuous message about bond trading. I thought, 'so what?'" To address this problem, some managers have begun demanding a "quick delete" key on their systems.

Other executives are not concerned about junk mail, feeling that miscellaneous, incidental communication keeps them in touch with the organization and justifies the effort of scanning through some irrelevant material. Beneficial's Caspersen expresses this point of view. He says, "Our next step is to get the system into all of our field offices. I'm sure I will receive an influx of messages from the field at that time, but as long as they're valid that doesn't bother me. . . . If someone wants to communicate with me, this is an open door invitation and frankly, I've always encouraged that. I want to make it easy and rewarding."[24]

Finally, some executives are uneasy about the possible impacts of the decline in interpersonal contact created by heavy EM use. Intuitively, they recognize the value of informal, unscheduled meetings, but as yet are unable to articulate what is lost by reducing the number of these exchanges. A manufacturing vice president expresses his reservations:

> If we all started using electronic mail a lot, I'm afraid we would stop telephoning each other, and we'd meet with each other less. That can be bad because there is only so much information you can put on a spreadsheet. And the English language, or any written language, is not capable of handling the innuendoes and nuances. You can write something on the screen and it can be interpreted four different ways by four different people. So, when it comes to automation, we must be conscious of manager-to-manager interfaces as well.
>
> I've had experiences where I have called another executive and said, "Hey, why the hell didn't you tell me this meeting was on?" And he said, "I did. I sent you a note on E-mail." But I didn't access the mail system that day. That's a problem.

Access To News

Electronic mail is by far the most significant capability offered in OS-based executive support systems, but other applications are also having an effect on how executives work. One such application provides access to internal and external news.

By "news" we mean generally-circulated information about what is happening inside a company, as well as summaries of external events relevant to the business. Internal news often appears in an automated company newsletter or electronic bulletin board. External news is provided through commercial news organizations such as Dow Jones News/Retrieval or United Press International, or through stock quotation services such as Dow Jones Stock Quote Reporter. We make a distinction between an application that provides access to sources of *general* news, and one providing structured access to external data about the firm's competitive position, performance, or potential in the market-place. The former is discussed here. We will deal with the latter in Chapter 6.

Access to general internal news is marginally useful for top management. Where it is available, executives may find it of interest, but not critical to their function. One sales director uses an internal videotext service which links his region's 28 sites and provides information on company activities, such as planned marketing events. "I use the system for browsing and to see what people are doing," he says.

External news summaries are generally seen as more valuable than internal news. Corporate executives at Boeing use the system to monitor stock prices, and to review a "morning report," a daily summary of current events relevant to the company, filed out of Boeing's Washington, D.C., office. The executive vice president of a consumer products firm finds computer access to a data summary of the *Wall Street Journal* to be very useful. The director of sales mentioned earlier gets news bulletins on takeover and merger activities involving his major customers. In another example, the vice president of corporate affairs for a Chicago-based conglomerate monitored Reuters and Dow Jones News/Retrieval Service for news that might affect his corporation's stock price. And, he followed the firm's as well as competitors' stock prices on a Quotron terminal.

One senior executive who often accessed news items in the trade press is Lee Paschall, former CEO and president of American Satellite Company. He began using computers in the mid–1970s, as director of the Defense Communications Agency, and continued his hands-on practice when he joined ASC in 1981. He says:

> At American Satellite I became an inveterate daily user of computers. In particular, I was using an external data base called Tele/Scope. Every morning when I went into the office at American Satellite, I accessed the data base and scanned the topics that had been entered the day before. Typically, there were 70 items in the topical headlines and I would read five to ten of them in detail.
>
> [Data accessing] enormously reduced the amount of paper I was reading. In the telecommunications industry, in particular

in the satellite communications business, there are an enormous number of technical publications and a myriad of stories each day in the trade press. Moreover, this greatly increased when we went through divestiture. The data base tracked an extensive number of publications—for example, the *Washington Post*, the *New York Times*, The *Financial Times* of London, as well as all of the trade press such as *Communications News*, *Aviation Week*, *Data Communications*. It also tracked the public releases of the FCC and the state public utilities commissions. I simply could not have covered this many periodicals personally without the system."[25]

Is this access to news useful? Paschall points to a number of instances where timely access to external information made a big difference to the company:

There was one situation where an FCC order was expected regarding the orbital spacing of satellites. The order could have had a direct effect on our planning efforts. The legal staff at American Satellite had not expected an early decision on this matter. A very small, easily overlooked paragraph in the *Wall Street Journal* indicated that such a decision was imminent. I was able to alert the legal staff and we were able to react much more quickly than we otherwise would have. Other examples like this were prevalent in tracking the status of new products from other vendors of satellite equipment and services. A competitor would announce a new rate or service and we were able to begin to react that same day rather than a week or so later when their press release finally would get around to us.[26]

Brad Butler, retired chairman of Procter & Gamble, also scanned the headlines of major newspapers on his ESS. Butler noted that terminal access allowed him to "get through the scanning process in a fraction of the time it would otherwise take and to quickly determine which articles to read."

The monitoring of stock prices frequently turns out to be one of the most popular uses of an ESS. Not only do executives check their firm's performance, and that of competitors, but many use the terminal to monitor and analyze their own investment portfolios. Such personal interests are a blessing in disguise for ESS designers trying to make executives more comfortable with a computer terminal. At Firestone, access to Dow Jones was the first capability offered on an ESS. Today, it remains the most widely used application, even though performance monitoring and modeling capabilities have been added to the system.

The major benefit of computerized news is to provide a faster way of scanning the external environment for information relevant to the business. An ESS attempts to simplify the information-scanning process which, as noted by Isenberg, can help to free up the executive for more critical tasks. News can also provide a diversion for the harried executive, looking for a few moments of "downtime" to relax between stretches of intense work.

Word Processing

One of the most common but least-used applications in ESS is word processing. For the most part, executives do not have the time or the typing skills to sit at a terminal and create a document. There are exceptions, however, more likely to be found among staff than line executives. Three executives we interviewed, holding the titles of vice president for corporate affairs or director of public relations, use word processing for press releases, policy statements, and the like. Since these jobs require a great deal of writing, which often must be done quickly, word processing is a logical tool for the public relations executive.

"I used to sit at a typewriter, pound out a document, and then make twelve copies of what I had written. Then the document would get delivered two days later to the other buildings. Now it goes out throughout the company instantaneously," said the public relations vice president for Auto Electronics, who uses his system "98 percent" for word processing and electronic mail.

The vice president for public relations at a midwestern telephone company also uses both word processing and electronic mail. When asked to announce a major marketing reorganization, the public relations VP created a draft with word processing. Then he talked to the marketing vice president, who was traveling, via mobile telephone to get his input. Later that night, from home, the PR executive called the operations VP, also out of town, to discuss the text. Working at a DEC Mate terminal in his den, the PR executive made the final changes to his reorganization paper. He then dialed up the company's VAX and stored it in the computer so he could print a finished copy of the document at the office the next morning. When combined with electronic mail, word processing enables much faster creation, review, and delivery of documents.

Word processing is more widely used in the rare firm where the culture encourages executives to type. At Lincoln National, a few executives type some of their own memos. A young vice president of strategic planning insisted on typing all his memos and short letters claiming, "I type as fast as I talk."

A more common use of word processing is for special projects. The head of one division at ICL travels too much to use a terminal in the office, but he uses word processing at home to draft speeches and strategy papers, which he then gives to his secretary for editing later. "The main thing I use the PC for is typing longer documents," he says. "I don't actually think it saves me a lot of time, but it helps me edit and re-edit to get the thing right."

Boeing's president, Malcolm Stamper, also likes to write speeches on his IBM PC. He says, "The way I like to sketch out ideas it's impossible to dictate—it's even intimidating. I used to write things out by hand, but now, with word processing, it's much easier to organize my thoughts, to add and change ideas—it's increased my productivity substantially."[27]

Sometimes word processing is used by executives in a different part of the document–creation process. Managers will hand their secretary a memo or letter to input; and then, using a compatibile system, the executive will review and edit the document. One staff planning director uses his word processor to edit spreadsheets that are made into slides for presentations to the management committee. He offered an example:

> To show where we stand in international sales, management in a division laid out a huge spreadsheet showing the state of orders and potential customers. It was transmitted to my system and I used the word processor to personalize the headings on the spreadsheet so that the management committee, instead of looking at some gobbledygook, would know immediately that this was a report for Europe.

The degree to which word processing is used by executives depends on the nature of their work, their typing skills, their philosophy about typing as an executive task, and their writing style. Everyone has different preferences when involved in the creative process of writing. Some managers can only write longhand on legal pads. Others must dictate. Still others prefer to type.

While word processing theoretically allows faster creation and editing of documents, executive time pressures, poor typing skills, and personal preferences in the creative process all suggest that word processing is, at the present time, a very marginal ESS capability. It is very useful for a small number of senior managers, but it will remain irrelevant to most during the late eighties.

DATA ANALYSIS TOOLS

Spreadsheets

Spreadsheet capabilities (e.g., Lotus 1-2-3) are another common feature found in OS-based ESS. Spreadsheet capability is useful for planning and control purposes (Chapter 5), for improving mental models (Chapter 6), and for supporting miscellaneous data analysis which is carried out occasionally by executives. The latter use is discussed here.

Like word processing, spreadsheets are little used by the executives we surveyed. Moore, on the other hand, did find extensive spreadsheet use.[28] From the data he presents, however, it is clear that his sample of organizations was, on the average, less than one-tenth the size of our average company. As Dearden points out, the more operational focus of small company executives could explain this difference.[29]

We suspect there are two reasons why we found little spreadsheet use. First, spreadsheets have detailed command structures that can be time-consuming to learn. Even the use of templates requires learning a certain number of commands and input procedures. An executive vice president at the Sun Company took four days to teach himself Lotus 1-2-3, once he decided he had to understand the software in order to keep up with his subordinates. Almost all line executives we interviewed felt that they could not afford this kind of time to learn and relearn (command structures are easy to forget) an application that is useful only occasionally.

Second, as noted in Chapter 2, an executive's work involves few repetitive decisions that rely heavily on quantitative analysis. Even when necessary, analysis can be delegated to a staff analyst likely to be more practiced at using spreadsheet software. Add to this the often marginal typing skills and the difficulties of data entry for some spreadsheet applications, and it is easy to see why few executives use spreadsheets. We found only about a dozen spreadsheet users among some 100 senior managers in our field interviews.

There are, however, some spreadsheet applications that executives do find very valuable. The most common use we found is for salary and bonus reviews, which may require allocation of a bonus pool and are often too sensitive to delegate. At Auto Electronics, the general manager and personnel director use their spreadsheet package to determine what mix of bonuses should be given to the division's executives. The "what if" capabilities on the system allows them to do what had been an arduous pencil-and-paper task in one-third the time. Similarly, the vice chairman of a Big Eight accounting firm developed a partner compensation data base which he uses each year to determine profit distribution. Because of the spreadsheet software, he claims he is always the first one in the company to finish his annual reviews.

The director of ICL (U.K.) uses a spreadsheet package to analyze weekly or monthly performance. When he gets his numbers, he enters them into the spreadsheet himself. Using another typical spreadsheet application, the director analyzes trends in his firm's competitive position. He does so by comparing ICL's sales data with that of its competition, and allowing the computer to sort the companies into growth order. He concedes that some would criticize him for keying performance data into the spreadsheets himself, but the director insists that it is a trivial job, and that it helps him get a better grasp of the numbers.

The heaviest use of spreadsheets is by financial executives and others with a staff component to their jobs. They tend to have more repetitive tasks for which spreadsheets can be quite helpful. For example, John Dembeck, vice president and treasurer of the Olin Corporation, has become a devotee of spreadsheets. He has developed about 1,000 spreadsheet models on his PC to help him better understand tax, acquisition, and capital-management problems. In detailing Dembeck's computer use, Meyer and Boone report:

> The acquisition situation comes up often. "A company that does a lot of business with Olin was of high interest to us. We were considering acquiring it. Within minutes and after many alternative scenarios, I could tell how long it would take to pay back the investment and achieve the target rate of return. . . . The real beauty of the spreadsheet is that it allows us to examine more alternatives in less time. Timing is important. When an investment banker calls and tells us something is available, we're not the only one they're calling. By using the electronic spreadsheet, we can get back faster with a decision.
>
> "Computers also help me not to miss elements or components of a deal. When structuring a credit agreement, I'm dealing with five to ten banks, using up to a dozen different variable rate spreads. The spreadsheet allows me in a 'what-if' mode to see the effect of all of those alternative rates compared side by side. Missing the impact of one of these alternatives could easily cost us a million dollars. More important, if I miss that optimal alternative, an outsider's perception of management would be 'this guy can be had.' The fact is, that PC puts me ahead of most people out there."[30]

At senior levels, however, spreadsheet use is still limited. International Data Corporation's *Software Watch* stated the general case when it noted, "There is little evidence that the financial planning and modeling systems installed on large systems and these spreadsheets on personal computers have found application in executive suites or in the offices of line managers."[31]

In the end, mastering spreadsheet software takes too much time for most executives, considering how infrequently they use it. And, like most command-driven software, spreadsheets require frequent use or the commands will be forgotten.

ORGANIZING TOOLS

Automated Filing

A number of executives we studied make significant use of electronic filing capabilities through their ESS. Their Rolodex and tickler files are prime candidates for automation. The chairman of one large manufacturing company keeps a data base of more than 800 people, with notations of their business specialties. For example, the chairman says, "If I'm concerned with the housing situation in Phoenix I can go into my data base and see who I know in the construction business there. I can do this all over the world—when you travel you acquire a lot of calling cards."[32]

Boeing's Stamper stores his speeches in a company computer file so he can refer back to them. When he was asked to talk to some visiting NASA officials, he wanted to recall some remarks he had made earlier in the year at the Conference Board. He retrieved the speech from his terminal and skimmed through it just before he went down to meet his visitors.[33]

Stamper also takes his Hewlett-Packard 110 portable computer with him every time he flies out on a business trip. "Having the computer with me when I travel is like taking the office and my files with me," Stamper says.[34]

One of the more sophisticated tickler files we found was developed for the chairman of Northern Bank to track correspondence forwarded to various departments for their input or action. Response time to correspondence passed on by the chairman's office had averaged 15 days. To reduce this, the chairman's staff installed a terminal-based system to track correspondence and monitor response time. Each Friday, the system automatically sent a letter to departments with correspondence outstanding. At the end of each month, the system totaled and ranked the response time of each department, and this list was published. Responses to the chairman's correspondence quickly dropped from an average of 15 to less than 5 days.

At Teledyne, President George Roberts uses a program he wrote to type, store, and retrieve notes from telephone conversations with subordinates. Roberts works at a stand-up desk and keys in notes while he talks on the phone. Later he may retrieve the notes to aid him in follow-up conversations. Mike Harper, CEO at ConAgra, sometimes wears a headset when talking on the phone and often calls up a file for the individual with whom he is speaking. This aids follow-up and ensures that Harper remembers everything he wants to cover.

Filing the executive's notes electronically and automating a Rolodex are ways, in Isenberg's terms, of rationalizing personal systems to provide time for complex unstructured tasks. These ESS applications enable the executive to pay better attention to detail and to follow up more effectively. They also help to better utilize the senior manager's network of external contacts. An important difference between the two applications, however, is that maintaining the automated Rolodex can be delegated to a secretary, while inputting routine notes can be done only by the executive who is a facile typist, and who is willing to integrate a keyboard into the daily routine.

Calendaring

Another frequently mentioned but seldom-used OS application is calendaring. ESS designers often offer this to top management as part of an OS package, but only occasionally is it used. There are several reasons for this.

First, the software, which allows executives to manage their appointment calendars on a terminal, is often not easy enough to use to comfortably fit the needs of senior managers. It is easier to delegate responsibility for the calendar to a secretary.

Another reason calendaring is not more widely used is that, in some organizations, executives are reluctant to share their calendars with their colleagues. Appointments may be too sensitive (a meeting with a merger candidate) or too personal (a golf game) to risk exposure. In addition, sharing reduces control.

For example, revealing an opening on a Wednesday afternoon makes it harder to turn down a chatty subordinate when the time could be better spent elsewhere.

One benefit a few companies have gained by using electronic calendars, however, is that it is easier to schedule meetings because the system identifies when those attending are available. At Xerox, a master calendar is circulated to top managers notifying them of all scheduled management committee meetings. This has improved coordination.

At Phillips petroleum, Executive Vice President Robert Wallace insists that his managers keep their calendars on the group's PROFS system so that Wallace can have access to his subordinates' schedules. Wallace explains, "With all of my people on the system, if I need to know where they are, or if I'm trying to set up a meeting, my secretary can go into PROFS and run a program. In just a few seconds she can determine what days might be most viable for setting up a group meeting."

In the last few years, we have seen a growing number of executives, like Wallace, who are willing to automate their calendars, or at least let their secretaries do it. These calendars may or may not be shared with other managers. At ICL, four of eight executives who have ESS use calendaring as a personal support tool. It is no surprise that the two who use it most are excellent typists. The director of business operations describes his experience this way:

> I don't keep a paper diary anymore. My secretary maintains my calendar on her terminal, and every night she gives me a save of it, and I take the cartridge home and load it into my computer there. If I amend it at home, when I am in the next morning, she loads from the amended cassette.
>
> I find this calendar more easily updated, but in a sophisticated manner, like moving an appointment to another day while preserving the text of it. It gives me a better overview of my schedule and allows me to study it at home.
>
> For example, I might see that a certain weekly meeting always runs over on Thursdays, and we would do better scheduling them on Tuesdays instead. And, working under more peaceful circumstances at home, I could see whether I could change a whole pattern of meetings in future months. You'd never do that with a paper calendar. Reorganizing your life on a "what if" basis in

peaceful circumstances without having to erase everything is much easier.

The above examples notwithstanding, we would expect management team use of electronic calendaring to grow rather slowly. It will be a key application only in the few companies where the top executive strongly dictates its use. Otherwise, automated calendars appear to over-rationalize the fluid process of managing an executive's time.

CONCLUSION

Executive support systems built on standard office automation packages are a very common type of ESS. The applications are well understood and easy to install. Except for news and electronic mail, which have had a dramatic impact in some cases, OS applications have proved to be of limited value to most executives.

As OS-based ESS software matures, however, executives are bound to find more and more creative applications in an ongoing effort to rationalize routine office systems. The objective always is to increase efficiency so that more time can be devoted to critical business problems. By definition, however, the impact of these organizational tools on executives and the firm will be relatively limited.

NOTES

1. Barrie S. Greiff and Preston K. Munter, *Tradeoffs* (New York: Mentor, 1981), p. 163.
2. Peter F. Drucker, *The Effective Executive* (New York: Harper & Row, 1967), pp. 10–11.
3. Ibid., p. 34
4. Henry Mintzberg, *The Nature of Managerial Work* (New York: Harper & Row, 1973), p. 30.
5. Bruce D. Henderson, *Henderson on Corporate Strategy* (New York: Mentor, 1982), pp. 58–59.
6. Eliot Levinson, "The Implementation of Executive Support Systems," *Working Paper No. 119*, Center for Information Systems

Research, Sloan School of Management, MIT, Cambridge, Mass., October 1984.

7. Henry Mintzberg, "The Myths of MIS," © 1982 by the Regents of the University of California. Reprinted from the *California Management Review*, vol. 15, no. 1 (Fall 1972), p. 97. By permission of The Regents.

8. Donald G. Sundue, "Genrad's On-Line Executives," *DSS-86 Transactions*, Conference on Decision Support Systems, Washington, D.C. Published by The Institute of Management Sciences, Providence, R.I., p. 16.

9. James L. McKenny, "The Influence of Computer-Communications on Organizational Information Processing." Working paper, Boston, Mass.: Harvard Business School, 1985.

10. Ibid., p. 35.

11. Ibid., p. 8.

12. Ibid., p. 18.

13. Ibid., p. 23.

14. N. Dean Meyer and Mary E. Boone, *The Information Edge* (Agincourt, Ontario: Gage Educational Publishing, 1987), p. 220.

15. C.J. Murphy, "The Global Factory: Managing the 'New Realities' In Worldwide Manufacturing" Speech to Society For Information Management, Scottsdale, Arizona, March 6, 1986.

16. McKenny, "The Influence of Computer-Communications . . ." 1985, p. 29.

17. Meyer and Boone, *The Information Edge*, pp. 209–10.

18. Edward Nyce and Richard E. Groppa, "Electronic Mail at MHT," *Management Technology*, vol. 1, no. 1 (May 1983), p. 71.

19. McKenny, "The Influence of Computer-Communications . . . ," p.7.

20. William Bowen, "The Puny Payoff From Office Computers," *Fortune*, vol. 113, no. 11 (May 26, 1986), p. 24.

21. Ibid.

22. Henry Fersko-Weiss, "Personal Computing at the Top," *Personal Computing*, March 1985, p. 77.

23. Jeffrey H. Moore, "Senior Executive Computer Use." Unpublished working paper, Stanford Graduate School of Business, Palo Alto, Calif., 1986.

24. Meyer and Boone, *The Information Edge*, p. 212.

25. Ibid., p. 224.

26. Ibid., p. 225.

27. Fersko-Weiss, "Personal Computing at the Top," p. 75.

28. Moore, "Senior Executive Computer Use."

29. John Dearden, "SMR Forum: Will the Computer Change the Job of Top Management?" *Sloan Management Review,* vol. 25, no. 1 (Fall 1983).

30. Meyer and Boone, *The Information Edge,* pp. 214–15.

31. David Friend, "Executive Information Systems: Successes, Failures, Insights and Misconceptions," *DSS-86 Transactions,* Conference on Decision Support Systems, Washington, D.C. Published by The Insitute of Management Sciences, Providence, R.I., p. 39.

32. Fersko-Weiss, "Personal Computing at the Top," p. 79.

33. Ibid., p. 75.

34. Ibid., p. 77.

CHAPTER 5

THE USE OF ESS TO IMPROVE THE PLANNING AND CONTROL PROCESS

As this book is being written in 1987, computer-based office support for executives is growing. Yet this is not the most significant impact of executive support systems. The key application of ESS is in the redesign and enhancement of planning and control processes. Such systems have a pervasive impact on a firm, often changing the explicit or implicit measurement system which can strongly affect the focus of an organization.

Anthony's model for planning and control was outlined in Chapter 3. He divided the process into strategic planning, management control, and operational control. In this chapter we will focus primarily on management control—the efficient and effective use of resources to achieve organizational goals. Management control systems are used for planning, the process by which short- and medium-term goals are established, as well as control, the process by which data is collected and evaluated to ensure that the organization is on the track toward its goals. Changes in these systems affect the way the organization operates.

There are six ways we have observed in which executive support systems improve organizational planning and control. The first, and major, section of this chapter will be devoted to exploring those six ways in detail. We spend the final few pages looking at the significance of ESS for the management control process. Corporations have used ESS to facilitate:

1. Improvements in existing corporate or divisional reporting systems.
2. The redesign of management reporting systems to focus more strikingly on factors critical to managing the business.
3. Changes in planning and forecasting processes.
4. An ability to perform ad hoc analysis using customized information data bases.
5. The enhancement of personal communication links enabling executives to stay on top of critical activities in the organization.
6. Improved program management capabilities in project-oriented firms.

Let us examine each of these approaches to enhancing an organization's planning and control processes.

1. Improvements in Existing Corporate or Divisional Reporting Systems

While leaving the existing management control system essentially intact, ESS can improve reporting by:

- Changing the way performance data is physically collected.
- Improving data integrity.
- Speeding up reporting.
- Changing the method of report presentation.

Changing Physical Collection Methods

The controller of Diversified Electronics Corporation explained why his chief executive's request for better information led to a restructuring of the firm's data collection system. He explains:

> Prior financial control systems at the corporate level were awkward and slow. We couldn't explain what was going on out there. We were so busy trying to add up the numbers that we hardly had time to do any analysis.

Under the company's old system, to get a report eight days after closing, corporate accountants had to call the 21 operating units and take figures over the telephone. Meanwhile, corporate financial analysts had to make their own calls to get explanations of the numbers and variances. It took three and a half days just to roll up the accounting data and the analysis was very superficial.

A new system was designed when the president expressed concern that he wasn't getting the performance information he needed. To streamline the reporting system, a network of IBM PCs was installed in the 21 operating units. The primary purpose of the PCs today is to collect divisional data and load it onto the corporate mainframe. Each month the units report 200–300 line items, including P&L, balance sheet, cash flow, ROI, and some product line information. Also collected at the same time are a few cryptic lines of text explaining any variances between budget and actuals. All of this information is downloaded into the corporate mainframe by the end of the third day of the month.

Although this is, in effect, a routine corporate financial reporting and consolidation system, it was new to this highly decentralized, multi-billion dollar company. The financial staff did not have the power to get information quickly from the decentralized divisions until the president, recognizing his own information needs, issued instructions to develop the system.

The impact of the redesigned reporting system is substantial. As the controller notes, "The new system allows corporate financial analysts to focus their attention primarily on analysis instead of on more clerical data collection tasks. It also enables them to produce a set of reports for top management which are much more timely and more applicable to current executive issues."

The president now goes into his monthly review meetings with his group vice presidents armed with a "Summary of Operations Report," detailing each business unit's year-to-date results versus those forecasted. Previously, when the chief executive met with his subordinates he did not have the prior month's operating results or the current forecast. As a result, much of the meeting was devoted to bringing the president up-to-date. Often there was disagreement on the accuracy of the figures presented. The new ESS-generated operations report, however, provides the CEO and his vice presidents with the same information. "The system has taken away all emphasis on getting the numbers right," explains the controller. "Now executives are focused on what the changes mean for the balance of the year. As a result, less time is spent debating the numbers, and much more time is devoted to substantive analysis of operational problems, opportunities, and potential acquisitions."

The chief executive at Diversified Electronics has an IBM 3179 color terminal on his desk and uses it occasionally to check specific numbers. More often, however, he relies on his staff to develop reports and analyses for him. Because he was involved in creating the system, he understands the structure of the data base. Recognizing what data is readily available and how quickly his staff can perform analytic work, he now asks more complex questions of them. In this system, as in some others, time at the terminal for the top executive is of little importance.

Improving Data Integrity

In developing an executive support system, organizations can uncover major inconsistencies in data management and accounting policies. Correcting them yields substantial improvements in current reporting systems. At Firestone, the first attempt to build an ESS revealed data incompatibilities in the basic business systems. As a result, the designers curtailed their ESS development until an integrated financial planning and control system study was completed. This study indicated the need for a centralized accounting and consolidation system to replace the 30 different existing general ledger systems. Only then could executives be provided with "clean data."

A similar situation occurred at Northwest Industries where ESS developers had to backtrack in order to establish common data definitions across divisions. Before the ESS was complete, a great deal of money was invested in overhauling corporate data bases to provide top management with accurate and useful information.

Speeding up Reporting

Providing top management with computer support can lead to the speeding up of a firm's reporting processes. Diversified Electronic's financial system is one example of more rapid data collection which produced faster reporting. At Lincoln National Corporation, where 3,000 terminals now feed into the system, not only has data collection become faster, but, more significantly, Lincoln was able to shift from quarterly to monthly financial reporting when CEO Ian Rolland was surprised once too often by inaccurate predictions of quarterly results. Understanding the capabilities of the technology to provide data, Rolland did not hesitate to demand a shorter cycle.

The ESS at ConAgra has extensive monitoring capabilities that have collapsed reporting cycles from monthly to weekly. Each Monday morning top management gets financial reports that include the previous week's profit before tax (PBT) forecast versus actual, as well as previous actuals for historical comparison. The PBT analysis provides the key numbers on one screen to give executives the big picture. Operating detail two to four levels down is available.

Because of ConAgra's rapid growth from $1 billion in 1980 to about $6 billion in 1986, executives have needed fast, accurate information. In particular, executives have needed to track the progress of new acquisitions.

Before the ESS, weekly information was unavailable to top management, since there was no system to collect, synthesize, and present that information. The current system, however, allows management to take more short-term actions consistent with their long-term strategy. "Executives can react faster and see more cause and effect based on their actions," says Lynn Trimpey, director of systems and operations for ConAgra. "We don't change our strategy, we just fine tune it a lot sooner."

Daily reporting systems are not unusual with ESS. Derwyn Phillips, executive vice president of Gillette North America, looks at daily sales data. At United Virginia Bank, the most widely used application by the top three executives is daily balance sheet data.[1] Robert Wallace, executive vice president of Phillips Petroleum, describes his use of an ESS for daily reporting:

> For 30 or 40 minutes each morning I get into the daily graphs looking at what my market changes might be, what the trend lines are, what we've done over the last x number of days, how we're tracking against the spot crude, how we're tracking against competitive pricing. I also get a daily report from my refineries.

Most executives at my level have very little contact with the hardware down in the refinery, but I can scan mine in a couple of minutes. And I can tell you where my units are, where I've got some soft spots in the operation, where I'm on an upbeat with my units. I take it right off the machine. As a result, I have more information than I would have normally received had I called the vice president of refining, for example, and asked, "How are we looking today?" That would have probably taken me 10 minutes and I would have been less informed than I am getting it off the machine.

Changing Report Presentation
Finally, computers can affect existing reporting processes by offering a new vehicle for presenting management control information in graphic or tabular formats. Phillips at Gillette emphasizes graphics using Pilot Executive Software, an ESS package which draws upon information abstracted from the group's general ledger system and other sources. Executives access the new information data base, which is stored on a DEC VAX, through Pilot's menu-driven front end, which allows users to enter commands with a mouse or keyboard.

The main menu on Phillips' system offers a series of applications. "Daily sales activity" provides information on order activity for the current month. "Financial data" includes budgets and forecasts by reporting unit. "Current graphs" depicts daily sales, market share by operating unit, market data, and customer information. "External companies" allows the executive to monitor financial data from selected competitors and vendors. "Personnel" provides access to an organization chart and personnel files. Electronic mail and world news (a daily update from Dow Jones News/Retrieval) are among the other facilities available to Phillips.

The Pilot system, providing status access but not query capabilities, does allow the group executive vice president to see a significant level of detail. For example, under "financial data," Phillips can look at total Gillette North America sales, and then at breakdowns by division, and by products in each division.

A "friendly" monitoring system with tabular, text, and graphic formats, Gillette's ESS is viewed by top management as the group's primary reporting vehicle. It has replaced the traditional paper-based system.

In summary, developing an executive support system can have far-reaching effects on existing reporting systems, even when these systems remain fundamentally the same. Improvements in collecting and presenting information about performance are a common objective in ESS development. But other advantages become obvious only as the system is used. What is clear in both cases, however, is that executives' concerns about the information they receive has led to significant improvements in their reporting systems.

2. The Redesign of Management Reporting Systems

Although improvements in data capture, the speed of data access, data quality, and presentation methods are very valuable, a greater opportunity is presented by today's technology—the opportunity to rethink the information needed, and thus the content and structure of existing management control systems, in the light of current business conditions.

Four factors motivate the reconceptualization and, quite often, the major redesign of planning and control systems:

The faster "metabolism" of business today. The old quarterly and monthly periodic processes for planning and control, although still the standard, are just not appropriate to the increasing pace of business. Kodak Senior Vice President C.J. Murphy sums it up: "The speed of everything that happens is now much more rapid than it used to be. At the risk of dating myself, I can recall—and not too long ago—that if we had a problem, we could assemble our managers from around the world next month. Then, to get something started, we'd sit down and talk about what we wanted to do—the month after that! Nowadays that's much too slow."[2]

Although monthly reporting of accounting data will remain the workhorse of the control process, there is an increasing need for weekly and daily data, especially data on market conditions. Although one can argue the merits of information about such a short time span, an increasing number of senior executives are asking for it, perhaps more to increase their "comfort level," than for taking action. In some cases, executives are using this more frequent data to buttress their understanding of competitive marketplaces.

A changing perspective on senior management's role in coordinating operations.   There is an increasing perception by some executives that it is not only "all right," but quite effective, for them to make tactical use of information to coordinate operations throughout the firm. This appears even more strongly in smaller organizations such as Citibank subsidiary Banco Internacional. At Lincoln National and Kodak, executive support systems also provide the basis for direct action in critical managerial areas. While the trend toward decentralization in the past two decades has led to the belief that hands-off management by senior executives is good, those executives coordinating worldwide business functions, or deeply concerned about a critical area of the business, may increasingly demand computer-based access to key data. Wrapp sums up the problem this way:

> Top-level managers are frequently criticized by writers, consultants, and lower levels of management for continuing to enmesh themselves in operating problems, after promotion to the top, rather than withdrawing to the "big picture." Without any doubt, some managers do get lost in a welter of detail and insist on making too many decisions. Superficially, the good manager may seem to make the same mistake—but his purposes are different. He knows that only by keeping well informed about the decisions being made can he avoid the sterility so often found in those who isolate themselves from operations.
>
> If he follows the advice to free himself from operations, he may soon find himself subsisting on a diet of abstractions, leaving the choice of what he eats in the hands of his subordinates. As Kenneth Boulding puts it: "The very purpose of a hierarchy is to prevent information from reaching higher layers. It operates as an information filter, and there are little wastebaskets all along the way."[3]

The availability of new methodologies.   New methods to help executives think through their information needs for planning and control are now available. The "critical success factors" method is one of these.[4]

The rapid improvement in hardware and software capabilities. Improved hardware and software exist for data management, communications, graphics, and document handling. Any planning and control system design assumes an underlying information-handling technology. As this technology changes, it can be expected that the planning and control process will also change.

Today, in response to global competition, senior executives like Jack Welsh of General Electric and Dick Mahoney of Monsanto are tearing apart and reshaping organizations that essentially have been stable for decades. Manufacturing systems and marketing channels are being redesigned, as are other functions and management processes. It is, therefore, reasonable to expect that planning and control systems will change also.

A number of executives are using the most recent technology to redesign their approaches to planning and control. For some, reporting systems are completely revamped. For others, only parts of the structure are altered. Examples of systems which are undergoing significant change are described below.

Fundamental revision

One corporation in which the entire planning and control process is being vastly revised through the implementation of an ESS is Xerox. Chairman David Kearns and Chief of Staff Paul Allaire, now president of Xerox, envisioned the need to revamp the management planning and control process. According to Ken Soha, director of the ESS project, Xerox had always been heavily decentralized, with planning and control data forwarded by divisions in somewhat different formats and in different levels of detail. In particular, planning documents fit the individual needs of each division. "With regard to planning data, executives at corporate were tired of always playing on the division's home court," says Soha. "As competitive pressures increased, Kearns and Allaire realized that there was a need to change the way that we did business at the corporate level. A shift in the relationship of the corporate office to the various divisions was necessary. This required more standard formats, as well as the ability to manipulate the information received from the divisions more effectively. In addition, external information on customers and competitors in the industries in which Xerox participates was necessary."

Soha was charged with implementation. Starting with three people in 1984 and a budget of $700,000, by late 1986 Soha had ten people developing and supporting the ESS with a budget of $1.3 million. The first piece of the system implemented was the redesigned planning process (discussed later in this chapter). Revision of the control process, or reporting system, was subsequently undertaken.

Although Derwyn Phillips, as noted earlier, made several improvements in the information presentation process at Gillette, his more pervasive change involved a full-scale revision of management reporting. Phillips asked division executives to identify their business's critical success factors. From this, he identified the information needed to manage the units more effectively. Having previously supported a financially oriented planning and control process, reporting at the group executive level now focuses mainly on marketing. Market share data, major program data, and daily activity reports enable Phillips to return from lengthy trips and get a quick update as to the health of the business. Because of his familiarity with the information and sense of things "being visible," Phillips has been able to reduce the number of major business reviews for his three divisions from two to one a year.

In a few firms, executives have used information technology to drastically revise their planning and control systems, yet have no intention of using the computer to directly access the data. The president of the midwestern food distributor first noted in Chapter 2 has vastly expanded the monthly book of operations and financial reports for himself and his management team.

He changed from the traditional reporting system because the information he received was too limited and too heavily filtered by subordinates. The system that was once financially oriented has been replaced by broader (e.g., market, product lines), more detailed, and accurate reports. Mixing graphics, text, and tabular data, the new formats allow the chief executive to assimilate the information more effectively.

This desire for more information is not unusual. Several systems we observed provide increased operational information, enabling executives to monitor a wider set of business situations more closely.

Partial System Change—New Information Streams to Monitor Critical Areas

When information that is critical for executives changes frequently, the planning and control process must respond. An ESS can facilitate this response. In 1979, as interest rates rose to record levels, the life insurance industry experienced a dramatic increase in the number of policies surrendered. Loans taken out by policyholders soared as insurees took advantage of the availability of cheap money. For companies like Lincoln National, cash dried up in the torrent of outflows. With no information on short-term cash status and trend, Lincoln's top management had difficulty assessing cash management alternatives. Up to that time, it had been relatively easy to forecast Lincoln's cash flow, which grew steadily 5 to 10 percent each year as the insurance business grew. But, by 1979, the simple cash flow extrapolation method had become invalid because the business had lost its stability.

To deal with this problem, CEO Ian Rolland had his staff automate short-term cash status reporting. Thus, when Rolland logged onto the terminal he had immediate access to screens summarizing Lincoln's short-term position. The first display showed the company stock price, yesterday's Dow Industrials Average, the pound Sterling exchange rate, and Lincoln's short-term investments. Another screen showed a menu of reports dealing with short-term cash status. These included: pool borrowing/deposits, commercial paper report, commentary on short-term cash flow strategy, cash position report, long-term cash objectives, and monthly cash objectives (as developed by the SBUs).

Rolland monitored these reports daily as long as high interest rates continued to threaten the company's cash position. Providing a better grasp on cash movements, the information helped him adjust the firm's strategy. But, as the problem became more manageable and less critical, Lincoln's chief executive used these reports less and less. Today, he rarely looks at short-term cash reports, leaving this area to subordinates.

In the Missile Systems Division at Raytheon, one critical factor in the engineering process is "investigation requests" (IRs). These represent technical problems identified in a missile program. Every IR is assigned to an engineer who is responsible for planning and implementing a solution to the problem within a specified period of time. In 1984, the manager of Raytheon's Bedford Laboratories was having trouble tracking IRs on the Patriot missile program.

Traditionally, IRs had been stored on file cards, and there were often inaccuracies in the data. Providing an executive with a status report on IRs could take seven people up to three weeks of sifting through what were usually thousands of IRs in the system at once.

The general manager of the Missile Systems Division (MSD) added an IR monitoring capability to his executive support system, and made it accessible to his staff to help monitor investigation requests. The system was soon utilized by all MSD program managers to stay current on the status of IRs in their units, and to prepare for questions from the general manager.

At Kodak, Senior Vice-President C.J. Murphy, who was in charge of manufacturing for the company in the early to mid–1980s, sponsored an executive support system. Aimed at providing his worldwide management team with the information they needed to focus on effective manufacturing management, it provides data on inventories, productivity, plant loading, quality, and costs in eight international locations. The data can be utilized both by individuals and by the managerial team working together. In a 1986 speech, Murphy noted, "In the offices of key managers and their staff, these systems form the basis of a rapid exchange of manufacturing performance information. . . . Today, what's needed is the ability to pull information in quickly, understand it quickly, make decisions quickly, and get things moving. That's the speed of response and control issue that we're faced with."[5]

At The New England, a financial service company whose products traditionally have been insurance-related, Executive Vice President Bob Shafto uses an ESS to improve his understanding of the performance of the firm's 100 general agencies. He says:

> When I'm meeting with general agents, it's a very valuable tool. I use the system to raise my knowledge level about the current performance of their agencies. What matters is how quickly I can get a comprehensive overview and draw conclusions from the data. The ESS, particularly with its graphics, helps me do that much faster. The system also allows me to see things at a more detailed level and to focus better. Normally, I tend to focus at a summary level, but the system lets me quickly access information at a lower level, to see what's really happening in particular agencies.

There are many other examples of ESS developed to monitor critical business factors.

- At one manufacturer, the increased importance of field stock and other inventory levels required weekly instead of monthly discussions by executives. An ESS made these weekly reviews possible. "The increased frequency with which the data is reported provides more detail on a more timely basis, and helps top management recognize new interrelationships among the data elements," says the CFO.

- The general director of materials management at Michigan Motors, a division of a major automaker, uses his system several times a day to monitor orders received by his unit.

- At International Computers, Ltd. (ICL), in Great Britain, a director of manufacturing uses his terminal every week to review trends in delivery performance, quality, and inventory for his four manufacturing centers. Meanwhile, the director of the U.K. division monitors sales weekly, and sometimes daily, through his ESS.

Critical success factors vary from company to company, and executive support systems reflect this fact. What is critical varies not only from company to company, but from executive to executive. At Comshare, Inc., a $70 million software sales organization, which offers an executive support system among other products, the company's own internal ESS illustrates the divergence of information needs among the major officers. The controller is served by a financial consolidation system, while President Rick Crandall, although needing financial data, is equally if not more interested in monitoring how well the company hires and retains personnel—especially those people rated outstanding. He also uses the ESS to focus his management team on a commonly defined and easily tracked set of customer satisfaction measures. The CFO, who also functions as a group operating executive, has many interests. Yet he focuses heavily on tracking software problems and their resolution as a result of Crandall's emphasis on customer satisfaction. Don Walker, the chief sales executive, while interested in much of the foregoing, finds greatest value in tracking the progress of his sales force toward the closing of new business. "Like most other companies, we have a structured series of steps toward closing a sale," Walker says. "The system provides me with unparalleled visibility into our progress in each situation. It has become the 'bible' for us in this area."

Comshare's system is so personalized that Crandall can simply point at a number, text item, or graph component on the workstation's video "touchscreen" and move rapidly through the set of screens which are of most interest to him. By tracking his usage pattern, the system's staff has fit the ESS neatly into Crandall's information-seeking approach, while also providing him the ability to deviate from this pattern.

This same ability to scan a pre-defined set of screens is built into the system at Lockheed–Georgia. Houdeshel notes that, if desired, executives also can page quickly through a series of displays whose sequence is defined in advance. These sequence files can be created either by the user, or by the ESS development staff after they have studied the executive's monitoring habits.[6]

At the heart of organizational planning and control systems is a periodic—usually monthly—process of financial reporting. This basic process will remain untouched by executive support systems—except for faster data collection and improved accuracy. But this basic reporting process is being expanded significantly in ESS-based systems. The information available to the senior executive is broader in scope, more market oriented, and, more often, available on a daily basis for critical areas. The systems are more dynamic and tailored to the needs of the individual executive. Thus, each executive can zero in on the factors which are currently most critical for managing the organization.

3. Changes in Planning and Forecasting Processes

Planning and forecasting, as yet, are only occasionally the primary focus of executive support systems. But, in many cases, improved control processes seem to lead to a new focus on the planning function. *Planning systems,* as used here, are systems which produce targets expected to be met by the organization. They produce front-end targets against which results are measured by the control system. *Forecasts,* on the other hand, merely produce estimates which are utilized in planning.

One company where improved planning was an initial objective is Xerox. In early 1985, a strategic planning system, known as the Business Resource Management System, was installed to improve planning. The new system requires business units to submit their plans in a well-defined five-page format through a network of Xerox workstations. Senior management now has more time to review the plans and ask questions of division management. And the uniform formats imposed by the system make it easier to compare plans across units. Because planning documents move considerably faster on the computer-based system, strategic planning has become a more iterative process at Xerox. "This system has substantially enhanced our understanding of the business," says Xerox Chairman David Kearns.

Ronald Compton, president of American Re-Insurance Company, uses his ESS to chart non-financial objectives and subjective data, as well as more traditional financial information. He explains, "The subjective data is handled by charting each objective as to the date it should be completed and how far work has progressed to date. I create project planning schedules directly on line and revise them frequently. As the principal planner and strategist for this organization, I can add changes and see where we are. At a glance I can see if someone's putting things off. I spent years trying to figure out if people were meeting objectives on projects I had given them. With this system, I can immediately determine how a project is progressing."[7]

In another case, the chairman of a large manufacturing company uses his ESS to challenge forecasts developed by his subordinates. Working with Lotus 1-2-3 and a Focus database, he has created models that provide different perspectives on the marketplace and allow him to test the validity of the firm's sales forecasts and forecasting assumptions. The models sharpen his scrutiny of sales targets and allow him to better estimate their effect on inventory levels, field stocks, and manufacturing production levels. The chairman explains, "The main thing I do with the computer is look ahead, ask questions, and look at our alternatives. I don't use the system to go back and analyze the past. I get others to do that."

In the Investment Division of Lincoln National Corporation, Senior Vice President Jon Boscia uses the corporation's computer facilities to support both strategic and tactical planning. Strategic planning capabilities include access to competitive analysis data bases. Action plans to implement Lincoln's strategy are developed utilizing the system, as are all financial projections for each division and for their products.

Competitive analysis is a major part of Lincoln's planning process. Boscia uses electronic mail to communicate with field salespeople who collect information on the competition and enter it on pre-formatted screens. Providing information to the firm's strategic planners in these automated and uniform formats cuts down analysis time by weeks, says Boscia.

Building a profile of each competitor's strengths and weaknesses, he identifies the factors critical for each line of business, and then ranks each competitor's capabilities in those areas, along with those of his own firm. Boscia asks: "Are we weak in the critical factors needed for success in this particular product line? Do we have a plan to strengthen ourselves in that area?

"In the meantime," he explains, "we make sure we develop a marketing plan that focuses on our key strengths, one that will lead to increased sales, while steering away from our weaknesses." Boscia also distributes the marketing plan over the electronic-mail system to the corporate office, which consolidates it with plans from the other eleven business units. The consolidated five-year plan goes to the CEO and his staff for approval. Boscia explains that Lincoln's system has allowed enforcement of uniform formats for business-unit plans, making it easier for top management to compare them.

Lincoln's Investment Division has also used this top-management-initiated planning system to gain a tactical advantage over the competition. For example, in the southeast region, a Tennessee-based competitor was consistently outbidding Lincoln's Atlanta office on a particular product. The sales force could not figure out why they were being underbid, nor did they know what to do about it.

Boscia used the competitive-analysis system to collect information from the Atlanta sales force about the cases they were losing to the Tennessee competitor. He then calculated the other firm's costs, drawing on the competitive-information data base, and determined that they were earning only 6 percent return on equity for these particular products. Because Lincoln demanded 15 percent ROE on its products to remain in a particular business, reducing premiums to compete on price was not a viable alternative.

Boscia's analysis, however, also showed that the Tennessee competitor was making up its lost revenue by padding profit margins on other product lines. Highlighting the competitor's weak spots for the Atlanta office, Lincoln altered its sales stategy and immediately began taking volume business away from the competition.

Executive support systems frequently evolve from initially focusing on improved control to focusing on improved planning, as at Lincoln. We found a few systems like the ones at Xerox and the large manufacturing company where the purpose of the ESS at the outset was to improve forecasting and planning. But they are rare.

At Diversified Electronics, the tighter management-control system enables financial analysts to revise short-term forecasts more effectively than in the past. For example, according to the corporate controller, if a division exceeds its forecast in the first month of the year, considerable attention is devoted to revising first-quarter and year-end expectations. Corporate analysts now have both the lead time and the capability to advise executives on the "issues at risk" and the opportunities influencing the forecast, so that top management can make more informed judgments about the quality of operating units' forecasts.

The initial purpose of the ESS at Banco Internacional de Colombia, a Citicorp subsidiary, was also to improve the control process. The president, Mike Jensen, wanted access to detailed operations data. Using his terminal, Jensen could look at customer information, including current accounts, loans, certificates of deposit, account profits, and similar data. In addition, he could see a report on commissions and expenses in critical areas, a balance sheet updated daily, as well as a graphic display of profit versus goals and forecasts. By the time Keen studied the South American bank's ESS in 1983, Jensen was well in command of current operations and was using the data to look forward. "I have enough day-by-day normal information to run this organization," said Jensen. "Eventually, I want to be able to see the dynamics and movements of everything."[8]

As with Diversified Electronics, once the bank's management had automated the control function, their interests in further developing the system became more future oriented. Noting this, Keen writes:

> Both Jensen and his senior managers rely on the system to help set goals and make plans. [The ESS] allows a combination of top-down planning (products, market segments) and bottom-up goal-setting (by the account officer).
>
> [The system] continues to evolve in the direction of better information about the future. One impact it has already had is to get Jensen and his managers more focused on "dynamics" and trends. In the interviews they all speak of a clearer sense of where things are going and a longer time-horizon for their planning.[9]

In some cases, executive support systems have contributed directly to improved forecasting. The vice president of business operations for a computer company is responsible for negotiating with other executives to establish manufacturing schedules based on predicted sales. He describes how his access to historical data has changed the forecasting process:

> The thing that has probably transformed [manufacturing scheduling] meetings most is graphs of historical statistics that are now

easily available. These graphs allow us immediately to detect whether something is an aspiration or a probability. We can now look backwards at what has happened in the past and say, "What you are projecting and using to justify this $75 million of capital spending doesn't make sense. Those kinds of discontinuities just don't happen that way."

In summary, there are three types of ESS that affect organizational planning and forecasting:

1. Systems like the one at Xerox which automate some aspect of the planning process;
2. Applications like Lincoln's strategic planning and competitive analysis that have evolved as communications and data retrieval systems mature;
3. Systems like those at Diversified Electronics, Banco Internacional, and ICL, which, although originally oriented toward managerial control, subsequently matured to the point at which executives began utilizing the systems for technical and long-range planning.

4. An Ability to Perform Ad Hoc Analysis Using Information Data Bases

Most of this chapter has been oriented to the development of reporting systems, whether for planning or control. Because these have rather limiting formats, however, executives need another way to access information. ESS designed to provide management with information outside of the standard reporting systems do so through an *information data base* (IDB). Data is usually transferred to an IDB from internal systems and from external sources of both text and data. An IDB, with a relational structure and a command language for access, gives management users the flexibility to manipulate performance information most critical for control and planning, and then to format their own reports.

Information data bases affect planning and control in several important ways. First, they provide a source of raw information which can be used by analytical executives to perform their own analysis. For example, the new vice president of operations for United Retailing, which had become unprofitable, was greeted by a sorely inadequate, paper-oriented management information system. The 1,000-store chain suffered from problems of poor image, dusty low-value merchandise, and outdated merchandising. The operations VP knew major changes were needed to make the company profitable again, including the closing of several hundred stores. But the existing sales reporting system was so slow in providing data, and so inflexible, that it was impossible for him to perform the analysis necessary to understand which stores should be closed.

An ESS, implemented to support this analysis, included the following information: (1) sales reported by the stores each week; (2) store financial data, such as budgets and salaries; (3) store characteristics, including store class, square footage, and district; and, (4) special pricing information for particular stores about to close for refurbishing, or which had recently reopened. With access to this information, and the analytic capabilities provided by the System W data base software, the operations VP was able to do executive ad hoc analysis. In a short period of time, he was able to pinpoint troubled stores as he worked to make the company profitable again.

In like manner, a computer company executive, responsible for one of the firm's largest sales territories, uses his system to evaluate the forecasting capabilities of his sales managers. With a spreadsheet he tracks the sales of his seven districts, showing historically what each unit manager forecast, the sales budget, and what was actually delivered. Looking at this information graphically over time, the sales executive can clearly see the forecasting tendencies of his managers. Some consistently forecast below budget but deliver sales over budget, while others forecast below budget and deliver below forecast. Other combinations exist. These analyses help the sales executive to estimate more confidently his expected sales. In addition, confronting his managers with graphic evidence of their forecasting tendencies helps improve forecasting skills, or at least the reporting accuracy.

Perhaps the most impressive example of an ESS used by a senior executive for analysis was at Northwest Industries. Before the company was sold to Farley Industries in 1985, Ben W.

Heineman, president and chief executive officer, used a system that he developed for himself and his staff. The system was undertaken in 1976 when Heineman decided that he needed a specially tailored data base to aid him in monitoring, projecting, and planning the progress of his nine operating companies. A great believer in "not being the captive of any particular source of information," Heineman wanted to be able to analyze various aspects of the business himself but saw little opportunity to do so without a computer-based system to reduce data-handling chores.

In January 1977, Heineman was given an experimental system to retrieve more than 70 reports and perform limited analysis. By February, he had reached the limits of the system's capabilities and was demanding more. Additional capabilities came in the form of a new access and analysis language, EXPRESS, which facilitated simple file handling and data aggregation, as well as extensive modeling and statistical analyses of data series. To complement these improved capabilities, Northwest developed an extensive executive information data base including:

- 350 financial and operational items concerning planned, budgeted, forecasted, and actual monthly results for each operating company for the past eight and next four years.
- 45 economic and key ratio time series.
- Several externally subscribed data bases, including Standard & Poor's Compustat and DRI services.

Working with the system was an everyday matter for Heineman. With his knowledge of the business and newly acquired ability to write programs, Heineman saw great value in working at a terminal himself rather than handing all assignments to staff personnel. "There is a huge advantage to the CEO to get his hands dirty in the data," he said, because "the answers to many significant questions are found in the detail. The system provides me with an improved ability to ask the right questions and to know the wrong answers."[10]

The management reporting system (MRS) at Firestone is also anchored by an information data base. The MRS draws information for top management from the centralized consolidation fed by the new general ledger system and provides about 200 operations reports. In addition, a menu-driven report generator allows executives to design customized reports from the EXPRESS data base by defining columns (e.g., monthly, quarterly, YTD) and rows (e.g., line items). This system is used occasionally by the president, but he has come to rely on the corporate controller, who accesses the system daily, for most computer-based analysis.

One of the advantages of a relational data base is the ability to continually add and eliminate tables of data as the executive learns what is important. The president of the bank in Colombia describes the design process in this manner:

> I wanted a computer by my desk. But what the hell did I want for information? I wanted [data] (1) not just on a monthly basis but over time; (2) who're the biggest clients, overdrafts, etc.; (3) and to answer a hundred questions.
>
> I asked Daniel [ESS designer] what he thought I should know. He gave me a list. I stretched it. It was interactive. I prioritized the list. We didn't see the whole picture at the beginning. We came out of a tunnel and saw the light and just kept moving towards it.[11]

Because the decision as to what ESS data is stored in an information data base is critical, the executive must be concerned with specifying the contents of the data base. Using either a top-down or prototyping approach, as in the example above, the executive designates what he or she believes is relevant to the business.

An information data base affects planning and control by enhancing executive access to management control information. It also can improve the quality of analysis for both manager and staff. More importantly, the definition of the information data base allows the executive to put a personal stamp on the organization's planning and control system by raising the visibility of particular information.

5. The Enhancement of Personal Communication Links

The use of electronic mail is another ESS capability that affects planning and control. Electronic mail, discussed in Chapter 4 and mentioned in the section on planning and forecasting, deserves attention here because of its unique role in affecting the communications component of the management control process. Where use of electronic mail by executives tightens communication links with the rest of the organization, top management's informal control and influence over subordinates is increased.

Anthony characterizes management control as a "periodic process," but the process involves more than just formal periodic reporting. There is informal follow-through by telephone and unscheduled meetings. Management control is really a dynamic process; because of this, electronic mail provides a great benefit.

Electronic mail facilitates ongoing monitoring in a number of ways. The director of European operations for an automated equipment testing firm says, "I find that I monitor a lot more information now than I used to be able to monitor. I can see from a number on the spreadsheet and from electronic mail messages where problems are occuring in the divisions or subsidiaries. Now I can take action sooner when I see a problem is growing."[12]

The chief executive of one company wanted his firm to remain non-union for strategic reasons, and he needed intelligence on potential problems in this area. He asked his personnel department to pass on copies of all electronic mail messages they received that gave any hint of worker discontent or potential union activity in the company's district offices.

At ICL, the director of information systems uses EM to speed along reports he uses to monitor important projects. He says:

> I get regular reports on a dozen key projects via electronic mail. Either my secretary prints out hard copies for me to review, or I look at them on my terminal at home. I receive these reports every other Monday now, but when they came by mail I wouldn't get them until Wednesday, so the review period was already a third over. There's also an extensive distribution list so everyone gets them at once. The reports are just summary level, so I can get a feel for whether or not I've got a problem. They show me progress vs. milestones on projects such as new mainframe or major application implementations.

Beneficial's chairman Finn Caspersen focuses on how EM's speed of response improves his ability to know what is going on and to provide his input to others in the organization.

> For me, the computer is a communication device, and the primary function of the chairman is to communicate. . . . I use it both to send and receive all my internal mail. I generate 90 to 95 percent of my electronic mail by typing it myself, despite the fact that I'm a very poor typist! It allows me to operate in a whole different time frame. Instead of having a memo wind its way through the system for five to seven days, I can get a response in half an hour.[13]

Electronic mail also facilitates the querying that is an inevitable part of the management control process. At Boeing, one executive says, "Usually I read the status of things first thing in the morning, as opposed to the afternoon, because now the information is available earlier. . . . And it's so much easier to ask a question about something I see in the status reports now that I've got electronic mail."[14]

6. Improved Program Management Capabilities in Project-Oriented Firms

Another common ESS application in project-oriented firms is program management. At Raytheon, Charles Jacobs, general manager of the Missile Systems Division, created an ESS for quick access to up-to-date information about missile programs in his division. This system gave Jacobs a pipeline into both the operational and financial data concerning program status.

Through a series of menus, Jacobs could access more than 400 screens or files of data. First, he would select a program, then an area of interest such as financial, quality, production, or delivery. Successive choices provided greater and greater detail, often supported with narrative text. In fact, the most striking feature in the system was the requirement for program managers, on a daily basis, to enter textual updates for Jacobs on significant changes in program status. Although this ESS feature was not popular with all his program managers, Jacobs insisted on it. Another system feature notified the user as to which files had been updated since that individual last logged onto the system.

This program management application proved to be a good way for the general manager to get timely, well-organized, and accessible information to aid in day-to-day management. When queried by customers or superiors, Jacobs could use the ESS as a quick reference system for such things as delivery dates, test results, types of contracts, and quality and quantity of production for the various programs.[15]

At Boeing Aerospace Company (BAC), an operating division of Boeing, an ESS enables executives to monitor program cost data directly from the cost collection data base, instead of waiting for it to filter up through the organization a month later. Over time, the system has gained a range of users from an executive vice president to first-level supervisors. All use menus to access successive levels of detail which can be viewed or summarized to create budget versus actual performance tracking at almost any level. In addition, some executives have departmental and program activity reports sent to them on the system. These reports summarize current project status focusing on schedules and critical issues.

A major benefit of the system is time saved. One user says, "I spend a lot less time now in program status reviews trying to wade through a bunch of charts someone else thinks I need to see. Now I can sit down at my terminal and look at the charts that are important to me. The standard formats help me pick up the trends immediately. It's a real time saver."[16]

A vice president comments on the value of accessing standardized, unfiltered data through the system: "We don't argue anymore about whether the data is correct or not, like we used to. Now we discuss what we're going to do about it. That has made for much faster decisions. No, not just decisions, for much faster actions."[17]

To one Boeing vice president, access to cost data, especially where overruns exist, is very valuable. He explains, "There was a specific program where my looking at the charts every few days and riding the program manager turned a bad trend around and kept the overrun from adversely affecting my division's performance. Without the system, I would not have seen the trend until it was too late to do anything about it, and we would not have made our cost targets."[18]

At yet another aerospace firm, program information is equally important to executives for marketing purposes. Houdeshel and Watson write:

> Lockheed–Georgia markets its aircraft worldwide. In response to these efforts, it is common for a prospective buyer to call a company executive to discuss a proposed deal. Upon receipt of a phone call, the executive can call up a display which provides the following information: the aircraft's model and quantity; the dollar value of the offer; the aircraft's availability for delivery; previous purchases by the prospect; the sales representative's name and exact location for the week; and a description for the status of the possible sale. . . . All this information is available without putting the prospective customer on hold, transferring the call to someone else, or awaiting the retrieval of information from a file.[19]

In a fourth example of program monitoring, an executive vice president in a $6 billion telecommunications company uses an ESS to monitor dozens of development projects. This senior manager, who used to get hundreds of status reports on paper, now accesses the same information on his terminal. One advantage of the system is that it makes information accessible when it is needed by the executive. He observes:

> Periodic reporting information tends to arrive at times when it is of little interest. When a report arrives, I'm usually involved in something else. It's better that, when I get the urge to look at something, it's there so I can get at it. I do less fumbling with this system. It has eliminated my prior frustration of not getting the project information I wanted, when I wanted it. Now I know where the information is and that what I am seeing is the most up to date.
>
> When I'm in the office, reading something will trigger a thought such as, "I wonder where they are with Project Plastic"—that's installing credit-card capabilities in pay stations. Now, if I want to know the status of that project, instead of calling the project manager, I'll look on the terminal to see how many locations we have implemented. If I don't like what I see, *then* I'll make a phone call.

Program management capabilities provide a number of advantages. First, the systems provide quicker access to information. Project status information becomes available to executives faster than through traditional channels, as at Boeing where program cost data became available in two days instead of 20. The actual retrieval is also faster. Now the executive hits a few keys on the terminal instead of rummaging through a pile of reports.

Second, program status systems allow immediate input of text, along with data or graphics, to help an executive understand the meaning of the numbers as interpreted by subordinates. This explanatory text helps avoid what Lockheed–Georgia's executives refer to as "paper tigers," numbers which appear to represent serious problems, but which have a logical explanation that makes them acceptable.

Third, program management capabilities generally provide access to more detailed information. At Raytheon, the system allowed the general manager to recall delivery dates, test results, and contract details on different missile programs. In effect, these systems expand the "memory" of senior managers.

Program management systems are only as good as the data entered into them. For senior management, however, computer systems can provide quicker access, multiple formats of input, and more detail. By tightening the feedback loop from operational activities to executive overview, they allow increased visibility into operations and faster corrective action.

THE SIGNIFICANCE OF EXECUTIVE SUPPORT SYSTEMS FOR MANAGEMENT PLANNING AND CONTROL

In the previous pages, we have discussed how executive support systems are used to improve management planning and control. It is clear that executive-driven systems are changing the formal and/or informal management control processes in an increasing number of companies. Having looked at *what* is being done, we now turn to *why* the presence of executive support systems appears likely to have a considerable impact on the design and operation of management control systems.

For a number of senior executives, the availability of computer-based information support has led them to do some or all of the following:

- To think through what is important to the business in the process of determining their own information needs.
- To redirect the emphasis of management planning and control from a historical, financially-based process to a forward-looking, marketing-oriented one.
- To revise the reporting process dynamically.
- To expand operational monitoring and coordination and hands-on direction of the firm's activities.
- To improve the management of data in the corporation.

Determining Their Own Information Needs

Historically, senior executives have given little attention to their own information needs. With the limited time available, they have addressed issues in marketing, production, finance, competitive strategy, and other areas critical to the firm—areas where an allocation of executive time could make a difference. The little time devoted to information has usually been used to address problems with the information systems department, or to discuss the computer needs of a particular function.

Until recently, most executives who considered using computer-based systems for their own information needs moved away from this fruitless line of thinking. They knew that the firm's computer staff and equipment were heavily backlogged. Available hardware and software appeared to have no relevance to the executive suite. Failed executive "war rooms" were frequently described in the popular press. And, even if the executive wanted to think through his information needs, there was no approach that seemed to help.

As a result, senior managers were usually recipients of information determined to be important by key personnel at the corporate or divisional level. Financial data dominated the reporting process. It was routinely collected, quantifiable and, after all, provided insight into the company's bottom line. Corporate-wide standardized data on staffing levels, orders, market shares, and so forth furnished the rest of the standard fare, providing adequate, if not rich, periodic information for the senior executive.

In the last few years, however, many executives have perceived a new set of conditions which, for the first time, facilitate the development of systems responsive to an executive's information needs. First, supporting hardware and software are now available. Second, many information systems departments have set up separate support groups to meet the needs of end users, particularly executives. Third, methodologies for determining information needs, such as critical success factors, are now available and supported by major consulting firms. And data, both internal and external, is increasingly available on the computer. These supporting conditions are demonstrated increasingly in successful executive support systems installations. Despite some system failures, an increasing number of senior executives are becoming convinced that efforts toward determining and fulfilling their own information needs are, today, not just a waste of time.

It is true that most executive support systems have not been built as a conscious effort to re-examine a manager's information needs. Rather, they have been initiated to provide access to data concerning a business problem or opportunity.

Increasingly, however, some executives are using the process of developing an ESS as an opportunity to think through their own information needs and to build systems to support them. As noted earlier, Derwyn Phillips, executive vice president of Gillette North America, personally used a CSF exercise and encouraged his division presidents to do the same, as a basis for designing GNA's ESS. Now several years old, the system has undergone many changes. But it continues to reflect Phillips' carefully developed vision of his managerial world and the information he needs to operate effectively in this world.

In a less formal manner, a vice president of manufacturing for a large high technology company identified the half-dozen factors reflecting his unit's performance. He explains:

My objectives for the year are, first, delivery performance to our customers—getting them the right board at the right time; second, quality yields, which measure the number of defects in production and are an indicator of cost control; and third, inventory performance. Knowing these and two or three other factors were my own specific key indicators of performance, it was easy for me to tell my IS people, "These are the reports I want."

A major issue in defining information needs is the level of detail desired. This varies by industry, organization, and managerial approach. Yet, surprising amounts of detail are found in many executive systems today. As we have noted, daily sales, sometimes broken down to the product line level, are not unusual. Significant programs, as well as problems and opportunities, are monitored closely. Data once gathered through telephone conversations is now routinely provided to the executives through electronic mail or data links.

In a sense, executive support systems are an attempt by executives to rationalize and structure the information that flows to them. The effects of this travel throughout the company. Even if not an explicit aim, the change in information flows to the top will send implicit signals to the rest of the organization.

Redirect Focus of Management Control System from Historical/Financial to Future/Market Perspective

Although financial data is a common feature of executive support systems, senior line executives have expressed to us their enthusiasm for the market-oriented segments of their systems. An explanation for this may be found in today's turbulent markets, where the need to understand customer and competitive trends is perhaps the crux of the executive's job.

Unfortunately, most management reporting systems have been almost exclusively based on historical information. David Friend, chairman of Pilot Executive Software, expresses the problem this presents for executives:

> When a manager says, "I want results," he is usually referring to measures such as profits or revenue. The problem is that these measures truly are *results* and consequently by the time they are observed, it is already too late to do something about them.

The good manager knows that trying to run an organization by monitoring these kinds of results is like trying to drive your car by looking in the rear-view mirror. A good manager should be attempting to control his exposure to surprises (which are always adverse) rather than to react to them after the fact.

There are managers who seem to be able to *control* events, and there are those who seem to *react* to events. These differences are also evident in their information systems (mostly manual or verbal) and the "actuals" that are tracked. I have observed that many managers are tracking the wrong actuals. In most cases there are clearly factors that could have *predicted* the actuals being tracked. These factors, if tracked, could have allowed management to control the outcome, rather than react to it.

For instance, I was very interested recently in seeing the [ESS] at two major banks, one of which is in deep trouble with foreign loan exposure. The one that is in trouble had lots of good reports showing the bad news in great detail, color graphics and all. The one that has skirted trouble has not quite as good historical reporting, but has a great deal of political and economic analyses and numerical information on leading economic indicators for each country. For instance, by betting that oil prices would decline, this organization was able to improve its position in oil-sensitive markets like Mexico and Venezuela. In this case, measurable oil prices were somewhat predictive of "actuals" (meaning loan problems).[20]

In an attempt to look forward, executives are using ESS to scrutinize market factors such as competitors, industry segments, and the economy. Examples noted earlier in this chapter include:

- Phillips of Gillette, who monitors the financial performance of his organization's closest competitors. His system also provides news service reports on product announcements made by the competition.

- Heineman of Northwest, who used extensive industry, historical, and forecast data to develop his own predictions of the future path of his product divisions.

- The chairmen of two large manufacturing companies who download data from major economic forecasting services. One follows the key economic factors affecting his industry. The other utilizes the data to test the assumptions underlying the sales forecasts made by subordinates.

- Best's on-line data base is used by insurance companies like Lincoln National. It includes detailed data on costs and revenues of most insurance companies, broken down by products offered.

Dynamic Revision of Management Reporting

It is difficult to change the information flows in an organization. Internal forms and procedures must be changed. If the information needed is available internally, the "owners" of the data must be identified. New pipelines through which this information will flow must be developed. In many cases, external data bases must be sought out. Organizational resistance must be overcome. And, staff must be dedicated to developing the new systems. Either explicitly or implicitly assessing the cost-benefit tradeoffs, senior executives all too often are reluctant to set in motion what they perceive to be a difficult and costly effort to develop the reporting systems appropriate to changing business conditions. To change the system, as needed, on an ongoing basis, is seen by most as "out of the question."

The advent of ESS has changed this. Increasingly, senior executives are learning about the availability of external data and text. They perceive that changes in graphs or report formats are simpler to make and less expensive with the new technology. They are also more aware of the many data bases that are available electronically. Finally, an increasing number of senior managers have the benefit of ESS support personnel who are familiar with the task of delivering new types of information in new formats.

Thus, there is a growing sense on the part of the executives we interviewed that dynamic revision of the data available to them is possible. It is reasonable to expect, therefore, that the management control process will become increasingly responsive to changing business conditions, and to the changing information needs of senior executives.

Increased Operational Monitoring, Coordination, and Direction of Actions

Perhaps one of the most interesting uses of ESS is to increase the executive's influence on the direct operations of the firm. A more hands-on approach to management from senior levels is evident in the design and use of some of these systems. At one level, the need to effectively coordinate the worldwide operations of its manufacturing facilities drove the development of Kodak's ESS. Electronic mail, for many executives, provides the capability to stay in touch and to determine when to be further involved.

At a second level, however, some senior executives in particular roles are utilizing the technology for active decision-making. Breaking the general mode of management described in Chapters 2 and 3, they are clearly involved in day-to-day operations. Jensen of Banco Internacional operated in this manner. Another of these executives is Dave Myerscough, described by Jacobson and Hillkirk as one of the "top two Xerox marketing executives in the United States." (He has since become director of marketing for Rank Xerox, the company's European operating unit.)

> Dave Myerscough has a wide range of contacts during his normal business day. He negotiates directly with the copier and systems division on prices and sales targets for copiers, supplies, Memorywriters, electronic printers, and workstations. He determines how many machines to move through the Xerox direct sales force and how many through alternate channels. When he sets his strategy, he tries to think the way his competition does, whether it be the Japanese and their dealer allies or Kodak. "He's got to be the brain trust of this organization," Dwight Ryan says of his number-two man.
>
> Myerscough, a twenty-year Xerox veteran, will also get right on the phone with a customer to cut a deal. He is a primary example of how Xerox has become more entrepreneurial and fast-moving in its traditional business. The computer on Myerscough's desk contains data on every major Xerox customer. While he is on the phone, he can look at the number of Xerox and competitors' machines a customer has, the copy volumes on those machines, the contract terms, and when the contracts run out.

He sometimes knows the customer's operation better than the customer.[21]

There are other examples of such direct operating control. Will this mode of operation grow? Will management control in the future more closely resemble operational control? In the very largest companies at the very top levels, the answer is probably no. But in smaller companies, at the divisional level in larger companies, and for some particular responsibilities in even the largest organizations, we expect to see increased computer access for operational purposes.

Improve the Management of Data in the Corporation

Thus far we have been talking about improving the *process* of planning and control. To do this, some *structural* features of the organization must also be improved. One of these is the management of data. With the exception of accounting data, data definitions in most companies have received little management attention. In many decentralized corporations, for example, a task force is needed to put together total sales figures for the organization's largest customers, since each division has its own customer coding system. Even terms such as *return on equity* or *sales backlog* may have definitions that vary from division to division.

The advent of an executive support system brings these and other data issues to light. Executives working with ESS have highlighted problems with data meanings, coding schemes, and data quality. At Northwest and Firestone these issues had to be faced squarely as executive systems were built and utilized. For global organizations working in increasingly competitive markets, "cleaning up" data is often a favorable side effect of executive systems. We will discuss this problem further in Chapter 8.

CONCLUSION

Executive support systems are in their early stages. A number of key uses for these systems in the area of planning and control are evident today. However, we expect these uses will change dramatically over the next decade. Even today, it is clear that computer-based support for senior managers is having significant, positive effects on the planning and control processes in many firms. Of most interest, workstation-based access is merely the visible tip of the iceberg of the deeper systematic changes being engendered and accelerated by these systems.

NOTES

1. John R. Dick, " 'Automating' Your Chairman," *The Magazine of BANK ADMINISTRATION*, July 1986, p. 38.
2. C.J. Murphy, "The Global Factory: Managing the 'New Realities' In Worldwide Manufacturing." Speech to *Society For Information Management*, Scottsdale, Arizona, March 6, 1986.
3. Copyright © 1967 by the President and Fellows of Harvard College; all rights reserved. Reprinted by permission of *Harvard Business Review*. "Good Managers Don't Make Policy Decisions," by Edward H. Wrapp, September-October 1967, p. 92.
4. See "Chief Executives Define Their Own Data Needs" by John F. Rockart; "A Primer on Critical Success Factors" by Christine V. Bullen and John F. Rockart; and "Engaging Top Management in Information Technology" by John F. Rockart and Adam D. Crescenzi. All reprinted in *The Rise of Managerial Computing*, John F. Rockart and Christine V. Bullen, eds. (Homewood, Ill: Dow Jones-Irwin, 1986).
5. Murphy, "The Global Factory...."
6. George Houdeshel and Hugh J. Watson, "The Management Information and Decision Support (MIDS) System at Lockheed–Georgia," *MIS Quarterly*, vol. 10 no. 5, (March 1987), p. 132.
7. N. Dean Meyer and Mary E. Boone, *The Information Edge*, (Agincourt, Ontario: Gage Educational Publishing, 1987), p. 217.
8. Peter G.W. Keen, "The On-Line CEO: How One Executive Uses MIS." Unpublished working paper, Micro Mainframe Inc., 1983, p. 20.
9. Ibid., p. 19–20.
10. Copyright © 1982 by the President and Fellows of Harvard College; all rights reserved. Reprinted by permission of *Harvard Business Review*. "The CEO Goes On-Line," by John F. Rockart and Michael E. Treacy, January–February 1982, p. 86.
11. Keen, "The On-Line CEO . . . , p. 14.

12. Meyer and Boone, *The Information Edge,* p. 221.
13. Ibid., 209–210.
14. Jeffrey L. Turner, "Executive Support Systems: A Comparative Study." Master's thesis, Sloan School of Management, MIT, Cambridge, Mass., 1985, p. 39.
15. Margaret Dickerman, "The Evolution and Diffusion of an Executive Support System: A Case Study." Master's thesis, Sloan School of Management, MIT, Cambridge, Mass., 1985.
16. Turner, "Executive Support Systems. . . ."
17. Ibid., p. 37.
18. Ibid., p. 38.
19. Houdeshel and Watson, "The . . .(MIDS) System at Lockheed–Georgia, p. 136."
20. David Friend, Pilot Executive Software, personal correspondence, July 21, 1986.
21. From XEROX AMERICAN SAMURAI by Gary Jacobson and John Hillkirk. Copyright © 1986 by Gary Jacobson and John Hillkirk. Reprinted with permission of the publisher. (New York: Macmillan Publishing Co., 1986), p. 82.

CHAPTER 6

HOW ESS ENHANCE
MENTAL MODELS

The most common early executive support applications were the office support area. The most dramatic impacts of ESS currently are seen in changes in the planning and control process. However, in the long term, the most significant effect of computer support for executives may be in the enhanced mental models of the systems' users.

As noted in Chapter 3, a mental model is "a cognitive construct" that describes a person's understanding of a particular segment of the managerial world.[1] McCaskey identified the fact that everyone has mental models developed through a process he calls "conceptual mapping."[2] McCaskey stresses that all of us live in a complex world which we need to simplify and organize if we are to operate effectively. He writes:

> At any moment we have only a limited, tangible physical reality around us—the office, the hallway, and the elevator, for example. We see chairs, walls, lights, color, and other people. We have names for, and knowledge about, all of these familiar objects. Most of this knowledge lies in the background of our attention, to be called to the foreground as needed. Our sense of reality, however, is not limited to the world immediately before us. We can visualize buildings, spaces, people, and events beyond our eyes. We can picture current and historical events around the world and use tools to extend our senses. These images, our names, our knowledge of how things fit together and what causes what to happen, constitute our "map." *A map is an interconnected set of understandings, formed by frequently implicit views*

of what one's interests and concerns are, what is important, and what demands action and what does not. It is a cognitive representation of the world and ourselves in it. (author's emphasis)

Each of us has unique maps that have grown out of our experiences and needs. Of course, we also share some maps more or less closely with family, office colleagues, neighbors, members of a political party, and with other groups of which we feel a part.

The recognized and named "world" is complex and ever-changing, and so we need to organize what is important and what is trivial, what is safe and what is dangerous, what is associated with what, and what causes what. The mental process and the product of this *organizing of reality*, this creating and maintaining a frame of reference, is what we call "conceptual mapping."[3]

The purpose of this chapter is to examine how executive support systems are used consciously and unconsciously to enhance conceptual maps. There is little hard evidence that executives use ESS to enrich their mental models. In fact, enhancing one's perspective of the business environment rarely was cited in our research as a *primary* motivation for developing an ESS. The evidence is limited to a few cases.

Improving his mental models was the objective stated by Ph.D. scientist George Hatsopoulos, chairman of Thermo Electron, an energy equipment manufacturer. Hatsopoulos developed computer-based models of his firms's operations, the industries in which the company competes, and the U.S. economy. He then adjusted his thinking in light of what he learned by watching the flow of data through the models.

The chairman of a large manufacturing company developed a series of forecasting models using historical data and business indicators, such as consumer confidence and building starts. These models allow him to assess sales forecasts from different perspectives, taking into account different variables. Over time, computer models have helped the chairman better grasp the relationships between the diverse factors that affect sales. The models also help in challenging the assumptions of his subordinates and help ensure that their forecasts are as realistic as possible.

While few executives talk explicitly of using ESS to improve their mental models, our interviews and the available

literature reveal many comments which suggest that an underlying conceptual model is being exercised by the executive in
looking at data. This manager's comment is typical:

> I bring a lot of knowledge to the party. Just scanning the current
> status of our operations enables me to see some things that those
> with less time in the company would not see as important. Al-
> though the resulting telephone calls undoubtedly shake up some
> of my subordinates, I think in the long run this is helpful to them,
> too.[4]

This executive implies that his view of the company and
industry enabled him to spot problems and opportunities not
obvious to others, who lacked the same conceptual map which
was built through years of experience.

Executives, it appears, do use many models in the managerial process. Pounds, in "The Process of Problem Finding,"
notes that problems and opportunities are recognized by managers through a process of comparing "current status versus
model." He says, "For the most part, these models are nonex-
plicit. The manager 'carries them in his head' or 'just knows'."[5]

Validating or helping to simplify the world that is "in his
head" is a major benefit of ESS for some executives. The desire
to improve their mental models, however, is rarely referred to
directly. Rather, phrases such as "I need to improve my understanding of the business," or "It gives me a better grasp of what's
going on in the company," are used to explain the reasons behind
some computer systems.

Applications which enhance the executive's fundamental
understanding of the business show up in many forms. One
executive served by a stream of information on his industry's
leading economic indicators says, "This is the linchpin on which
I operate. The better I internalize the status of these numbers,
the more confidently I can act." A utilities industry executive
who keeps a display of network status on his desk notes that it
improves his grasp of company operations.

For better understanding, some executives even turn to programming. Ronald Compton, president of American Re-Insurance Company, says, "By helping to create the software and by

using the computer myself, I understand the assumptions that go into what is on the screen and in the reports. I used to have someone else do it, but now I'd feel very uncomfortable [in not doing it myself] because it gives me a much more in-depth understanding of what's really going on in the company I'm in charge of."[6]

For William Smithburg, chairman and CEO of The Quaker Oats Company, an increased understanding of the firm's competitive environment is a striking advantage of his ESS. His Comshare and IFPS-based system provides him with easy access to Dow Jones News/Retrieval and extensive financial and marketing data bases. He says:

> With the computer, I understand better what is going on in the marketplace. I have a better grasp of both the world as reported by Dow Jones and the specifics of what my internally generated financial and marketing data tells me. I get the data faster, it tells me more about the world I am in, and it does it in a format that allows me to think about the information and interact with it. In the end, the system helps me understand more about the world that exists around a given business for which we are making a decision.

Better understanding of the company environment is also the goal of other executives. As one says, "By working with the data I originally thought I needed, I've been able to zero in on the data I actually need. We've expanded our data base significantly, but each step has led to a better understanding of our company and its environment."[7]

Charles Bowerman, vice president of marketing at Phillips Petroleum, also stresses the increased understanding of his marketplace that both data and text access provide for him. A key decision area for Bowerman is the pricing of petroleum products. Several electronic pricing services had historically been available to his staff, as had sales data. But they had never been drawn together on one system and, more importantly, this data had never been available to him for his own perusal. Bowerman says:

> The availability of pricing and sales data puts me in the middle of the managerial process. If there is need for a change in pricing

strategy both my staff and I are looking at common data. They don't need to take time to bring me up to date. The background data allows me to effectively take part in the decision where they have recommended a change. It also provides the capability, as I analyze what I see, for me to initiate change.

The key to this is having the background information available on a continuing basis so that I can better understand our markets. In addition to the pricing and sales data, I have a wealth of other information, which gives increased meaning to the sales data. API inventory figures and news briefs are readily available and important in supporting the management process. As more marketing managers receive computers, electronic mail "conversations" with the field managers will give me an improved understanding of what is actually going on in the marketplace.

Each morning, I look to see the impact of our price changes the day before. We can follow our sales rate every day. We have some 250 terminals through which we sell refined products. Making effective price changes strongly affects our bottom line.

The president of Diversified Electronics, who upgraded his management control system (discussed in Chapter 5), enjoyed this new opportunity for in-depth analysis:

Now that I've got accurate, available, and accessible data, the real joy of this system is it allows me to probe deeper into the data to enhance my understanding of the dynamics of our business. Instead of asking what happened to the sales in division A last month, I can ask: When we consolidate divisions A and B, what kind of profit do we get on product X? I can pose a lot more "what if" questions to understand the business, instead of just asking why sales are off.

Communicating the way an executive thinks is another benefit. A senior manager at Boeing says:

My subordinates have gained a better understanding of how I think. [With ESS] the data is so flexible and easy to manipulate that I don't mind changing my mind about what I want after I see the output to get it just the way I want it. That phenomenon is drawing the subordinate and the boss closer together. It's a little like mind reading. Because they know how I think, I'm getting better information on the first request.[8]

HOW ESS SUPPORT MENTAL MODELS

Other executives had similar comments. They emphasized their more robust understanding of the economy, their industries, and the business as a whole as a result of ESS. An analysis of their comments suggests six attributes of ESS most important in enhancing mental models:

1. Improved access to external data.
2. Ability to combine data from multiple sources.
3. Data presented in more meaningful formats.
4. Improved analytic and modeling capabilities.
5. Ability to surface and test assumptions about the business.
6. Off-hours data access.

Improved Access to External Data

Improving access to external data increases the effectiveness of the manager's environmental scanning by providing more relevant data quicker. Senior executives do much of their own scanning. Most see it as one of their primary tasks. In his study of Silicon Valley executives, El Sawy notes:

> CEOs in the high technology environment are very systematic scanners, and the surveillance activity, although seeming haphazard to the outside observer, is in reality well planned. They monitor information sources which they know have the likelihood of yielding strategic information. There are certain habitual sources that the CEO monitors and consults, especially for verification.[9]

The increased speed and payoff of computer-based scanning helps the executive justify doing it personally instead of delegating it to staff. Senior managers often find great value in filtering external data through their own mental models. Here are some typical comments.

> Because I'm a CEO I have to focus on what is going on outside the company. In terms of my time at the computer, I probably

spend two-thirds of it looking at the Dow Jones news service. I get a great deal of information about what's going on in the food industry this way. It is much easier than having my secretary watch newspapers and clip stories. For example, if someone says there was a product announcement today, I just go over to the computer, hit several keys and a few seconds later I'm reading the story. It saves a lot of time. —William Smithburg, chairman and CEO, The Quaker Oats Company.

I find the external information, such as world news and competitive information, very helpful. I can scan the headlines and read the stories that look interesting. I don't have to wade through a lot of irrelevant material. Also, I find that the system focuses my attention, and I actually get better comprehension and retention of the information. —Derwyn Phillips, executive vice president, Gillette North America[10]

I do a lot of scanning myself . . . there may be subtleties that others won't see — CEO of a high technology firm.[11]

If someone else did my information screening by clipping articles that he or she felt were pertinent to me, I would lose a lot of control. That person would have to judge what's important to me, and he or she simply wouldn't have my level of experience to know what nuance in a story may have long-term implications.—Lee Paschall, former CEO and president of American Satellite Company.[12]

Those commenting above represent a growing number of top managers using an ESS to collect information about the external environment. We found others as well:

- The chairman and vice chairman of a major health care company monitor the Dow Jones News/Retrieval Service for information about competitors, new drug releases, foreign exchange rates, international news, and major business stories that affect the company.

- A sales director at ICL tracks merger and acquisition activity involving his major customers.

- The vice president of corporate affairs for Northwest Industries monitored business news, and stock market activity of his competitors.

These executives who do much of their own scanning are not atypical. El Sawy found that chief executives resist delegating environmental scanning because their cognitive maps are more complete and more sophisticated than those of subordinates. As a result, senior managers will perceive information differently than those at lower levels of the organization.

El Sawy categorizes one type of strategic information executives get through scanning as *accommodation information.* He describes it this way:

> Accommodation information causes an individual's cognitive schema (loosely interpreted as the individual's frames of reference) to accommodate and change.
>
> *Accommodation information* is general surveillance information which is not necessarily coupled with a specific threat or opportunity. This is usually information of a very general nature. This information is important in that it enabled CEO's later to interpret specific information differently, and perhaps better identify threats and opportunities. In other words, it is "wisdom-increasing" information. CEOs referred to this information as "Information that molds the way in which we think in a broad sense like the *Wall Street Journal* and *Business Week.*"[13]

Accommodation information is, however, far from the most significant information for an executive. Viewing it in another dimension, El Sawy differentiates between "personal" information communicated specifically to an individual and "impersonal" information found in periodicals and speeches. He and other researchers observe that managers rely more heavily on personal than impersonal sources for strategic information.

Combining impersonal external sources with more personal staff analysis is a feature of a small, but growing, number of ESS. ConAgra's executives, for example, have direct access to commodities markets information and Dow Jones News/Retrieval. Reports are also provided by internal financial and economics research departments on critical factors such as weekly crop conditions and interest rates.

At Phillips Petroleum, staff analysts summarize relevant economic and political news from around the world three times a day for top management. Executive Vice President Robert Wallace, who accesses these updates regularly through his ESS, says:

> I'm normally in my office by 7:45 in the morning, and the first thing I used to grab was the *Wall Street Journal*. Now, instead, the first thing I look at is the business highlights worldwide on our system, so that by 8 o'clock I have literally looked at all the critical external factors for our business. I've been clear around the world with that business summary, and I have a very good feel before my day starts of what kind of environment I'm operating in right now. That is extremely valuable for an executive at my level.

Computer-based executive support can provide a substantial advantage in processing external information, as illustrated by the examples throughout this section. Access to external data bases not only provides standard information faster than print media (e.g., news summaries and stock quotes), but, as Lee Paschall of American Satellite contends, it also makes additional information available to the executive—information that previously was too time consuming to obtain. He says:

> When we put together a long-range plan for American Satellite, I used the data base to search through two years of information on fiber-optics. It would have been hopeless to try and find all this information by hand. We got a complete story of what has happened in fiber-optics; we determined the plans, financing, and actual implementation of various fiber networks. I was able to give the Board a very comprehensive report on where fiber-optics is going and what they should do about it.[14]

El Sawy points out that the importance of environmental scanning should increase as the business environment becomes more complex and interconnected. Thus, we expect the use of ESS in collecting this type of strategic information to increase as well. But, to facilitate this, two things must happen.

First, the software used to access external information must improve. Executives need an interface that allows them to log onto external data bases quickly and to search fluidly without having to remember large sets of commands. Although much of the software to date has been awkward for the casual executive user, more and more interfaces are being offered that require a minimum number of keystrokes to access and search commercial data bases. At present, much of the external access is provided indirectly by ESS support groups which bring information onto the executive's system, thus making it more easily available.

The other change that will increase executive use of ESS for environmental scanning is the availability of more high-level, industry-specific data bases. Most commercial data bases today contain information that is too raw and unsynthesized to be of much value to executives. Again, to get around this, some IS departments are taking on the responsibility of synthesizing external data to make it more useful to executives, and some small vendors have sprung up to address this problem.

One such company, Strategic Intelligence Systems, offers competitive intelligence data bases for 18 different industries, including financial services, aerospace, and food. These data bases, updated monthly, abstract and analyze information from over 500 publications. Topics covered include market activity, industry trends, legislation, new product development, and so on. "This enables us to scan many more publications," says Jim Figura of Colgate-Palmolive, "but the biggest barrier in this area is getting expert knowledge out of the executive's head in a very abstract and free-flowing form and down to the people scanning the data sources so they can recognize what is useful."

Ability to Combine Data From Multiple Sources

Access to external data is only one ESS capability that improves executive understanding. Combining data from multiple sources enables executives to explore new relationships and improve their grasp of the business. Gerald Viste, former president of Wausau Insurance Companies, describes this benefit:

> We have extended the resources of the [ESS] to include a large library of public data on our competitors and the industry. This has been particularly useful when matched with our internal data and has significantly deepened our insight into the problems and opportunities which challenge us as managers. We also couple

the information from DRI's industry model with these other resources.

Was this same information available before we had terminals in our offices? Of course it was. But it was a burdensome task to assemble it from the volumes of books and reports into formats which matched the problem areas under scrutiny.[15]

In another case, a vice president for product development and marketing uses a multiple-source management review system. Product/sales data is extracted from a corporate data base which consolidates product information from around the world. Expenditures are pulled automatically from the general ledger system. Data on product quality is extracted from yet another system, and still more information, such as product development milestones, is collected manually from department files. This information is synthesized monthly into a set of graphs and charts created in a standard format.

The vice president describes his use of the system in management review meetings this way:

> When looking at data on the screen we have an immediate perspective on the trends that are taking place because we see the information for previous months and previous quarters, so there is generally instant agreement about the trends and where things are going.
>
> I couldn't have intensified the review process without the technology because there was such a mass of data that it was extremely difficult for me to form a view about the implications of all the data without spending an awful lot of time studying it.

Another example of how ESS enable executives to combine and review data from disparate sources was discussed in Chapter 5. To analyze a competitive situation, Jon Boscia, senior vice president at Lincoln National Corporation, combined internal sales data, competitive activity, reports from his field sales force, and financial data on the competitor from an external industry data base. Boscia used this information to analyze a competitive situation and to develop a plan of attack. Without the technology, Boscia feels that it would have been virtually impossible for him to have collected the data and prepared the necessary analysis.

Data Presented in More Meaningful Formats

Presenting data in flexible formats, combining text, numbers, and graphics, helps many executives understand their businesses by highlighting trends they might not have recognized with just tabular data. Ronald Compton, president of American Re-Insurance Company, explains it this way:

> I'm a very visual person—my first love is photography. So graphics is a wonderful tool for me. I can understand them quickly and so can others. I always say that graphics is a language you can teach anybody. I'll tell you, before we got this system, it could take an entire day to see the trends that are contained in one graph we're looking at.[16]

Another executive observes:

> I think graphically. It's so nice to be able to easily graph out the data in which I'm interested. . . . And it's especially nice to be able to adjust the display to see the data in the exact perspective that best tells the story.[17]

The availability of new presentation formats—particularly graphics—has an important impact on the way executives think about information. But graphics is not the only formatting advantage provided by the computer. The CEO at one major food distributor took advantage of the computer's ability to combine tabular, text, and graphic data on the same page to satisfy his idiosyncratic way of viewing performance data.

Most commonly, graphics are used for standard performance reports or to present the results of ad hoc queries. The president of Banco Internacional found that a graphic display of profits versus goals and forecasts provided a picture over time and revealed dynamics of the business he had not previously recognized. Derwyn Phillips, Gillette's executive vice president, implemented his ESS largely to view performance reports graphically. Phillips believes that executives can get too caught up in minor variances when looking only at numbers. The key is in seeing trends, he says, not minor blips, and graphs help management do that.

At The New England, another financial services company whose products traditionally have been insurance-related, Executive Vice President Bob Shafto says the most valuable aspect of his ESS is the graphics capability which allows him to more fully comprehend performance trends over time. Built with Comshare's ESS software package, Shafto's system tracks the monthly performance of the company's 100 general agencies. He can view a series of graphs showing different dimensions of each agency's performance. "It's being able to see all these dimensions at once and the relative changes over time that's so valuable," he says. "Before, I only had a gut feel from talking to people that the trends were there, but now with the graphs I can verify what is actually happening and effectively communicate this understanding to other officers of The New England."

Like Phillips and Shafto, a regional sales director at ICL finds graphic information easier to absorb. He says, "I have a propensity for graphics. I'm a poor reader, and I find pages and pages of numbers difficult in helping to understand what's going on."

This search for understanding—the ability to recognize trends and patterns in the welter of data which buffets executives—is stressed by Horton in his profile of eight chief executives. He writes:

> The effective CEO is constantly in motion, dashing off to get first-hand information—visiting company sites, conversing with employees and customers, reconnoitering the outside environment, all the while testing the validity of the information that has been heard back at headquarters. One CEO in this book referred to his unannounced visits to company sites as "reality testing."
>
> Despite the prodigious amounts of data that arrive at the CEO's desk, there is an unquenchable thirst for more. The volume and fire-hose velocity of this information would overwhelm most executives, but the successful chief develops the capacity to stand to the side, sampling chunks of data as they rush by, looking for patterns and incongruities. To draw meaning from a mass of data in motion requires a capacity to synthesize—an ability to convert data into information and information into knowledge.[18]

Wausau president Gerald Viste sums up the benefits of graphics in this process:

> Although the flexibility and efficiency with which one can develop tabular reports is a convenience, the ability to graph the data is of far greater importance. I have found that graphic presentations are much more effective than the tabular format in determining stability or volatility, direction, change and observations in our operations. To see data as a graphic time series rather than as a column of comparisons really highlights significant situations.[19]

Improved Analytic and Modeling Capabilities

In addition to providing data from new sources in new formats, ESS enhances the executive's understanding of the business by providing analytic and modeling capabilities. These systems allow exploration of the cause-and-effect relationships which underlie the firm's business environment. They bring enhanced spreadsheet analysis and DSS modeling capabilities to the senior manager, although the actual number crunching may still be done by staff members. While some comprehensive models have been built for or by senior executives, most analytical work addresses particular problems. Former Procter & Gamble Chairman Owen Butler is a good example of an executive who learned to program and build financial models on his own. He says:

> It's much more efficient to think through a problem at the same time you are working on it—in this way you interact directly with the thought process. Sometimes I get to the point where I realize I want to change a model and I can do it right then and there. If someone else was building it this wouldn't be possible.[20]

Butler is one of a number of executives who found building formal models helpful. David Davis, president of a $100 million British company, is another. Writing to the *Sloan Management Review* to rebut an article by John Dearden, which stated that computers were useless to executives, Davis described one of his personal computer applications:

> A commodity that could not be perfectly hedged accounted for a major portion of the cost of our products. This commodity had

a significant impact on the cost of production, could materially affect the contribution on sales, and, in conjunction with currency and other commodity movements, could cause a major shift in the location of the most profitable marketplace. The price of this commodity had to be followed closely. Although this was possible, but time-consuming on a manual basis, the personal computer made it easy to evaluate the current position more rapidly and to explore the various probabilities in detail.[21]

Exploring alternative scenarios on-line is an application used infrequently by senior managers, but we did find several examples. At Firestone, the president works closely with his controller, who accesses the ESS to explore future scenarios; e.g., "If we raised our equity in our French affiliate, what impact would that have on . . . ?" This modeling-system approach to "what if" scenarios allows management to use actual financial data base information without disrupting official financial and accounting data.

John Dembeck, vice president and treasurer of the Olin Corporation, has similar sessions with his chairman:

> The Chairman frequently comes into my office and poses a question or problem. We look at the screen together in order to evaluate the problem. In this way we try a wide range of alternatives, scenarios. If an analyst were coming in here to make a presentation relating to a problem we gave him, we would probably be much more limited as to how many alternatives we gave him. If we constantly changed our minds, he'd go crazy. And we might be embarrassed to ask for an analysis of some of our wilder ideas.[22]

All of these executives are doing analysis that would not be practical without a computer. One bank executive, however, sounds a temperate note on this newfound cognitive capability. He says, "Where we used to do two what-ifs in two days, we now do ten in an hour. It doesn't necessarily lead to better decisions, but you feel more secure."[23]

David Davis adds, "Until the last few years, I had viewed most of the more complex quantitative techniques that I learned at business school as so much spare baggage; I now find that I have used more of them in the last two years than I had in the previous ten."[24]

Does increased analytic and modeling capability help a manager improve his mental model(s) of the business? We really do not know. But an increasing number of top managers say it does. And the concept behind modeling—to abstract the fundamental structure of a complex environment—points in that direction.

Ability to Surface and Test Assumptions about the Business

Surfacing and testing assumptions about the business is a major but usually unforeseen benefit of ESS. ESS provide data to challenge the assumptions that underlie a manager's mental model. By definition, changing assumptions changes the executive's understanding of the business. In a large food distributor, a system was designed at the request of the CEO to improve the firm's management control process. But the reports emanating from the system also challenged the chief executive's assumptions about the future direction of the company. He says, "When I looked at graphs of revenues in our SBUs, and saw the three core businesses standing out, while the other units were flat and the new businesses were negative, that had an effect on me. I realized we needed to put more support into the core businesses. The system changed my assumptions about diversification because it confronted us with hard data."

An ESS enables senior management to question more readily their assumptions and those of their subordinates. The need for executives to surface and test assumptions is well established in the literature.[25]

But, what is the relationship between assumptions and mental models? Wagner answers this way:

A mental image of the business environment is developed. That image is an imperfect simplification of the environment, based on limited inputs and mental processes—it is a mental model which guides the organization's actions. My definition of assumptions is that they are the components of that image.

In this sense, assumptions include beliefs, values, hopes, dreams, comfortable illusions, and familiar habits of thought.... Many assumptions together—in an individual's mind or in the collective mind of a managerial group—form the mental images on which decisions are based. My point is that a deep, fundamental need of senior management is for technology to help externalize, communicate, understand, challenge, arrive at consensus upon, and own *assumptions*.[26]

Assumptions are key building blocks of mental models. When assumptions are challenged, the model may be affected. Henderson et al. have argued that the primary role of ESS are to manage the executives' assumptions about the business. They note:

> The management of assumptions . . . can not be delegated. The assumption set is the domain of executive management and the responsibility for ensuring the validity of assumptions rests clearly with executive management.
>
> We suggest that a major implicit reason for existing ESS is to support executives in the analysis of critical assumptions.[27]

The management of assumptions may be a reason for the ESS, but it remains implicit with only one or two exceptions. Yet, as a by-product of the ESS, it can be very significant.

Sometimes, executives use ESS to challenge assumptions directly. At Thermo-Electron, Chairman George Hatsopoulos had doubts about one division's claim of 80 percent market share in a specialized segment for industrial furnaces. Hatsopoulos built a data base to check the claim and discovered that division management's assumptions about market share were wrong. The share was lower in the industrial furnaces segment, but higher in another part of the market. As a result, the division shifted its strategy to build on its market leadership.[28]

Off-Hours Data Access

Many executives are frustrated by their dependence on others for information they need on a particular issue. An ESS gives an executive access to corporate or external data "after hours" without relying on staff or secretarial support. One senior manager describes how this helps:

Some of my best ideas come at fallow times between five in the evening and seven the next morning. Access to the relevant data to check out something right then is very important. My home terminal lets me perform the analysis while it's at the forefront of my mind.[29]

Being able to check on a particular item late in the evening can mean the difference between pursuing a line of thought or putting it aside. Since many executives feel they do their best thinking outside the work day routine, having immediate access to corporate data can facilitate this cognitive process.

Ronald Compton, president of American Re-Insurance Company, expresses this succinctly. "An idea could come to me at any time," he says. "With a PC at home, a lap portable to carry along when I travel and when I'm on my sailboat, and one here at the office, it's always close at hand."[30]

William Smithburg, chairman and CEO of The Quaker Oats Company, had a workstation installed at home where he has much more time to access his ESS. He explains:

First of all, I travel a lot so I'm not in the office much anyway. When I am in the office my work is strictly communication, either in meetings or on the phone. I don't have time to sit down and do interactive work with a computer, except to spend a few seconds checking a number or reading something on Dow Jones. So my computer time in the office is minimal.

But, when I'm home, I can really sit down for an hour and think about our long range plans or how a given brand is doing. Often at home I use the corporate data base when I have a recommendation before me for something that will come up at the next day's management committee meeting. I like to go into the historical data base for the products involved to get a better understanding of the situation. It's a lot easier than calling my controller at home on Sunday night and saying, "Have this in my office tomorrow morning."

Support for off-hours thinking does not directly improve an executive's understanding of the business, but making information available at times when some of a manager's most reflective thinking is done is bound to prove useful.

CONCLUSION

To reiterate, the management literature shows that mental models are an integral part of executive work, but just how ESS supports this cognitive process is less clear. Nevertheless, executives point to six ways in which computer use enhances their understanding of the business. The technology provides them:

- Improved access to external data.
- Ability to combine data from multiple sources.
- Data presented in more meaningful formats.
- Improved analytic and modeling capabilities.
- Ability to surface and test assumptions about the business.
- Off-hours data access.

Perhaps the most interesting of these is computer modeling. The potential value of modeling techniques for top management has been identified by Mintzberg[31] and many others. To date, these techniques have proved to be of limited value. But, with improved software and data access, as well as increased computer literacy, the number of senior managers who find computer modeling a valuable aid is likely to increase.

We have now examined the range of applications derived from executive support systems. In Chapter 4 we looked at the office support applications designed to improve the efficiency and effectiveness of individual managers. Changes in an organization's planning and control processes were identified in Chapter 5. Finally, in Chapter 6, we reviewed ways in which ESS assists the cognitive processes so critical to top management performance. The next five chapters will be devoted to the critical factors in implementing executive support systems.

NOTES

1. John M. Carroll, "Satisfaction Conditions for Mental Models," *Contemporary Psychology*, vol. 30, no. 9, (1985), p. 693.
2. From McCaskey's THE EXECUTIVE CHALLENGE: MANAGING CHANGE AND AMBIGUITY. Copyright 1982 by Michael

B. McCaskey. Reprinted with permission from Ballinger Publishing Company.

3. Ibid., p. 17–18.

4. Copyright © 1982 by the President and Fellows of Harvard College; all rights reserved. Reprinted by permission of *Harvard Business Review*. "The CEO Goes On-Line" by John F. Rockart and Michael E. Treacy, January-February 1982, p. 8686.

5. William F. Pounds, "The Process of Problem Finding," *Sloan Management Review*, Fall 1969, p. 7.

6. N. Dean Meyer and Mary E. Boone, *The Information Edge* (Agincourt, Ontario: Gage Educational Publishing, 1987), p. 218.

7. Copyright © 1982 by the President and Fellows of Harvard College; all rights reserved. Reprinted by permission of *Harvard Business Review*. "The CEO Goes On-Line" by John F. Rockart and Michael E. Treacy, January-February 1982, p. 86.

8. Jeffrey L. Turner, "Executive Support Systems: A Comparative Study." Master's thesis, Sloan School of Management, MIT, Cambridge, Mass.: (May 1985), p. 28.

9. Omar E. El Sawy, "Personal Information Systems for Strategic Scanning in Turbulent Environments: Can the CEO Go On-Line?" *MIS Quarterly*, March 1985, p. 58.

10. An Interview with Donald Palmer, Controller, Gillette, N.A. (Boston, Mass.: Pilot Executive Software, 1986).

11. El Sawy, "Personal Information Systems for Strategic Scanning . . . , p. 56.

12. Meyer and Boone, *The Information Edge*, p. 227.

13. El Sawy, "Personal Information Systems for Strategic Scanning . . . ," p. 57.

14. Meyer and Boone, *The Information Edge*, p. 226.

15. Gerald Viste, "Executive Use of Interactive MIS." Speech to American Assembly of Collegiate Schools of Business, Phoenix, Ariz., May 3, 1984.

16. Meyer and Boone, *The Information Edge*, p. 217.

17. Copyright © 1982 by the President and Fellows of Harvard College; all rights reserved. Reprinted by permission of *Harvard Business Review*. "The CEO Goes On-Line" by John F. Rockart and Michael E. Treacy, January-February 1982, p. 86.

18. Thomas R. Horton, *What Works for Me* (New York: Random House, 1986), p. 388.

19. Viste, "Executive Use of Interactive MIS," p. 6.

20. Henry Fersko-Weisiss, "Personal Computing at the Top," *Personal Computing*, March 1985, p. 71.

21. Reprinted from "Computers in Top Management," by David Davis, *Sloan Management Review*, Spring 1984, p. 63, by permission of the publisher. Copyright © 1984 by the Sloan Management Review Association. All rights reserved.

22. Meyer and Boone, *The Information Edge*, p. 215.

23. Peter Nulty, "How Personal Computers Change Manager's Lives," *Fortune*, September 3, 1984, p. 44.

24. Reprinted from "Computers in Top Management," by David Davis, *Sloan Management Review*, Spring 1984, p. 63, by permission of the publisher. Copyright © 1984 by the Sloan Management Review Association. All rights reserved.

25. See Richard O. Mason and Ian F. Mitroff, *Challenging Strategic Planning Assumptions: Theory, Cases and Techniques*, (New York: Wiley, and Sons, 1981); Pierre Wack, "Scenarios: Uncharted Waters Ahead," *Harvard Business Review*, vol. 63, no. 5, (September-October 1985); and Peter Senge, "Catalyzing Systems Thinking Within Organizations," working paper, Systems Dynamics Group, MIT, Cambridge, Mass., 1987.

26. G.E. Wagner, "DSS: Dealing With Executive Assumptions in the Office of the Future," *Managerial Planning*, vol. 30, no. 5, (March-April, 1982), p. 4.

27. John C. Henderson, John F. Rockart, and John G. Sifonis, "A Planning Methodology for Integrating Management Support Systems," *Working Paper No. 116*, Center for Information Systems Research, Sloan School of Management, MIT, Cambridge, Mass., September 1984, pp. 15, 23.

28. Mary Bralove, "Some Chief Executives Bypass, and Irk, Staffs in Getting Information," *The Wall Street Journal*, January 12, 1983, p. 22.

29. Copyright © 1982 by the President and Fellows of Harvard College; all rights reserved. Reprinted by permission of *Harvard Business Review*. "The CEO Goes On-Line" by John F. Rockart and Michael E. Treacy, January-February 1982, p. 86.

30. Meyer and Boone, *The Information Edge*, p. 218.

31. Henry Mintzberg, *The Nature of Managerial Work* (New York: Harper and Row, 1973).

CHAPTER 7

IMPLEMENTATION: OVERVIEW
AND SPONSORSHIP ROLES

One of the major barriers to the spread of ESS has been a lack of understanding about the implementation of these systems. For more mature IS applications, such as transaction processing and decision support systems, implementation methods have been developed based on years of experience and much trial and error. Unfortunately, these methods cannot be transferred directly to the ESS domain. The fragmented nature of executive work, the high degree of environmental uncertainty at this level of the organization, and the political ramifications of providing top management with more and better information, as well as other factors, make implementing ESS a special challenge.

Factors in ESS Implementation

There is a substantial body of literature on information systems implementation.[1] While particular approaches differ, the fundamental processes for designing and installing transaction-processing systems are well understood. For DSS, however, the people, tasks, and the development process itself are all different and thus require a new approach to implementation.[2] Similarly, for executive support, the users, applications, and organizational and technical issues are all different from those faced either in transaction processing or DSS; thus, the approach to implementation must differ. In these next five chapters, we focus on the factors critical to the implementation of executive support systems.

We do this, however, mindful of the limitations of factors research. We have no doubt that our initial description of critical factors in ESS implementation will be refined by other researchers as the field evolves. Further, the variables we identify here provide a *structural* approach to ESS development and increase the likelihood that an ESS project will be successful. They shed no light, however, on the *dynamics* of the implementation process.

Keen and Scott Morton addressed this problem when writing about decision support systems almost a decade ago. Their comments are still relevant for ESS:

> The conclusion to be drawn from . . . the [DDS] factor research is not so much that we lack any basis for a conventional wisdom as that there are obviously very few absolutes. It is this fact that makes it so hard to study implementation and learn better ways of increasing chances of success.
>
> The most obvious point is that we just do not understand the *dynamics* of implementation.
>
> Implementation is a *process*. This cannot be stressed too much. One reason the [DSS] factor studies have not found any general factors that affect implementation is almost certainly because the dynamics of the process swamp particular structural aspects of the situation. For example, it may well be that top management support is a critical facilitator in implementation because it provides a power base, credibility, and momentum for action. However, the *behavior* of the parties in the implementation can either erode or build on this support. What determines the quality of the outcome is the designer's ability to identify the key constraints of the situation, to then match the formal technology to those constraints, and to work with the people to whom they apply. This is a complex process and very few rules can confidently be applied.[3]

Keen and Scott Morton make two significant points with regard to DSS implementation. First, each implementation is unique, different from every other DSS project because it takes place in a dynamic organizational setting. Second, throughout years of DSS research, no statistically meaningful set of key factors for implementation, replicable from study to study, has been found. This is understandable. Organizations are not scientific laboratories. Each system is different and affects different organizations in different ways.

Yet, in a new field, we must have a starting point. In organization after organization, we observed eight areas which appeared to be most important for effective ESS implementation. In several follow-on case studies, we found that both executive sponsors and IS staff involved in ESS agreed that these areas were very significant. Therefore, although mindful of the words of caution noted above, we present these eight critical factors. The reader, however, must determine the relative importance of each factor within the context of a specific organization, while watching for other factors that may be of equal if not greater importance in a particular firm.

The eight factors critical to successful ESS implementation are:

1. *A Committed and Informed Executive Sponsor.* This is an executive who has a realistic understanding of the capabilities and limitations of ESS, and who values the system enough to spend considerable time and energy guiding its development.

2. *An Operating Sponsor.* To leverage the time of the executive sponsor, it is often necessary to have an operating sponsor designated to manage the details of implementation from the user's side. This person is usually a trusted executive subordinate (often the CFO or controller, or an executive assistant) who is well acquainted with the executive sponsor's work style and way of thinking.

3. *Appropriate IS Staff.* As in any project, the quality of the ESS project manager on the IS side is important. This person should have technical as well as business knowledge, and the ability to communicate effectively with senior management. The support staff also must be sophisticated enough to interact with top management. In addition, this ESS design team should have a workable relationship with the rest of the IS department.

4. *Appropriate Technology.* The choice of hardware and software has a major bearing on the acceptance of a system. An early barrier to executive support was the lack

of hardware and software that fit the demands of highly variable executive work styles and environments. More products, however, are now being designed for the ESS market.

5. *Management of Data.* The ability to provide access to reliable data, from both external and internal sources, is a major issue in ESS development. Aggregating, accessing, and extracting data from production data bases in a corporation with multiple suborganizations can be a roadblock to ESS implementation.

6. *Clear Link to Business Objectives.* The ESS must solve a business problem or meet a need that can be addressed effectively with IS technology. There should be a clear benefit to using the technology.

7. *Management of Organizational Resistance.* Political resistance to ESS is a common cause of implementation failure. An ESS alters information flows, and this can shift power relationships in a company. Anticipating and managing the political ramifications of an ESS will remain a potential problem throughout the life of the system.

8. *Management of System Evolution and Spread.* An installation that is successful and used regularly by the executive sponsor usually produces pressures for rapid expansion of the system as the user quickly recognizes and demands additional applications. A useful ESS also produces demands by peers or subordinates for access to a similar system. Managing the process of "spread" means identifying the technical orientation and work style, as well as specific job function and information needs of potential users, and taking these into account when expanding the system.

It is worth pointing out that these implementation factors are essentially descriptive, based primarily on a research sample of 30 cases. Most, or all, of the eight factors were relevant during the implementation of systems deemed successful by executive users and developers. While it is unclear that favorable handling of these factors will guarantee system acceptance, there is substantial evidence that failure to consider these issues increases the chances of system failure.

In the balance of this chapter, we discuss the key roles of executive and operating sponsors in the implementation process. Chapter 8 will be devoted to IS resources—staff, technology, and data. Linking ESS technology to specific business objectives is the focus of Chapter 9, while anticipating and managing problems of organizational resistance is the topic of Chapter 10. Finally, Chapter 11 covers problems encountered in managing the evolution and spread of an ESS. The last two chapters are devoted to some initial observations concerning organizational impacts, and a few final ruminations on ESS.

A COMMITTED AND INFORMED
EXECUTIVE SPONSOR

The executive sponsor is the most senior user of an executive support system. This is the person who initially requests the ESS. He or she also manages or monitors the implementation process. While this sponsor's role is well-defined, the way the role is fulfilled varies depending on the individual's personality, management style, technical orientation, and perception of the business. Here are five different executive sponsors:

• Firestone's CEO, John Nevin, is described by his staff as the consumate accountant, but not a hands-on analyst. He has a fascination for the technology, and a great penchant for accounting detail. This chief executive, however, would say, "This is *our* data base, not mine, and I want my management groups to understand the importance of using it." He lives through his managers, challenging everything, dotting i's and crossing t's, but he is fascinated more by what the numbers indicate than by the technology. He, therefore, depends on his controller to do most of the computer analysis.

• Charles Jacobs, former general manager of Raytheon's Missile Systems Division, is described as a "good engineer" knowledgeable about IS. Jacobs needed a system to put data at his fingertips because he found it impossible to remember all the information he needed to stay on top of a large number of programs. Moreover, he was not inclined to take notes during discussions with subordinates. His style was informal, pursuing issues on an ad hoc basis. His system supported this. The ESS was initially designed for him with no thought about use elsewhere.

• Bruce Armstrong, a director of manufacturing operations for ICL, has a relatively hands-off approach to managing his plants. He believes managers should be given quantifiable objectives and then left alone unless something goes wrong. Armstrong relies on his line managers to solve daily problems while he focuses on trends week-to-week. For this reason, he wanted an ESS that provided trend information which would tell him instantly if an operation was on track. "I don't want to look at detail," he says. "I pay other guys to do that."

• Mike Jensen, former president of Banco Internacional, believes in strong direction from the top. At the bank, he kept constant pressure on his managers and had a clear vision of where he wanted the bank to go. Jensen knew what he wanted in an executive support system, was dedicated to making it happen, and was its main user, beginning each day at the terminal. Jensen's system and the data it monitors reflects his view of the organization and its strategy.

• The chairman of a large manufacturing company is an engineer by training and learned Fortran programming early in his career. ("It gave me a terrible dull headache.") Today, he can easily write queries to a Focus data base. "I've never had trouble visualizing formats, or mental flow diagrams, and I like to manipulate data myself," he says. "The question is: Does the PC fit into your style of management? I don't think many executives will do what I do. I spend lots of time at home working with the PC."

One can define ESS as a management concept which reflects the unique perspective and style of its sponsor and the business. Just as there is no typical executive, there is no typical ESS. The major thing the five managers above have in common is that they all wanted a computer-based support system badly enough to champion its development. But the similarities end there.

Sponsors have different technical orientations, ranging from the hands-off approach of Firestone's chief executive to the manufacturing company chairman who used to write Fortran programs. This technical orientation is reflected in the way the sponsors use their systems. Firestone's CEO, John Nevin, leaves virtually all use of the system to his subordinates, relying particularly on his controller for analysis, while Mike Jensen at Banco Internacional sat at his terminal every day, monitoring bank activities.

In many ways, ESS design and use reflects different sponsor styles. For example, Jacobs at Raytheon was not detail-oriented, yet his need for detail was a strong motivation for developing the system. On the other hand, Nevin at Firestone is "the consumate accountant," dotting i's and crossing t's, and he found value in an executive support system as well.

Finally, we see in these five executive sponsors a different sense of system ownership and purpose. Jacobs viewed his as a personal system at the outset, as did many other early ESS users, while Jensen, Nevin and Armstrong saw their systems as having organizational implications. The sense of system ownership and purpose can vary widely among sponsors.

Of the 30 companies we studied in detail, executive sponsors held the following positions:

13 presidents/CEOs.

2 chairmen.

1 vice chairman.

2 executive vice presidents.

2 senior vice presidents.

4 division general managers.

1 chief financial officer.

3 vice presidents.

2 no executive sponsors.

No matter what position the sponsor holds, there is a correlation between the degree of executive involvement in implementation and the use and ultimate impact of the system on the organization. There are two stages of sponsorship: initiating and driving the system into existence, and using the system. Those who push hardest to develop a system usually end up using it actively, too. Most of the time this increases the impact of the system and encourages its spread throughout the organization. But there are exceptions to this rule. An executive may drive a system into existence, then delegate most of its use to others, as in the case of the CEO at Firestone.

Whether or not the executive makes hands-on use of the system, however, it is virtually impossible to install one successfully without a strong, committed sponsor who will focus time and energy on the project.

At Gillette North America (GNA), Executive Vice President Derwyn Phillips is a prototypical executive sponsor. One subordinate described his involvement this way:

> Derwyn initiated the system by asking if we couldn't use computer graphics to portray key trends for him. Then he was very patient going through some of the initial hardware and software issues. There were many technical problems and limitations in the system at first. Derwyn functioned as a pilot operation and as a test site, and committed his time and support to do that. In addition, he continually reviewed the objectives of the system, which changed over time, and reviewed the progress we were making, adding specific requests, comments, and observations as we went along. Finally, he took a leadership role in stressing the importance of using the ESS in all operations of Gillette North America.

Paul Allaire, senior vice president and chief of staff at Xerox at the start of the ESS project, served as executive sponsor in a similar fashion. At Xerox, however, the initial problems for the sponsor were more organizational than technical. Xerox was developing an ESS for its entire senior management team at corporate headquarters, and Allaire recognized the potential for resistance among the corporate staff who might feel threatened by the new system.

Allaire wanted to implement the system as part of an overall strategy to improve the management processes in Xerox. His role is described by Ken Soha, ESS project manager:

As general manager of corporate headquarters, Paul was the senior management advocate. He had to be the spokesman for the vision of the ESS. He had to be a prophet, advocate, and supporter. In important meetings, he had to make key statements about his vision of the ESS that were clear and unambiguous. He also had to use his influence as a supporter, facilitator, and peer pressurer to help us get things done. As a result, Paul began influencing both top management and staff. The vision for the ESS became part of his life.

One of the critical things Allaire did in his role of executive sponsor was to keep the ESS project highly visible in the organization so that those involved would recognize it as a priority for top management. The corporate management committee, which consists of the firm's six senior executives, has a top-ten list of key projects, and Allaire kept the ESS project on that list for two years. This ensured the resources and political support needed for the system to survive.

In ESS implementation, only the executive sponsor has the influence needed for the system to be created and used. Although the day-to-day management of the project can be delegated to an operational sponsor (see the next section), the leadership rests with the senior executive user, and this responsibility cannot be delegated.

For Lack of an Executive Sponsor...

At Auto Electronics, the general manager was described as someone who would "run the world from a terminal if he could." He installed an ESS that consisted largely of office support applications. He pushed his executive team to use the system, installing terminals in their offices and homes. He communicated constantly by electronic mail and expected his subordinates to do the same. This general manager had a clear idea of how he wanted the system used. But he was promoted, and his successor believed each executive should decide what applications to use and refused to push for further development. The system languished.

Similarly, at Stowe Computers the ESS project had good visibility initially under the direction of the CFO. Before the system was installed, however, the CFO decided he did not have enough time to oversee the project, and he delegated it to the director of information systems. This sent an unintended message to the organization that the ESS was no longer important. As the system's designers lost direct access to senior management, the ESS lost the political support needed to succeed.

In one Boeing division, the director of operations initiated an ESS, but when he was reassigned his replacement did not have the same interest in the system. Sponsorship was ultimately taken on by a group of executives who formed an ESS "steering committee." The system did not survive.

At a regional telephone company, the IS department tried to implement an ESS without an executive sponsor. In fact, no executive had even expressed interest in a computer system. Asked to characterize the commitment of top management, the ESS project manager said, "There was no commitment. It was strictly a bottom-up operation. It was a sales pitch from us." This system has had virtually no impact, limping along with one moderately interested executive user and lots of resistance from others.

The Executive Sponsor's Roles

In our experience, ESS without strong, active champions have virtually no chance of success. There are too many responsibilities to be fulfilled by the lead user that cannot be delegated. The three major responsibilities include: (1) make the initial request for the system; (2) stay on top of the system's development, providing direction and feedback about proposed applications; and (3) communicate strong and continuing interest to those with a stake in the system, such as key staff groups and line managers supplying data. While making the initial request is easy, monitoring the system's development and communicating its importance to the organization takes more time and energy.

Two general managers committed to their system's development by writing "implement an ESS" into their job performance objectives for the year. Other executives set challenging deadlines for developers and continued speaking to subordinates about the importance of installing ESS.

One pattern we found was that of strong executive sponsors who initiated the system properly; yet, failing to comprehend the difficulties of implementation, set difficult, sometimes unrealistic deadlines for the development team. At Xerox, Allaire initially wanted the system operational within six months. When Ken Soha, ESS project manager, argued that this was impossible, Allaire resisted, saying, "I don't want a big IS project." Soha assured him it was just a prototype but that it still would take time. However, Soha notes, "It was not until Allaire got into the political issues that he started to understand why we needed the time. He saw that at other companies, where they had put systems up too fast, the stuff didn't stick." In the end, Allaire understood both the technical difficulties and the need to handle organizational resistance, so he extended the installation deadline. Even this deadline would not have been met had Allaire not served as a buffer between the design team and other senior managers, each of whom had his own list of desirable applications.

At Stowe, on the other hand, the chief executive pressured developers to install a prototype before the technology was sufficiently developed. When the system was demonstrated, an executive commented, "It's painfully slow and too awkward to use. Too many keystrokes are needed. If I have work to do, I can't work at that speed." The developers knew the computer's response time was too slow to be useful to management, but because of pressure from the sponsor, they installed the system anyway. Of course, it was little used.

The executive sponsor, in monitoring the development of an ESS, must walk a fine line between setting unrealistic deadlines and setting very loose or no deadlines at all, thus communicating a lack of interest.

Patterns of Executive Sponsorship

In our research, we did not find an effective ESS that had been initiated solely by the information systems department. Although we recognize in rare instances this might happen, executive users as a rule must want and ask for the system themselves. To be effective, the executive sponsor must commit time and energy to the ESS project. In addition, the sponsor's expectations for the system must be in line with the limitations of the technology and data access.

Finally, the sponsor should be realistic about the implementation process and what the organization must go through to develop an effective ESS. The executive must at some general level comprehend: (1) the human and financial resources needed for the project; (2) the organizational impacts of the system; (3) the inevitable multiple sources of resistance to the system's perceived impacts; and (4) the probable need for an operating sponsor.

Three patterns of ESS sponsorship emerged from the 30 systems we studied. The first is a strong executive sponsor, who commits considerable time and energy to the process and works directly with an IS development team during installation. This relationship works best when the executive will be a heavy user of the system. We found this pattern in 12 of the 30 sites. CEO Ben Heineman at Northwest Industries; Mike Jensen, president of Banco Internacional; CEO Finn Caspersen at Beneficial; and the chairman of the manufacturing company who programs in Focus are good examples. They were heavily involved in all phases of the initial development of the system.

A second pattern of sponsorship is one with a weak executive sponsor, or a sponsor who leaves during implementation, with the result that the system drifts along steered only by the IS department. This occurred in five sites. It is no surprise that these were the least successful systems we studied. A large proportion of all attempts at ESS development undoubtedly are made with half-hearted sponsorship, but only a few such cases exist in our sample, which was biased toward "successful" systems, or those which initially showed promise.

The third pattern of sponsorship, and one we feel represents the trend of the future, occurs where a senior executive sponsor designates an operating sponsor to represent the business side and work with the IS department handling day-to-day issues of implementation. The earliest ESS users were ambitious innovators who took control of the implementation process. But as new waves of executives who are less intrigued with the technology want to develop systems, their need for an operating sponsor will become more significant. We will discuss the operating sponsor in the next section, but we found this executive/operating sponsor relationship produced some of the most effective ESS, including those at Gillette, Xerox, and Phillips 66. One advantage of the operating sponsor's role is that it provides someone who has the time and knowledge to translate the executive's needs into specific applications, as well as the time and capability to attend to the technical and political hurdles that can be so time-consuming during ESS installation. It is to this role that we now turn our attention.

OPERATING SPONSOR

The task of managing ESS development is frequently, but not always, delegated to a trusted subordinate who becomes the operating sponsor.[4] Ideally this sponsor communicates easily with both the executive user and the ESS designers. He or she serves as a go-between, helping to match business needs with technical capabilities.

Operating sponsors carry no consistent titles. Sometimes, where the CEO is executive sponsor, operating sponsorship falls to the CFO or controller. This was the case at both Gillette and Diversified Electronics. At The Quaker Oats Company, Verinder Syal, vice president of corporate planning, filled this vital role, interpreting the chief executive's information needs so that Frank Hemmige, manager of the information center, could lead the project to build the ESS and provide the appropriate data. The thirteen operating sponsors that we identified in other companies filled diverse positions including "assistant to the GM," "division planning and control manager," and "vice president."

Operating sponsors are often difficult to distinguish from executive sponsors. The roles may blend, particularly when the operating sponsor is a senior executive who is functioning at the request of the president or CEO, but who also may be developing a system for himself at the same time. As a rule, the executive sponsor is the most senior person taking an active interest in the project, and the operating sponsor is the person asked to play a significant role in system design and to manage the implementation details from the business side. This was the case at Phillips Petroleum, where Executive Vice President Robert Wallace asked Gene Batchelder to manage the ESS project. Wallace explains his reasoning:

> I wanted a person who is responsible for the operational analysis and control function, which is primarily a controller operation. I also wanted to put him concurrently over the management information system, tying them together because I don't want to approach management information and operational analysis and control from two separate viewpoints. I wanted them pulled together so that I could tie the operational analysis and control processes which analyze business performance to the management information systems.
>
> I picked Gene Batchelder because of his experience. First, he had very good accounting qualifications. Second, he had been a controller in one of our smaller business units, so he already had a fairly good—and I had checked this out very carefully—understanding of business information, as opposed to lower-level functional information. So he gave me accounting credibility. At the same time, although he had very limited exposure to data processing, I felt he was broad enough that that might be an attribute in my contacts with the data processing people.
>
> Historically, the DP people tend to be too technical. They drive development from such a strong technical position, they scare the user off a bit. I felt that Gene would look at the system more from a lay viewpoint of providing information in a manner that we could utilize.

Another operating sponsor is Vince Ficcaglia at The New England, a financial services company. Ficcaglia, who serves as both head of the firm's research department and as staff assistant to Executive Vice President Bob Shafto describes his role as operating sponsor for Shafto's ESS:

> My job is often to take what is in Bob's mind conceptually and translate it into a deliverable system. He can think very abstractly, so taking his concepts and getting them onto hard copy or a screen so they are of value to him is a major challenge. One advantage I have is that we have worked closely together for four years, so

I know his business style quite well. There has to be some chemistry between the two people in this situation. Fortunately, we have similar backgrounds and similar working styles. Both of us were in consulting, and we work from the same "get-it-done" mentality.

Don Palmer, controller for Gillette North America, is the operating sponsor for the system supporting Executive Vice President Derwyn Phillips. He explains his role as follows:

The executive needs an operating sponsor to act in his stead, someone who is in an executive function himself, and who understands how the person for whom the system is being designed operates. There's a problem when you don't have a person to fill that role, because it's difficult for the IS manager to understand the executive's operating focus. The role of the financial manager is a logical place to expect someone to respond to these information needs. Doing this was interesting to me because of my curiosity about computers and also my frustration with the limitations of our current financial reporting system.

Stan Bernstein, assistant to the general manager at Raytheon's Missile Systems Division, is another example of a hands-on operating sponsor. Bernstein was brought in by GM Charlie Jacobs to help implement an ESS. His role was described in this way by one observer:

Bernstein had been Jacobs' "right hand man" on the Patriot program when Jacobs was Patriot program manager, before becoming general manager... Bernstein said he already had the experience of being Jacobs' "executive support system," and so was able to appreciate how the information needed to be arranged to be helpful to him. Bernstein had also formed a close personal relationship with Jacobs and his family over the years.

Bernstein's experience was in program management so that he knew what information was relevant and how to get it, as well as how to present it to Jacobs ... Bernstein is a charming raconteur who is very sensitive to individuals and their needs. His strong marketing sense enables him to identify for managers ways in which [the ESS] would be helpful to them in solving problems and in explaining their difficulties to Jacobs.[5]

In a few cases, the IS project manager qualifies as operating sponsor because of an extensive business background and close relationship with top management. This is the case at Xerox where Ken Soha, the IS department project manager, was previously a divisional controller who had experience in finance and administration and was closely tied to many of the senior executives at Xerox.

There are two types of operating sponsor. The first is the manager or staff person developing the ESS for a senior executive. Batchelder, Palmer, Soha, and Bernstein fall into this category. Although they may make some use of the system themselves, their emphasis is on building the system to serve the executive sponsor and other senior executives.

The other type of operating sponsor is a senior manager who will be using the system, but who is designing it at the request of the chief executive, and is, therefore, developing the system with the CEO's needs also in mind. For example, when the general manager of Michigan Motors wanted an ESS, he made it known around the company that he was relying on the vice president of planning and IS to guide the development process. This was no surprise since this vice president and the GM were close associates, and the VP was known as "assistant GM." In another case, CEO Ian Rolland at Lincoln National asked the senior VP of administration to oversee ESS development. In both situations, the operating sponsors became active ESS users, although the systems were initiated and utilized by the chief executive.

The operating sponsor's responsibilities take varying amounts of time and effort depending on the degree to which the executive sponsor is involved in implementation, the complexity of the applications, and the capabilities of the ESS design team.

Overall, one of the operating sponsor's primary tasks is making certain that adequate resources are allocated to build the system. This includes funding, usually $100,000–$500,000 for the development phase, as well as access to personnel with technical and business knowledge needed to design the system.

If the executive sponsor cannot make sufficient time for the project, the operating sponsor takes responsibility for determining the specific content of the initial applications. These decisions may determine whether the system is accepted or rejected by the users. Don Palmer at Gillette comments:

> What does the executive really want? That's the gut of it. You have to get the initiating sponsor to articulate exactly what it is that he really needs. But, often, the executive has only a rough sense of it and cannot specify reports or graphs in more than a general way. And that is your toughest job—to figure out, and to help him figure out, exactly what he wants.

In addition to identifying and designing applications, the operating sponsor pries data loose from the organization to support the system. Often, line and staff managers are reluctant to provide new or existing data for the as yet unknown system.

Fighting for access to data can be a major function of the operating sponsor, one that consumes immense amounts of time in working through the labyrinth of organizational politics. Ultimately, however, the operating sponsor's success will depend in large part on that individual's relationship to the executive sponsor and how the organization perceives the relationship. Where the operating sponsor is effective, he or she is seen to be very closely aligned with the executive sponsor.

At United Retailing, the operating sponsor, seen as an alter ego for the executive sponsor, had great leverage negotiating with managers who resisted the system. "If I had to step on toes or go through locked doors, I just did it," he said. "I got away with a lot."

This hard-line approach was seen in a few cases, but more often, the operating sponsor chose to "sell" the system to the organization. At Xerox, Ken Soha identified those most affected by the ESS, then met with each stakeholder to explain the system and deal with any objections. This selling process can be long and time-consuming, but it is necessary if the system is to have the support it needs and overcome the resistance it generates in most organizations.

The amount of coaxing needed to install an effective ESS is related to the complexity of the applications and the changes they threaten to bring about. It is obviously much easier to install office support applications, such as electronic mail or word processing, than a redesigned financial control system. The more apparent impact a system will have on the organization, the more political groundwork must be laid by the operating sponsor.

As mentioned earlier, a responsibility that may inadvertently fall to the operating sponsor is protecting the design team from top management pressures. If too many executives try to influence the design of a system, this "building-an-elephant-by-committee" approach can paralyze the design process or produce an ESS that pleases no one. Thus, the operating sponsor must serve as a buffer between the designers and executives, making sure they have constructive interactions and communicate clearly.

The operating sponsor's role does not disappear once an ESS is in place. In fact, it becomes even more critical if the system spreads throughout the organization. Negotiating access to new data sources, deciding who gets terminals, and developing new applications are some of the functions involved in ESS administration. At Gillette, Don Palmer estimates that 25 percent of his time is spent managing the group's ESS, even though executive sponsor Derwyn Phillips has had a terminal for several years. The system continues to evolve.

In conclusion, operating sponsors are not essential if the executive sponsor invests extensive time and effort in developing an ESS. But the realities of executive work and the time required for implementation, combined with increasingly sophisticated applications and data management problems, are factors that conspire to make it virtually impossible for the senior executive, especially a CEO, to manage system development alone.

NOTES

1. For example, see Tora K. Bikson, Barbara A. Gutek, and Don A. Monkin, *Implementation of Information Technology in Office Settings: Review of Relevant Literature* (Santa Monica, Calif.: Rand Corporation, 1981); Henry C. Lucas, Jr., *The Analysis, Design and Implementation of Information Systems* (New York: McGraw-Hill,

1981); Ralph H. Sprague and Eric D. Carlson, *Building Effective Decision Support Systems* (Englewood Cliffs, N.J.: Prentice Hall, Inc., 1982); M. Lynne Markus, "Power, Politics and MIS Implementation," *Communications of the ACM*, vol. 26 no. 6, (June 1983); and G.B. Davis and M.H. Olsen, *Management Information Systems: Conceptual Foundations, Structure and Development* (New York: McGraw-Hill, 1985).

2. Peter G.W. Keen and Michael Scott Morton, *Decision Support Systems: An Organizational Perspective* (Reading, Mass.: Addison-Wesley, 1978); Steven L. Alter, *Decision Support Systems* (Reading, Mass.: Addison-Wesley, 1978); Ralph H. Sprague and Eric D. Carlson, *Building Effective Decision Support Systems* (Englewood Cliffs, N.J.: Prentice Hall, Inc., 1982); John L. Bennett, *Building Decision Support Systems* (Reading, Mass.: Addison-Wesley, 1983).

3. Peter G.W. Keen and Michael S. Scott Morton, *Decision Support Systems: An Organizational Perspective*, (Reading, Mass.: Addison-Wesley, 1978), pp. 196, 199.

4. Eliot Levinson, "The Implementation of Executive Support Systems," *Working Paper No. 119*, Center for Information Systems Research, Sloan School of Management, MIT, Cambridge, Mass., October 1984.

5. Margaret Dickerman, "The Evolution and Diffusion of an Executive Support System: A Case Study." Master's thesis, Sloan School of Management, MIT, Cambridge, Mass., June 1985, p. 28.

CHAPTER 8

IS RESOURCES—PEOPLE, TECHNOLOGY, AND DATA

In addition to strong executive and operating sponsors, three essential IS resources serve as building blocks for every successful executive support system. These are adequate IS human resources, appropriate hardware and software technology, and effective data management. This chapter will address these three factors, beginning with human resources.

IS RESOURCES: PEOPLE

We observed a number of different ways in which human resources were structured to support ESS development, some more successful than others. The experiences of four companies illustrate these patterns and many of the IS human resource issues which arise in the implementation process.

Gillette North America
When Don Palmer, controller at Gillette North America (GNA), was asked to become operating sponsor in developing an ESS for the group's executive vice president, he enlisted the support of the R&D group in the Corporate MIS department. Working with this creative group of information systems personnel had its pluses and minuses. Palmer explains it this way:

> Going in, most of our experience had been in dealing with the way in which MIS traditionally functioned. We filled out a work request and waited six weeks to get a product back. This negative

feeling about the process came from a long experience in working with MIS on classical accounting systems. There was a great deal of natural animosity between MIS and finance. So, as we approached this ESS project, we had quite a few reservations as to how the working relationship with MIS would evolve.

We found out, to our pleasure, that the people in the research environment were different in their orientation than those in traditional systems development. They were responsive and anxious to provide a product. They took a prototyping approach, and we were able to gain their commitment to the project.

However, the research orientation of this group, in contrast to production-oriented information systems people, brought special problems, as Palmer soon discovered. He explains:

The weakness in the process was my inability to control the priorities and the number of IS people working on the project. We could never be assured that we had the right number and right kind of people. And they were working on a number of different programs, pursuing their own technology and their own solutions to the issues that we were raising. So they were reinventing some of the things that were available from outside vendors. We had two problems really. First, competing for the number of IS people to work on the project, and, second, once we got those people, getting them to focus their time and attention on what we needed.

We solved those problems, in part, by making them an integral part of our team, trying to make the R&D group believers in the importance of executive support systems by exposing them to how it would work. We tried to get them to buy into the project with their hearts and minds, as opposed to just letting them focus on interesting technical problems. The IS people were extremely intelligent and competent and, when they were focused on what we wanted them to focus on, we got a good system. Working in a research environment, however, they placed less emphasis on deadlines and adhering to specifically what we asked them for. The support of MIS was critical to the success of our team effort.

International Computers, Ltd. (ICL)

Alan Rousell, managing director of ICL [UK], the firm's largest sales and support group, also chose a non-traditional route for the development of his ESS. Rousell bypassed the information systems department and worked directly with an analyst, known at ICL as an "information engineer," to develop his applications. One of Rousell's colleagues spoke about this new type of staff member:

> This was a role that we talked about theoretically at first, but which has proved to be very practical. What becomes clear is that its incumbent is not a new type of individual. He is actually someone who is an accountant, or who is responsible for monitoring figures anyway, but instead of using a pencil and paper, he is now using the technology. We took someone who was enthusiastic and who understood what we were trying to do in getting information from around the company, and who understood how we needed to review it. He trained himself in how to use spreadsheets and how to strip data off the company's financial data base. He learned about the technology. Then he applied it to the business, using his business knowledge as his source of strength.

Raytheon

At Raytheon, Bob Ferrara, manager of advanced technologies, was appointed by the the head of the division's traditional MIS group, Information Processing Services (IPS), to implement the ESS for General Manager Charlie Jacobs. (Stan Bernstein would not be brought in as operating sponsor until a few months later.) Ferrara did several things that were unexpected by his IPS colleagues, who had a strong allegiance to their IBM mainframes, and who were used to handling large projects with long lead times.

First he set up a "quick-response team," which experimented with quickly constructed prototypes, taking advantage of feedback from the general manager to refine the system. The fast feedback, user involvement, and early availability of some parts of the system proved eminently successful in this environment.

In addition, Ferrara decided to build the ESS on the division's Control Data Cyber computer, located in a department independent of IPS. Although there were good technical reasons for choosing the Cyber, Ferrara's decision had serious political implications for IPS and its relationship to management.

Predictably, there was strong resistance among the IBM-oriented IPS group, but Ferrara felt these two unorthodox courses of action were necessary to implement an ESS.[1]

Xerox

When top management decided they wanted an ESS, the head of corporate IS brought in Ken Soha, a vice president and controller of one of Xerox's operating units, to manage the project. Although Soha's small team worked closely with the IS department, they were never viewed as a typical IS development group. Soha says, "To install an ESS, we needed a small bunch of hard-hitting marines, so the project wouldn't get bogged down." Soha started with a team of three developers that grew to nine people within two years.

These cases provide good examples of the organizational issues encountered in developing an ESS. Such projects require a combination of skills not usually found in traditional IS design teams. Designers must work faster than in other types of IS development and must be responsive to the executive's needs and desires as they become clearer during implementation. New types of people often handle these non-traditional design needs. At Gillette, Don Palmer used IS R&D people, while at Raytheon, Bob Ferrara formed an independent quick-response team.

An ESS project team needs sophisticated business knowledge to identify executive needs. At ICL, the information engineer had both the technical skills and business knowledge to design an ESS. At Gillette, Controller Don Palmer supplied the business expertise in his role as operating sponsor, as did Ken Soha at Xerox.

It is impossible to talk about IS human recources without considering how they interact with executive and operating sponsors. There are three sets of players in this process, and four different ways they work together. There is the executive sponsor, and sometimes other members of the senior management team. Often an operating sponsor is designated by the executive who initially rquests the system. In addition, people with technical IS skills, usually from MIS department, are assigned to create the system.

The ESS development personnel we saw came from one of two places in the organization. Some were a part of the "mainstream" MIS department, drawing freely on the resources of their colleagues and accepted by the department's culture. This was the case at Xerox. The IS people at Gillette, although part of an R&D group, also fit in this category. A second group were "fringe" ESS project teams, which may report to IS management on paper, but which, far too often, are not accepted by the mainstream IS culture and may even be politically ostracized by their colleagues. The quick response team at Raytheon and the information engineers at ICL were not part of the mainstream IS organization.

Given these players, we identified four patterns used to implement an ESS:

1. *Executive sponsor—operating sponsor—mainstream IS*. A mainstream IS team working with an operating sponsor to develop an ESS for an executive sponsor is a pattern we found in ten companies. Six of these systems were highly successful, three modestly so, and one had little impact. The one that failed did so mainly because of a weak executive sponsor. Ironically, the firm had a relatively sophisticated IS department.

2. *Executive sponsor — mainstream IS*. Another common pattern was a mainstream IS team working directly for an executive sponsor, either because no operating sponsor had been designated or the role was filled inadequately. There were twelve such cases, including eight which were judged successful by the executives using them. One was modestly successful, and three were unsuccessful. Five of the eight successes, however, were individual systems driven by strong executive sponsors. The three unsuccessful attempts were all organizational systems, and they were among the worst failures we saw. Again, weak executive sponsorship was the primary flaw which, combined with lack of an operating sponsor, left no chance of success.

3. *Executive sponsor—operating sponsor—fringe IS*. Four systems were developed where executive and operating sponsors worked with IS designers who were not part of the mainstream IS culture. Three were successful. The system that fell

short was Stowe Computers, where the operating sponsor abdicated his role in the middle of the project.

4. *Executive sponsor—fringe IS.* Of the four companies where executive sponsors worked with a fringe IS group, only one was very successful. That was ICL, where executives worked directly with information engineers to design individual ESS. The other three cases were only moderately successful at best, because there were no operating sponsors to overcome relatively weak executive sponsorship and IS department resistance.

Some tentative conclusions can be drawn from this small but interesting sample. If systems are to be used by a broad range of executives and have wide impact on the organization, their chances for success are greater when developed by a mainstream IS team working with a strong operating sponsor. Executive sponsors working directly with analysts, as at ICL, can produce effective individual systems, but generally lack time to deal with the technical and political issues of an organization-wide ESS.

If the IS department does not have the capability or willingness to support an ESS project, it is much more difficult to build around the IS department because it can create barriers to accessing telecommunications networks and data bases. Only very strong operating sponsors, such as Stan Bernstein at Raytheon, can manage their way around or through resistance in the IS department.

As a rule, executives are better off with mainstream IS support and a strong operating sponsor. The more complex and broad-based an application is, the more an operating sponsor is needed. The exception is an office-support-based ESS, which is easier to install.

Fringe IS teams can produce effective systems only with a strong operating sponsor, unless the system is being designed for an individual executive and will have a relatively narrow impact. An executive sponsor does not have time to overcome the political obstacles that a fringe IS team must cope with. In the end, we found that fringe teams usually join the mainstream IS group once the political value of the system becomes evident to IS management. Only in this way can ESS developers get the support needed from the IS department.

Issues in Managing IS Human Resources for ESS

Some executive support systems are less successful, not because of inadequate executive or operating sponsors, but because the IS organization is not capable of implementing a system for top management. The question for executives considering ESS is: What human resource factors promote or inhibit development of these systems? We have identified three elements essential to successful design teams, as well as three that can impede development.

Elements of a Successful Design Team

ESS design teams combine the skills of the executive and operating sponsors, as well as the IS group. What makes these teams successful are: (1) adequate human resources to complete the project; (2) the right mix of skills; and (3) the level of sophistication necessary to work with executives, given the mix of sponsorship, IS experience, and application complexity. The interplay of these elements depends on the objectives of a specific system (e.g., office support versus strategic planning), and the individuals on the team. Let us look at each element separately.

Adequate human resources.   Throughout our research we found that management frequently underestimated the number of IS staff needed to design, install, and maintain an ESS. It takes an extraordinary amount of resources to customize hardware, software, and data to meet the needs of individual executives. At Gillette, the operating sponsor was frustrated by his inability to get enough IS people for essential development tasks. A similar problem developed at United Retailing. As the ESS took hold, IS management needed to step back and develop an ESS strategy to establish priorities for allocating its resources. This was because executives' demands for new applications were straining existing IS resources.

For the systems we studied, design teams ranged from one to about 12 people. At ICL, where systems were largely personal, executives worked directly with an information engineer. At Banco Internacional, President Mike Jensen worked with a single systems analyst to design his system. At Boeing, however, an ESS in one division drew on a dozen people.

With ESS, the real support needs become evident only after the system is in use. At one consumer products company, the ESS manager summed up his experience, saying, "I underestimated the resources that we needed. I was driving the project in terms of 'let's get more information on the system' and, at the same time, I was littering the corridor out here with bodies and hours because we totally underestimated what kind of people-resource commitment was required to make the technology into an ESS."

Right mix of skills. Often what differentiates an ESS design team from other IS groups is the mix of skills needed. This is dictated by the number of organizational boundaries an ESS crosses, and the sophistication of its applications. Office support systems need fewer people than systems which provide financial modeling and broad data retrieval. For example, the team developing an organization-wide ESS for Michigan Motors included staff from DSS, data base administration, technical support, end user computing, and financial services groups. Obviously, the mix of skills on any design team varies from company to company, depending on the nature of the system and existing IS resources. The 12-person Boeing project team mentioned earlier included representatives from the finance department, who provided business knowledge and expertise about the cost data used in the system; divisional design analysts, who interacted with users and provided technical specifications; and programmers from the corporate computer services group.

In addition to the formal skills needed for the team, personal relationships between ESS designers and executives often play an important part in gaining access and time with the potential users. Since lack of access to executives is one of the major constraints in designing a system that will meet the user's needs, those with a personal "in" have an unplanned—but critical—advantage over IS staff unknown to the executive.

Some of the most successful systems we studied were created by people who had strong personal ties to the executive user. Ken Soha, ESS operating sponsor at Xerox, had worked for Chairman David Kearns many years ago when they first started at Xerox.

In one regional phone company, the operating sponsor had been with the firm for over 20 years and was well-known and well-liked by top management. He could "shoot the breeze" with the executives, even those most resistant to the new ESS. These personal relationships cannot be factored into any rational model of systems development, but they played an important role in at least a third of the systems we studied, and in a majority of the most successful ones.

Writing about how managers reduce uncertainty, Rosabeth Moss Kanter provides insight into why personal relationships play an important role in systems development for senior management:

> It was easier to talk with those of one's kind who had shared experiences—more certain, more accurate, more predictable. Less time could be spent concentrating on subtle meanings, and more time (such an overloaded resource for managers) on the task. The corporation's official language system and cryptic jargon . . . could be supplemented by the certainty that socially similar communicators would have more basis for understanding one another.[2]

Appropriate level of business knowledge. Knowledge of the business is important for DSS and OA development, but it is even more critical when working with top management. Understanding executive needs demands a business-savvy developer. Where the IS personnel lack business knowledge, an active operating sponsor must fill the gap. At United Retailing, an ESS was developed by two low-level programmers with an executive assistant serving as liaison between them and the operations vice president who would be using the system. The assistant, who understood the VP's information needs, translated the business issues for the programmers. In a regional telephone company with no operating sponsor, the technically oriented ESS design team developed a system that did not meet the business needs of the firm's executives.

Several organizations today are attempting to combine business understanding with technical competence in a single role, sometimes called "ESS coordinator," "information engineer," or "information analyst." Michigan Motors created ESS coordinators from staff analysts to help manage the evolution and spread of ESS in particular units. In a sense, these people become local operating sponsors, but they also have the technical knowledge to manage applications development. Similarly, at least four senior executives at ICL used an information engineer, which is a hybrid accountant/systems developer who can design user interfaces and work out mainframe connections. More importantly, however, that person is charged with understanding the executive's business, reporting systems, critical data, and desired presentation formats. The information engineer works directly for the executive user or unit's controller.

A related position has emerged at San Diego Gas & Electric, where internal consultants provide the top managers with support in accessing the company's "executive data cube." Rinehart reports, "These consultants are different from normal data-processing analysts. They will work with the executives to assist them in defining their data needs and developing the methodologies by which answers can be derived from this executive data cube .... They will train the executive to access this information and teach the executive to recognize the analytical routines that best fit the different types of analysis that have to be performed."[3]

Applegate's Harvard Business School case study on the Lockheed-Georgia ESS describes a new information analyst role as follows:

> Each Information Analyst was assigned to specific functional and program areas. They were responsible for attending meetings and developing effective information channels to assure that they "knew everything that was going on in that program or area." In short, they were responsible for actively gathering information throughout the company and developing and maintaining the displays in a manner that best suited the information scanning style and content required by each executive. As [one senior

manager] explained, "It is imperative that the Information Analysts understand the information that they enter into the system. Several actions are taken to ensure that this is the case. Most of the Information Analysts have work experience and/or training in their areas of responsibility. They are encouraged to take courses which provide a better understanding of the users' areas and they frequently attend functional area meetings, often serving as an important resource on the companywide perspective. They must determine . . . how to present the information, other data that are necessary to fully understand a display and finally, how to classify the information for access and control."[4]

IS Factors Impeding Development

In addition to the characteristics of successful design teams, we identified several factors that inhibit ESS implementation:

1. IS personnel may cling to traditional methods of system development that are not appropriate for top management systems.

2. IS personnel sometimes lack an understanding of the executive work environment.

3. Executives sometimes do not trust the IS department and instead turn to fringe groups. Conflict between IS and the fringe unit developing the system often results.

Clinging to Traditional Methods of Development.   Most ESS development teams ignore the standard IS development procedures. Rarely is there an implementation plan, the systems are virtually never cost justified, analyses of user needs are almost always incomplete, and the prototype is usually installed within a few months of the project's start. Most IS professionals are unfamiliar with such unstructured projects, where design and installation schedules can change at the whim of the executive sponsor.

The ESS project manager at a large telecommunications company says, "In our corporate systems group, variance is considered a sin. A project *must* finish on time, even if all the functions aren't in the system." To get around this cultural idiosyncrasy, end users created local development groups to do the necessary prototyping.

In another case, an ESS project manager at Boeing said, "The rapid prototyping method of development is contrary to our standard method of developing systems. There was a problem getting technical people to work that way. They had a concern that they were generating a poor-quality system."[5]

Lack of Understanding of the Executive Environment. IS personnel are frequently uncomfortable with the fact that, unlike other development efforts, they do not control the ESS implementation process. The process is usually driven by the sponsoring executive who can pressure designers to install a prototype prematurely. Rarely can IS dictate the development schedule for an ESS, as it can with other systems. Pressure from the users weighs much more heavily on the ESS design process than it does for lower-level systems.

At Beneficial Corporation, the data processing group planned to install an office automation system starting from the bottom of the organization. CEO Finn Caspersen, however, short-circuited that plan after trying the new office support system at home, asking IS to automate all senior executives first. Since IS had not yet done a pilot of the system, IS management was apprehensive about the sudden shift in implementation strategy. Nevertheless, within a year they had installed 600 terminals and trained the users, starting with the CEO and his management team.

Executive users must be treated with care, and they expect high-quality, "instant" support. For example, in one firm, the IS department installed a new version of an electronic mail package without first notifying executive users. The new software was more difficult to use and had a few bugs. One frequent user, a vice president, let IS know in no uncertain terms that he was displeased.

A senior manager in the firm observed:

> The implementation of an ESS is traumatic for MIS because they now have great visibility at the VP level. Those managers expect a level of performance that MIS has never been required to provide in the past. They don't want technical mumbo jumbo. As a result, we have been working to establish standards of perfor-

mance for executive support, to make sure that response times are adequate, data base updates happen when they're supposed to, and that communications lines to the data bases are dependable. Low-level end users never had the power to press on these issues. Customer service has never been an issue, but now MIS must manage it effectively.

Reliance on Fringe IS Groups. Pursuing an ESS project can also surface some smoldering resentment that executives have against their IS departments. At a major accounting firm, the vice chairman conceded he hadn't trusted his MIS group since they had "blown smoke in my direction," estimating a system development project at $200,000 but spending $600,000 before he pulled the plug on an unfinished system. As a result, he refused to use them for an ESS project.

Executives turn to fringe groups if they do not trust IS to deliver. When executives see their IS departments clinging to old design methods or lacking sensitivity to management needs, they are likely to prefer a smaller, more flexible design team. At Raytheon, the general manager shocked the IS group by choosing a prototype developed by Ferrara's quick-response team for $20,000, over a more complicated division-wide system projected to take the "IBMers" two years and $300,000 to build.[6] At Stowe, the CEO chose a small consulting team to develop an ESS after receiving a proposal from one of his large mainframe-oriented development groups that called for a 50-person project. This rejection of the traditional IS approach inevitably sets up tension between the two groups.

IS RESOURCES: ESS TECHNOLOGY

Computer technology continues to change incredibly fast. New generations of hardware and software appear on the market every year just as the existing technology is being assimilated. Nowhere is the technology evolving more rapidly than in the emerging field of ESS. For this reason, we will not deal with specific hardware and software configurations and problems because whatever we say will be obsolete in short order.

Only in the last few years have hardware and software products been designed specifically for senior management systems. Firms such as Comshare and Pilot have led the way in a technology niche destined to grow in the years ahead. In the meantime, there are lessons to be learned from those who have already had to cope with ESS technology.

Hardware Issues

The major hardware decisions deal with the choice of executive workstations and minicomputer or mainframe host. These choices are frequently straightforward, influenced heavily by the dominant vendor, and the capacity already available in the company. Where a particular vendor predominates in the firm's existing office systems, hardware choices often are seen as predetermined.

The major hardware decision at this level is whether to use the corporate mainframe or to invest in a departmental machine, usually a minicomputer. Given IBM's dominance in mainframe marketshare, it is no surprise that it is the overwhelming choice in the systems we studied when the host computer is a mainframe. However, at least half of the 30 companies studied built ESS on specialized hosts, independent of big transaction–processing mainframes and the traditional data processing environment. The size of hardware selected varies. At Raytheon, Ferrara chose the Cyber over an IBM mainframe, and Gillette runs its system on a DEC VAX. The primary reasons for this non-mainframe approach are the needs for instant response time and dependability. We found the mini to be a common choice among many of the more successful systems, but no one vendor stood out. Again, the main criterion was compatibility with the installed hardware base.

IBM dominated the choice of workstations. There were IBM PCs, XTs, and ATs, as well as models 3179 and 3279. Of 30 systems, the front-end hardware used was: IBM (15), Wang (4), Hewlett-Packard (2), DEC (2), Data General (1), AT&T (1), Xerox (1), Apple (1), ICL (1), and other (2).

Issues in choosing workstation hardware are compatibility, capacity, and response time. That compatibilty is desirable seems obvious, but it is sometimes overlooked. For example, the secretary for the director of engineering at Michigan Motors uses her boss's terminal to send long electronic mail messages because her terminal is not compatible with his mail system. At the same company, the general manager installed another vendor's PC at home but discovered that software was not available to access the firm's E-mail system.

Capacity is an important consideration because developers often do not anticipate how fast a successful ESS can grow. At the same time, however, there is a danger of overspending for unneeded capacity. At Banco Internacional, designers underestimated the demands that would be placed on their system. The system was chosen because it was easy to design screen formats, but it soon became overloaded and response time was too slow if more than a few people were on the system at once. In the end, the small minicomputer constrained system expansion just when interest in ESS was growing fast.[7]

At the other end of the spectrum, one company installed "loaded" personal computers, at a cost of $10,000 each, in the offices and homes of all 14 top executives. This proved to be technological overkill, as most of the managers had no use for so much computing power. A year later, the IS department replaced many of these with cheaper models.

In general, ESS developers are more likely to err on the side of undercapacity than overcapacity, as evidenced by the many complaints executives make about poor response time. The importance of instant response time cannot be emphasized enough. Managers will not use systems that take more than a second or two to respond, except when those systems provide high-value information that can be obtained from no other source. These latter situations, however, are rare.

"If I have to wait this long for the system, I won't use it," is a frequent reaction from executives when they are shown a slow-moving ESS prototype, which is what often happens when developers rush to get some kind of system in front of their sponsor. At Raytheon, use of the system started by Jacobs had grown so fast that in the early afternoon it could take two hours to scan four data bases, a procedure that took five minutes at 7 A.M. "You learned to plan your day accordingly," said one manager.

After an ESS had become an integral part of the management process at one firm, the system manager was called into a senior staff meeting to discuss why executives were experiencing reduced response time. He explained that budget cuts had forced him to reallocate computing capacity and he needed $600,000 to restore system response time. The CEO, without hesitation, made the commitment.

Software Issues

Choosing software may be the most important decision in assembling the building blocks of an ESS. Several factors should be kept in mind when making the choice. Because of the limited number of ESS software packages available in the early days of this emerging applications area, many ESS project managers have been confronted with a difficult "buy versus build" dilemma. The first thing that should influence this decision should be—but often is not—user needs. As we have already shown, executives want different things from computer-based support systems. Some want only electronic mail. Others are interested in monitoring, query, or analytic capabilities. These needs narrow the potential software choices significantly. Many good electronic mail packages are available, but there are fewer offerings of software suitable for executive-level status access or query systems.

A major factor in software selection should be its speed and flexibility as a prototyping tool. Because prototyping is central to ESS development, software should support fast and flexible design to allow developers to adapt quickly to management needs. At Stowe, the experience of the vice president of R&D illustrates the point. He says, "I made a nuisance of myself saying, 'I don't want a package.' Instead, I wanted project updates, but IS couldn't make the system flexible that way. They tried to give everyone the same package of capabilities. They didn't realize that we all wanted to do something different. The fact that getting new applications took six months was too long." Software that cannot be adapted quickly creates frustration for users, and for designers who are unable to respond fast enough.

Another factor that can influence software choices is the styles of executive users. In a division of Boeing, designers were frustrated because one executive, adept with personal computers, was willing to learn complex command structures for word processing and spreadsheet packages. At the same time, another manager resisted the suggestion that he would even have to learn a sign-on sequence. These two users presented significantly different design requirements even though they wanted to access the same data bases on the system.[8]

While a few executives will master complex command structures, a majority of the users we studied relied on menus to prompt them through applications. As infrequent users (e.g., several times a week), some executives can easily forget or confuse commands for a series of applications. Nothing deters an executive faster than struggling with a system whose commands are difficult to remember. One vice president of personnel said, "An ESS ought to take you quickly into the back woods of a data base. I have so many things to think about, having to worry about how I mechanically operate the PC makes me angry. I have enough problems with the business. I don't need an overlay of machine problems."

One paradox created by the reliance on menus for prompting is that executives who use a system frequently can become frustrated by the delays in having to step through menus designed for less frequent users. For this reason, an ideal system offers some way to bypass menus when not needed.

Like many decisions related to software design, building an ESS involves trade-offs. One of the most difficult is between user friendliness and security. An ESS must be fast, flexible, transparent, *and* secure. The objective, however, is *appropriate* security, a concept sometimes lost on designers and overzealous controllers concerned about data leaks. Such concerns vary from company to company, with those hurt by leaks being more sensitive to the problem.

Most ESS provide security with a user password system. In the case of Lockheed-Georgia, however, both executives and workstations are cleared to access specific levels of data. The president, for example, using his password, can access more sensitive data through the workstation in his office than through the terminal in a nearby conference room.

Home use, found among a high proportion of executives, is another area where software as well as hardware choices must be made. Often, home systems are identical to those at the office. If they are not, care must be taken to make sure the home and office workstations are compatible because, regardless of what executives say at the outset, they will almost inevitably want to tap into the firm's system from home. Many users find that this dial-up arrangement offers some of the system's greatest value.

An important consideration in home use is the transfer of highly sensitive company data. Will the executives be given secure lines? Will they use regular telephone lines or carry floppy disks home? Each company appears to have a different policy, depending on its sensitivity to security.

One other factor influencing software choices is the implicit philosophy the development team has about what it is providing to executives. Is the ESS simply a collection of software packages—i.e., "a tool box,"—from which executives choose applications that require extensive learning and sometimes end-user programming? Or, is the system a set of tailored applications designed to meet specific end-user needs with easy-to-use interfaces? The significance of this becomes more apparent in the next chapter when we discuss the problem of linking ESS to specific business objectives.

The tool-box approach usually includes a collection of OA applications, a spreadsheet, and possibly a fourth-generation language, while the tailored applications set can use any combination of software. The software-driven tool collection is, as a rule, less effective because it requires too much executive time and initiative to be useful. The design philosophy that provides predefined capabilities with easy-to-use front ends implies that more thought has been given to the specific needs of the user. Of course, many systems combine these two approaches, providing some raw tools as well as more polished applications, but those that lean toward the latter seem to be more effective.

Process Issues

In addition to specific hardware and software considerations, several overriding process factors related to technology affect the success of the system, independent of the vendors chosen. For example, a strong executive sponsor, often impatient for a prototype, may be unwilling to wait for a detailed vendor study. At Auto Electronics, the general manager refused to wait a month for vendor information which developers considered critical to their choice of hardware. Technology decisions are often made quickly when implementing ESS, in part because the IS department does not control the process. Don Palmer, controller and operating sponsor for Gillette North America's ESS, offers a classic example:

> After going to a seminar, Derwyn Phillips asked me what we were doing in graphic formats. He also asked the question of our MIS group. But, within two months, before MIS even had a chance to respond, Derwyn had purchased the software and had me developing graphs to show what could be done.

Because of the time pressures and the leading-edge nature of the technology, ESS designers are often forced to learn as they go. The chairman of a major consumer goods company wanted to use electronic mail to check with his office while on a trip to Japan. His support staff wasn't sure if that had been done before. For better or worse, an ESS can be the first place IS staff tries certain technical feats, simultaneously attacking problems of compatibility, networking, and data management.

And then there is the new hardware. "No one told us the workstation comes in 13 boxes," said the ESS project manager at Auto Electronics, who was under great pressure from his general manager to install computers for the executive team. "We were learning the technology on the fly and created a lot of problems for ourselves that way."

ESS frequently involve leading-edge applications, and the cost of failure in supporting the executive team is high. Because of this, many designers cultivate strong relationships with their vendors to get instant support when something goes awry. For example, Gillette chose to be a beta test site for Pilot's COMMAND CENTER so it could influence the product's final design.

In another case, once Auto Electronics had chosen its hardware vendor, the ESS project manager called the vice president of the vendor's office systems division. He reminded the vice president that future business from the auto manufacturer depended on how senior executives viewed the equipment. Thus, the project manager asked for special support during system installation. The VP assigned a high-level corporate manager to monitor the progress of the project.

The ESS manager was rewarded for developing this relationship with the vendor. As the workstations were being installed, it was discovered that they would not function with communications boards from another supplier even though both vendors had promised that the terminals and boards would be compatible. Calling the local service office produced little help, since the vendor's field-service people were inexperienced with this advanced application. The ESS project manager contacted the vendor's corporate office and was immediately connected with the key product managers who had designed the hardware. The product managers took the hardware home that night and solved the problem the next morning in a conference call with the ESS designers and the hardware and board vendors. Solving this problem through normal channels would have taken months, insists the project manager.

IS RESOURCES: DATA

The value of any information system for top management depends on the quality of its data—its timeliness, accessibility, accuracy, and completeness. But in attempting to provide high-quality data, executive support systems often bring existing data resource management (DRM) issues to light, and, at the same time, create new problems of managing data. While data management may not be a problem when an ESS prototype is first installed, the technical, physical, and political barriers to providing executives with the data they need can be a major roadblock in the evolution of an ESS.

At one major bank, the ESS manager says installing an ESS had a "therapeutic effect" on the firm, because trying to load the new system with data from existing production data bases exposed several major DRM problems. A researcher who studied the system reports:

First, when [the bank] developed the staffing portion of their system they had assumed that all the data was available from their existing systems. To their surprise, they discovered that there was no single production data stream which contained all the information that they needed. The full portfolio of human resource information was running on a variety of dissimilar systems. There was no easy way to link all the various components of the data. As a result, only a portion of the functions that are built into the staffing module are usable. Now they have begun a campaign to reevaluate the human resource systems.[9]

An ESS is only as good as the data it makes available. A general manager at Raytheon summed up the problem: "For a while, the system bordered on useless because the information in it was no good." It is easy to give data too little attention since hardware and software issues also pose challenges—challenges of particular interest to technically-oriented systems developers. With 20-20 hindsight, the president of Stowe said:

We were putting more management effort into that so-called decision support system than we were on trying to figure out how we could get our data faster, regardless of what format it was in. We were busy looking at the graphics and how to get it up onto screens, and how the LAN system worked, when, in fact, all the data we were looking at was three weeks out of date.

So our priorities were in the wrong place. What we should have been doing was spending all of our management effort making sure that we could get timely, appropriate data, and then figuring out how to use it.

The DRM issues facing ESS developers are not unique. In fact, they merely focus a spotlight on the overall state of data management in an organization. The issues are summed up well in the following comment:

An underlying problem with managing data in organizations today is the difficulty of integrating data originally designed to meet the needs of isolated applications, which were often developed in widely dispersed, almost autonomous, sub-organizations within a large corporation. This problem of decentralized development has led to discrepancies in data definitions, accuracy differences, and timing and coordination problems. The resulting lack of accessible, quality data today often limits managerial and staff access to information, hinders system development and maintenance activities, and even constrains the ability to undertake strategic initiatives.[10]

Information technology has removed barriers to data sharing between organizational units and individuals. As these technical barriers drop even further, executives and systems developers are faced with a number of issues relating to data availability, infrastructure, ownership, security, and management. The difficulty of coping with these issues can make data the key implementation challenge.

Data Availability

Unfortunately, in many executive support systems, merely obtaining the desired data is extremely difficult. The majority of computer systems in existence today were developed by accountants, order-entry supervisors, manufacturing personnel, and similar staff, for operational use or financial accounting. The data needs of these users, however, are very different from those of top management. While some accounting information is useful and summaries of operations are valuable, economic forecasts, industry trends, and competitive data are equally if not more valued. Much of this external data is not readily available. Therefore, system designers must search out and often convert data from outside sources, as well as data available internally but not already in electronic form.

Even when internal and external data are available, they are often fragmented, stored with incompatible codes and inconsistent data definitions. This unfortunate incompatibility is due primarily to the decentralized nature of system development for the past 20 years. At Boeing, for example, where data was incomplete initially, the effectiveness of the system suffered. Use of the corporate ESS was constrained by the lack of adequate data bases in the operating units needed to feed timely performance information to corporate. One executive said, "The lack of complete data bases was seen by many as the major shortcoming of the system and to complete the data bases was a priority for the future."[11]

Data Infrastructure

An organization's data infrastructure encompasses the policies under which data are structured and stored, as well as the physical location and technical representation of the data itself. Included among the policies are standard data definitions and coded schemes. Technical representation includes the choice of file structures and data formats.

Executive support systems tend to expose weaknesses in this infrastructure and frequently force a big investment in rebuilding data bases and cleaning up existing production systems. This happened at Firestone where the first attempt to build an ESS revealed a major problem in data integrity. It became clear there was inadequate central control over accounting procedures, and the company had to define new report formats and develop a consolidation system to replace the 30 different existing general ledger systems before undertaking the ESS project. An ESS can be a catalyst for rebuilding a firm's data infrastructure, which can be a costly and time-consuming project.

Firestone is far from unique. At a major consumer goods company, the CEO asked for a list of his firm's 50 largest customers. Each of the nine divisions quickly produced a list of *its* 50 largest customers. However, multiple coding systems and incompatible alphabetical storage of customer names necessitated a manual search through thousands of customer records to insure that the CEO received accurate data.

In another case, the installation of an ESS built with Pilot's COMMAND CENTER revealed some major inconsistencies in the way the underlying data was managed. According to the ESS manager:

> The Pilot system has been a catalyst for change. The hierarchy of the data structure in the feeder systems was in disarray. We found that we were not all together on how data was aggregated from the management unit to the regional level to the divisional level. What we needed to fill the Pilot data base, the feeder systems could not give us. Pilot has forced these people to get their act together.[12]

In many companies today, data needed for an ESS resides in flat files, hierarchical, or network data bases. Restructuring this data into a relational or quasi-relational data base is far from simple. Yet the relational format is ultimately necessary if executives and their staffs are to be able to probe beyond simple displays, which are a major but probably only early step in the development of ESS in the late 1980s.

Although it will happen slowly, this issue will become less of an obstacle over the next decade. Many organizations are working today to create an appropriate data infrastructure.

Data Ownership

Questions of data ownership are among the most controversial facing ESS developers. "Who controls the data is a key issue in ESS. The question is who gets what data and when," says the ESS manager in a large paper company. For good managerial reasons, organizations have been subdivided in the past into near-separate organizational entities. Encouraged to act on their own, many have developed procedures to optimize their own objectives.[13] Creating common access to information in a decentralized organization can be unsettling. Political power and corporate culture can play a big part in deciding who gets access to information through an ESS. But there is also a tradeoff between the value of sharing information vertically and across organizational units, and the risk of misuse.

One ESS manager described the problem this way:

> We wanted to encourage information sharing, but we didn't want to risk its misuse. We had to limit the information shared across divisions because of the political sensitivity to this issue. Our biggest concern was that the data would be misused. For example, in the case of a new product that was having only marginal success, if it was highly visible because information about its performance was being shared, then the product's future could be hurt by pressure and lack of support from other units.

At Lockheed–Georgia, developers had to confront the issue of data ownership directly. In Applegate's Harvard Business School case study of this ESS, known as the Management Information and Decision Support (MIDS) system, one executive explained:

> Early in the development of MIDS, we [the MIDS staff] were forced to confront two important policy issues. First, and most important, was a determination of who owned the data in the MIDS system. The second issue concerned the determination of who would be responsible for controlling access to information within the system and how that control would be enforced. We felt that a key factor in the success of the system was that the executives felt confident that the information they received from MIDS was unbiased and did not reflect the usual filtering that comes when the information source is in a position of defending his/her organizational unit's performance. We wanted functional area managers to have the same confidence in the system.[14]

Applegate goes on to report:

> The MIDS staff, with the approval of [President] Ormsby, decided that individual managers should control access to information specific to their functional area. To enforce this policy, the MIDS system was partitioned into two levels. The Executive MIDS system contained information available to all of the top executives of the company, based on their authorization status. MIDS subsystems were developed by specific functional managers who controlled access to their subsystem's data. No executive could view information in a MIDS subsystem without the approval of the subsystem manager. Access to a MIDS subsystem by other functional managers was controlled in a similar manner. Based on their authorization status, managers were given access to portions of the Executive MIDS system.[15]

Security

Data security is often a thinly veiled data ownership issue. Staff, as well as line departments, are not immune from concerns about sharing information they have traditionally "owned." Sometimes they will use security as the reason for refusing to share information with others.

Nevertheless, security can be extremely important because of the sensitivity of files such as strategic plans and executive bonuses, created and accessed by ESS users. At Boeing, a corporate vice president says, "When we started this system, computing security was unheard of around here. Now there are complete corporate-wide computer security procedures which have been heavily influenced by this system."[16]

Some firms take a conservative approach to the problem, such as one company with three to five levels of passwords for ESS users. Other firms feel uneasy about security, but are undecided about how to approach the problem. "Because we have a centralized DP operation, there are lots of concerns about localized PC applications and the resulting questions of security," said the director of corporate computing for a large manufacturer. "There is lots of talk and worry, but no action yet."

Most senior executives prefer "one-button" access to their systems. Comshare President Crandell had a strong dislike for log-on procedures, so he installed a simple device that allowed him to use his American Express card to identify himself.

Grady Baker, executive vice president at Georgia Power, summarizes the security problem this way:

> Executives don't remember long log-on sequences very well. I'm tied into the DEC, I've got an ID and a password. VM/CMS, I've got an ID and a password . . . . If you don't change the password every month, the VM/CMS won't talk to you.
>
> We've got all this security that somebody has spent a lot of money on, and it doesn't work because there's a three-by-five card over there with every password I've got to remember on it.[17]

We found that attitudes toward security range from extreme to nonchalant. Its importance seems to be a function of past experiences, corporate culture, and the political expediency of using security concerns as an excuse for refusing to release information to others in the organization. Security is likely to remain an issue in ESS development because there are important tradeoffs between security and the user friendliness of the technology.

Management of Data

If data ownership and security do not present problems for the ESS developer, the collection and maintenance of data almost always do. Procedures to ensure that the appropriate data is collected on time, refreshed when necessary, consolidated where applicable, and made available in appropriate formats must be instituted and kept current. These tasks are essential to the well-being of any ESS.

Issues of data availability and access appear early in the life of an ESS. Six months after installation of an ESS at Michigan Motors, the general manager was frustrated at not having more useful information: "There's not yet enough information on the system to make it worthwhile interacting with it. But executive support can be a chicken-and-egg thing. Until you get enough information on it, the system won't get used, but it won't get the backing to get necessary information until people find it useful." In these early stages, a committed executive sponsor and the management of expectations as to what data can actually be delivered are seen as extremely important by several ESS developers.

Once the initial hurdles are past, the ongoing collection of data must become routine with procedures set in place to capture new items. This example comes from one recent study:

> An extensive information data base used by the chief executive was fed by many operational systems from many divisions. The quality and consistency of the CEO's data base depended upon coordinating the update data from the divisions so that the data base reflected a view of the corporation at a single point in time. In order to manage what was becoming a difficult problem, the group in charge of the CEO's data base developed a "master data input calendar" for critical data files coming from the divisions. The MDIC specified the schedule of updates from each division, and the person responsible for data arriving on time. Thus it formalized the operational coordination problem.[18]

Discipline is also imposed on report formats, such as those used in the planning processes at Lincoln National and Xerox. Both systems assure that plans from the business units are consistent, making it easy for top management to compare information from different units. At Xerox, divisional business plans are submitted on five-page forms, which are communicated electronically from around the world on the firm's ESS. The new format eliminated the traditional planning book that top management found difficult to use. "Automating the planning process forces the SBUs to conform to the new format. Thus the information put in must be better thought through, and now corporate executives can compare apples and apples." says Ken Soha, ESS project manager at Xerox. "You can hide a lot in a one-inch thick report, but you can't hide anything in five pages."

The impact of ESS on data standards was also found at Lockheed–Georgia, where Applegate's case study of the system, known as MIDS, quoted one executive:

> The importance of standard definitions can be illustrated by the use of the word "signup." In general, the term refers to a customer's agreement to buy an aircraft. Before MIDS, different organizational units tended to use the term differently. To marketing people, a signup was when a letter of intent to buy was received. Legal services considered it to be when a contract was received. Finance interpreted it as when a down payment was made. In MIDS we defined a signup as a signed contract with a non-refundable down payment. Over the years, we have noticed that gradually all of the organizational units began to use the term signup in the same way that it was defined in MIDS. This has been true for many other terms where, before MIDS, the definition was vague and subject to wide ranges of interpretation.[19]

A role that is becoming increasingly common with the rise of executive support systems is that of data administrator. This individual is authorized by top management to maintain the quality of the data bases and decide who gets access to what data. At Firestone, the director of financial systems coordinates the data system, handling both maintenance and questions of data access. Although he reports to the controller, he stays separate from the corporate accounting group to keep his primary functions of data security, data integrity, and system development from being diluted by other special projects.

A strong operating sponsor, responsible for the initial development of an ESS, may take on the responsibilities of a data administrator after the system is installed. This is a logical, although often unwanted, evolution of the operating sponsor's role, especially if this person is a key staff member in the corporate office, such as CFO or executive assistant.

One operating sponsor who spends a lot of time on data management issues assessed his efforts: "To have an effect on the data bases, you must have people who are interested and able to make things happen. The MIS manager simply lacks the authority to drive the data bases. No one will push data up in the organization unless they are forced to. I use the implied authority of the CEO to make it happen."

In another case, a large telecommunications company appointed a data base manager at the executive level to address questions of data ownership and to manage access to corporate data. "We had to ask: 'Does the controller in the organization own the financial data?' We decided the data belongs to the company, not the function," says the IS manager.

Development of executive support systems generates few questions more volatile than "who owns the data?" Sometimes confrontations over control of performance information are unavoidable, but most often data ownership issues can be negotiated.

In summary, data management is a crucial issue, requiring significant managerial attention. The amount of time needed to develop data definitions and coding standards is often underestimated. So is the time required to set in place the processes which insure the timely arrival of data after it has been "cleaned up." The difficulty of obtaining new, often externally supplied data is also far from trivial. Perhaps most important in this lengthy process is effectively managing the expectations of the executive user who is eager for a new system but unaware of all these difficulties.

CONCLUSION

The developer's ability to overcome technical problems influences how well a system is accepted by executives and, ultimately, how effective it is. But technology is not the dominant issue in ESS implementation. In the end, if we are to rank the factors critical to success, technical concerns are of relatively small importance. The danger is that developers may let technology questions overshadow more important issues. One division vice president, after working with an ESS for a year, recognized this problem:

> Using a computer has convinced me the problem we are trying to solve is about getting information, and only secondarily about information technology. The problems of how we get the information to the office or home are really trivial. There is a general misconception that if only we can figure out how to connect the mainframe to the PC, and get into the right mail system, then we will have solved the "real" problem.
>
> The truth is that once we have solved all those technical problems, you see clearly that the problem is entirely about information, not the technology. The fact that there are a lot of technology problems tend to blind us to the fact that the real issues deal with getting the right information.

Chapter 9 will address the problem of linking ESS to particular business needs and, specifically, to identifying what information a system should provide.

NOTES

1. Margaret Dickerman, "The Evolution and Diffusion of an Executive Support System: A Case Study." Master's thesis, Sloan School of Management, MIT, Cambridge, Mass., June 1985.
2. Rosabeth Moss Kanter, *Men and Women of the Corporation* (New York: Basic Books, 1977), p. 58.
3. Gary D. Rinehart, "EIS In A Public Utility," *DSS–86 Transactions* (Providence, R.I.: The Institute of Management Sciences, 1986), p. 66.
4. From Lynda Applegate, "Lockheed–Georgia Company: Executive Information Systems," case 9-187-135, p. 15. Boston: Harvard Business School, 1987. Reprinted by permission.
5. Jeffrey L. Turner, "Executive Support Systems: A Comparative Study." Master's thesis, Sloan School of Management, MIT, Cambridge, Mass., May 1985, p. 34.
6. Dickerman, "The Evolution and Diffusion of an Executive Support System: A Case Study."
7. Peter G.W. Keen, "The On-Line CEO: How One Executive Uses MIS." Unpublished working paper, Micro Mainframe Inc., 1983, p. 14–15.
8. Turner, "Executive Support Systems . . . ," p. 65.

9. Hans Paal Bunaes, "The Anatomy of an EIS Development Tool." Master's thesis, Sloan School of Management, MIT, Cambridge, Mass., 1987, p. 75.

10. Dale Goodhue, Judith A. Quillard and John F. Rockart, "The Management of Data: Preliminary Research Results," *Working Paper No. 140*, Center for Information Systems Research, Sloan School of Management, MIT, Cambridge, Mass., May 1986, p. 4.

11. Turner, "Executive Support Systems . . .," p. 53.

12. Bunaes, "The Anatomy of an EIS Development Tool," p. 76–77.

13. See Graham T. Allison, *Essence of Decision* (Boston, Mass.: Little, Brown and Company, 1971).

14. From Lynda Applegate, "Lockheed–Georgia Company: Executive Information Systems," case 9-187-135, p. 8. Boston: Harvard Business School, 1987. Reprinted by permission.

15. Ibid.

16. Turner, "Executive Support Systems . . .," p. 58.

17. Avery Jenkins, "The PC Wit and Wisdom of GP's Grady Baker,"*PC Week*, May 27, 1986, p. 46.

18. Goodhue, et. al., *Working Paper No. 140*, p. 35.

19. From Lynda Applegate, "Lockheed–Georgia Company: Executive Information Systems," case 9-187-135, p. 10. Boston: Harvard Business School, 1987. Reprinted by permission.

CHAPTER 9

LINKING THE SYSTEM TO BUSINESS OBJECTIVES

Another critical factor in implementing systems for senior management is the linkage of applications to specific business objectives. Examining the links between ESS and their business objectives in 30 sites, we discovered that the 18 systems judged most valuable by their users tended to directly address a business need or problem. The seven systems judged moderately effective were, as a rule, more vaguely connected to business objectives. The five ESS considered ineffective were, for the most part, not linked to business needs.

Satisfying top management's need for better information was the most commonly expressed business objective for ESS. Sometimes the request was for specific information, but often the need was articulated only in general terms. Other objectives mentioned were reducing the number of support staff, and creating specific organizational and cultural changes. As is usually the case with management support systems, the anticipated benefits were not quantifiable, as they are with transaction processing systems where a streamlined process or fewer people translate directly into dollar savings. Rather, the anticipated benefits of the ESS reflected the executive's intuitive, qualitative assessment of intangible value that could not be directly related to the bottom line. In this chapter, we will first discuss the ways in which organizations ensure that their systems are meeting business objectives. We then turn to the issue of ESS justification in the final section of the chapter.

LINKING ESS TO BUSINESS OBJECTIVES

There are several different ways in which ESS technology can be linked to business needs.

1. Start with a specific business problem. These problems typically are related to the need for tighter management control, as in the case of Lincoln's cash management system or Raytheon's program management system.

2. Identify and prioritize the executive's overall information needs for managing the business with the help of a planning technique such as Critical Success Factors.

3. Use prototyping to elicit the specific requirements for information and communications capabilities which are needed to enhance the existing management control system. Through this trial-and-error learning process, the executive gains familarity with alternative screen formats and data elements, selecting the most valuable aspects of the prototype while having designers add and delete other capabilities.

These approaches are not independent of each other. In many cases, systems evolve through a mixture of these techniques and philosophies. Unfortunately, a fourth and relatively common approach to ESS design also exists. This approach was followed by six companies in our sample and, we suspect, by many others we did not visit. The approach, which most often leads to unused or low-value systems, is:

4. Delegate to subordinates the critical choice of the problems the ESS should address. In this case, the executive leaves it to staff members to design the applications—a decision that, as we will discuss later, often produces systems of little value to senior management.

We will now examine in more detail these four approaches linking business objectives to the technology.

Start with a Well-Defined Business Problem

It is easiest to identify the benefits of ESS applications that address well-defined business needs. In these situations, the link between the technology and the business objective is self-evident, which helps assure that the systems will provide value. For example, in one division of Boeing, a vice president was frustrated at waiting weeks for program-cost data which was being filtered by middle managers. He requested a system that provided him the data directly from the cost-collection system. Similarly, at Raytheon, the general manager of the Missile Systems Division identified the need for a system to help him monitor the status of the division's complex programs.

Focus Using Critical Success Factors

In many cases, the business objective does not focus on a specific area. Rather, the desire for an ESS reflects a belief that the entire management reporting process must be redefined and improved. In these situations, the executive sponsor can proactively plan the contents of the new systems using methods such as the critical success factors (CSF) approach. Some have done so.

The determination of a manager's critical success factors as the key to management reporting appears to be increasingly accepted. Critical success factors have been defined as ". . . the limited number of areas in which results, if they are satisfactory, will ensure successful competitive performance for the organization. They are the few key areas where 'things must go right' for the business to flourish. If results in these areas are not adequate, the organization's efforts for the period will be less than desired."[1]

This suggests that critical success factors are areas of activity that should receive constant and careful attention from management. The current status of performance in each area should be continually measured, and the information should be made available to an executive or the senior management team. The methods by which executives determine their CSFs are the subject of a growing literature.[2]

The CSF method provides a structured approach with which companies can organize and develop their executive information systems. The process begins by reviewing the strategic plans, if any, of the organization, and identifying the key goals of the organization and those of the executive being studied. The next step, given the strategy and goals, is to determine the

key areas of the business on which the executive should focus—
the critical success factors. These will vary with the executive's
particular responsibilities and will change over time.

The next step is to identify the measures that will enable
the executive to monitor the CSFs. Once a set of useful measures
is identified, the process can proceed to the design of the ESS.
A handful of companies, including Gillette and American Re-
Insurance, have used the critical success factors approach to
identify the information most needed by senior management.

Don Palmer, controller for Gillette North America and operating sponsor for its ESS, says, "From the beginning, we saw
[ESS] as a way of having a clearer insight into our performance
against some key measures that were inherent in our whole
strategic planning process. . . .

"For this reason, we spent a fair amount of time identifying
what our critical success factors were and how to measure them,
as opposed to simply taking the existing reporting system and
attempting to replicate that on a PC. Once that was done, it was
not a difficult process to accomplish the technical implementation."[3]

At American Re-Insurance, President Ronald Compton says:

> To make this system useful to me, I had to sit down and create
> a factor tree of critical success factors to this business. I asked
> myself what I needed to see and, together with others, we built
> the software to give me that information. Too many executives
> let the systems people determine what information they receive.
> It is absolutely essential that these executives first determine
> what is necessary to running the business properly—that is, to
> determine critical success factors. Then the system should pro-
> vide that information.[4]

At The New England, a financial services firm, Vince Ficcaglia, operating sponsor for EVP Bob Shafto's ESS, took his
boss through a "quick and dirty" CSFs exercise after deciding
that the initial application of the system should focus on monitoring the performance of the company's 100 general agencies.
Ficcaglia explained:

> Bob had a growing need for better, more comprehensive infor-
> mation about the organization. When the task fell to me, we
> decided to focus on a well-defined and manageable set of infor-

mation (agency performance) where we knew the computer could provide real value. In the past, others further down in the organization had tried to define the data for an ESS and each time the system died of its own weight because they tried to put too much in it. We did a CSFs exercise by asking Bob what his critical success factors were in monitoring the general agencies. We then asked the same question of the senior vice president in charge of the agency distribution system, and came up with a surprisingly similar list. These CSFs were the foundation of our early ESS.

While the CSF method can be an effective way to define the information needed in an ESS, the realities of implementation and individual management styles often do not provide the time needed for such a reflective process. In fact, ESS have rarely been designed with the objective of overhauling an executive's entire management information system, although we feel this is changing. Rather, the systems have been focused on specific problems (e.g., getting sales or cost data faster) or needs (e.g., improving communications). As a result, "quick and dirty" approaches to creating a link between ESS technology and executive needs usually have been more appropriate. This leads to prototyping.

Get to the Specifics by Prototyping

The most common way of finding how the technology can provide value for the executive is through prototyping. With this flexible design approach, developers create a series of sample screens and present them to management, and the executive selects what has value through a process of trial and error. The screens are revised based on management feedback, and presented again to the manager in what becomes an iterative process. Prototyping requires ongoing executive interest in the project or the effort will languish.

Commenting on the value of the prototyping at Lockheed–Georgia, Houdeshel and Watson write:

> Initially identifying a complete set of information requirements is difficult or impossible for systems which support decision making. The evolutionary nature of [the ESS'] development has al-

lowed users to better understand and evolve their information requirements. Having seen a given set of information in a given format, an executive is often prompted to identify additional information or variations of formats.[5]

George Houdeshel, one of the designers of the Lockheed–Georgia system, further describes how his team decided what information to put in the prototype. "In talking with the president's secretary, we learned that one of the major things Ormsby got each month was a 104-page overhead report. We knew that he couldn't be looking at the whole thing, so we asked the president what he used and built part of the prototype based on the figures he indicated were most important."

Pilot Software's David Friend relates another prototyping experience:

> The president of a large insurance company was asked what were the first ten things he would want to look at after coming back from vacation. Two weeks later they gave him an EIS that consisted of one menu with ten choices on it. While this system was very limited, the user loved it because it took no training since he immediately recognized all ten items. And, by definition, every item on the system was a nugget of useful information. Naturally, it did not take too long for the user to complain about the limitations of the system, but it was also very easy for him to articulate what he would like to see in the next iteration. As a result, the company has been engaged in several years of constant prototyping. The president has a system which he uses every day and which he could not part with.[6]

One of the most difficult tasks in the prototyping process is getting top management to communicate its specific information needs in order to give designers a practical place to start. Donald Sundue, corporate director of MIS at Genrad, comments on the problems of identifying user needs in the early phases of an ESS project:

> Defining requirements and specifications at this stage was difficult. The users' creativity was constrained by the only system they knew, primarily existing printed reports. Common expressions of user requirements included: (1.) I'd like to have just one button to press and see anything I want . . . (2). There are too many reports; make it all fit on two pages . . . [and] (3.) I want instant access to all the relevant data.[7]

The most common approach used in order to get beyond these general goals and define specific requirements is interviews with executives. Developers frequently try to interview potential users to clarify what they want and need in a system. These interviews or questionnaires have met with mixed success, however. Their effectiveness is a function of top management's commitment to the project and understanding of the design process, and the sophistication of the interviewers. Ken Soha, the operating sponsor and ESS manager at Xerox, for example, conducted a very successful round of interviews with top management which helped identify what they really wanted in a system. Soha was able to do this because of his extensive business experience and longstanding personal relationships with many of the executives. In addition, management understood the importance of the system to the company. In some cases, however, executives do not see the need for such interviews and, as a result, refuse to spend time with ESS designers in order to think about what their system should contain.

Resistance to the interviewing process may come, in part, because executives are hard pressed themselves to say what information they want on the system. When approached by ESS designers, Lockheed–Georgia President Robert Ormsby responded. "I use a lot of soft information, one-time information, and temporal information, so it is hard to know what to tell you."

Delegate Identification of Business Objectives

Among the ESS studied, six systems were only justified in general terms such as "improve decision making," or "educate executives about technology." These were systems where top management delegated decisions about applications design to their staffs. And, because the general goal was not translated into specific business needs and applications requirements, the systems had only moderate if any impact.

When executives refuse to be involved in the process of linking the technology to their business needs, the system suffers. Subordinates usually lack the perspective that only top management can offer systems developers. And, in the end, staff members almost inevitably try to design a system to answer the types of questions the boss asks *them* when, in reality, those may not be the questions the executive needs answered by an ESS. The result tends to be a system used only by the staff, if at all, because top management does not see value in it, and the interfaces acceptable for staff users are usually too complex for busy executives.

James Hardwick, ESS manager at R.J. Reynolds, encountered the problem of assigning staff to define business objectives for an ESS: "Over time we have discovered that it is best to design around the unique, expressed needs of particular individuals rather than try to logically analyze what they *should* want for a particular business function."[8]

JUSTIFYING THE ESS INVESTMENT

Past system justifications have typically followed a formal process developed by the IS department for transaction processing systems. The effort takes on a different cast for justification of ESS whose value is not quantifiable in terms of people and time savings or other efficiencies.[9] So different is it that not one company we studied performed a traditional cost/benefit analysis either before or after installation of an ESS.

David Scotting, information services manager for a unit of The Bechtel Group, Inc., an international engineering and construction company, offers a common perspective on ESS justification:

> It is very difficult to link the new [ESS] capabilities directly to contract wins or the detection of a potential project overrun which can then be controlled. Although it only takes a few successes to pay for the system many times over, we are not likely to prove direct causality. For this reason, it is especially critical to have commitment and understanding of these realities at the very top. In this way, we can get on with the business of providing support without getting overly concerned about proving its worth.[10]

This departure from traditional justification methods is evident in the following statement by John Dembeck, vice president and treasurer of Olin Corporation:

> The PC opens up a wide spectrum of new alternatives for me. What price do you pay to extend the mind? It's something whose

value can only be determined by the creativity of the mind that uses and directs it . . . I have instructed every person who reports to me to get a PC. I justify it from the standpoint of being and staying ahead. The person who has to have a number to justify purchasing a PC shouldn't be in management.[11]

How then does one weigh the value of ESS? Often expressed qualitatively, the primary value of ESS to management is increased management effectiveness. This can be seen in the way several executives assessed their systems. Ronald Compton, president of American Re-Insurance says:

They've clarified my thinking, they save me time—both in thinking and being able to send messages to many people at once. By using the PC myself, I have improved my understanding of the business. I see it in my performance, and all indications are that my boss sees that improvement as well . . . As I look at our performance over the last two years since we got the microcomputer in the . . . system, I realize that relative to what our performance would have been without the tools it's much, much better.[12]

The controller at Diversified Electronics says: "You put more dollars in, but you can do x times more work than before. Our justification was to improve the quality of information and control. There was no cost/benefit analysis. How much is speed, time, or quality of information worth in getting the job done?"

Beneficial's Chairman Finn Caspersen offers this assessment:

What we're talking about here is the productivity of your executives. People are able to produce more, to react more quickly, and they also tend to work longer hours—particularly when they use their computers at home. The accuracy of the information they use is greater. All these things have significant effects on executives. There were many skeptics in the beginning, but as far as I know there are no skeptics now. People can't live without it; they can just get so much more done in a shorter amount of time.[13]

Increased management effectiveness also justifies Xerox's system, says President Paul Allaire: "I am convinced that what we have is cost justified, although I have not insisted on cost justification for individual applications . . . The cost of an ESS is small compared to executive salaries. If we are going to improve our executives' effectiveness and save them time, this is a hell of a lot cheaper than a corporate jet."

If increased management effectiveness justifies the system for some, for others the value judgement is strictly intuitive. Raytheon's former general manager Charles Jacobs put it simply: "I saw value in building the system."

Commenting on how Lockheed–Georgia's president Robert Ormsby justified his ESS, known as the Management Information and Decision Support System (MIDS), Houdeshel and Watson contend, "The justification for MIDS was informal. No attempt was made to cost-justify its initial development. Ormsby felt he and other Lockheed–Georgia executives needed the system and mandated its development."[14]

Intuitive judgements took on a slightly more quantitative form at Diversified Electronics, where the controller says the question was whether or not to spend an extra $300,000 for the next two years to develop an ESS, instead of just continuing to spend $1 million a year for an MIS that "wasn't doing top management much good."

One additional justification for ESS was directed at gaining competitive advantage. The vice president for manufacturing at Auto Electronics says, "We can't justify it in dollars and cents, but to compete we must be in this game. ESS will be common five years from now, so I look at this as an investment in the future." At Michigan Motors, the general manager also acknowledged the competitive motivation for his ESS: "If we don't do it now, five years from now we're going to pay for it," he says.

NOTES

1. John F. Rockart, "Chief Executives Define Their Own Data Needs," *Harvard Business Review*, vol. 57, no. 2 (March-April 1979), p. 85.
2. For more on CSFs see "Chief Executives Define Their Own Data Needs," by John F. Rockart; "A Primer on Critical Success Factors," by Christine V. Bullen and John F. Rockart; and "Engaging Top Management in Information Technology," by John F. Rockart and Adam D. Crescenzi, all reprinted in *The Rise of Managerial Computing*, John F. Rockart and Christine V. Bullen, eds. (Home-

wood, Ill: Dow Jones-Irwin, 1986). See also Andrew C. Boynton, Michael E. Shank, and Robert W. Zmud, "Critical Success Factor Analysis as a Methodology for MIS Planning," *MIS Quarterly,* June 1985.
3. Michael Sullivan-Trainor, "Gillette Buys its EIS, Firestone Builds," *Computerworld,* October 27, 1986, p. 38.
4. N. Dean Meyer and Mary E. Boone, *The Information Edge* (Agincourt, Ontario: Gage Educational Publishing, 1987), p. 218.
5. George Houdeshel and Hugh J. Watson, "The Management Information and Decision Support (MIDS) System at Lockheed-Georgia," *MIS Quarterly,* March 1987, p. 136.
6. David Friend, "Executive Information Systems: Successes, Failures, Insights and Misconceptions," *DSS-86 Transactions* (Providence, R.I.: The Institute for Management Sciences, 1986), p. 38.
7. Donald G. Sundue, "Genrad's On-Line Executives," *DSS-86 Transactions* (Providence, R.I.: The Institute for Management Sciences, 1986), p. 15.
8. James Hardwick, "Information Support For Senior Executives," *DSS-86 Transactions* (Providence, R.I.: The Institute for Management Sciences, 1986), p. 22.
9. For more on non-quantifiable approaches to justifying management support systems see Peter G.W. Keen, "Value Analysis: Justifying DSS," *MIS Quarterly,* vol. 5, no. 1, (1981).
10. "ESS in the Real World: A Roundtable Discussion," *Insights,* issue 15 (New York: Booz Allen & Hamilton, 1986), p. 10.
11. Meyer and Boone, *The Information Edge,* pp. 215–16.
12. Ibid., p. 219.
13. Ibid., p. 213.
14. Houdeshel and Watson, "The . . . (MIDS) System at Lockheed-Georgia," p. 129.

CHAPTER 10

ANTICIPATING AND MANAGING ORGANIZATIONAL RESISTANCE

ESS development is an intensely political, as well as technical, process. "If you aren't aware of the politics, you're dead," says Xerox's Ken Soha. ESS implementation is political because it presents the potential for significant change in the organization's power structure. Information is power, and changes in the information flow almost always create countervailing efforts to maintain the status quo. To successfully install a system for top management, sponsors and designers must anticipate and manage this resistance. Failure to do so can result in lack of cooperation, delays in releasing information, and more subtle sabotage, all of which ultimately reduce the effectiveness of the system.

Resistance to computer systems can have many causes. Markus[1] identifies three major ones—people problems, weaknesses in the technology, and issues springing from the interaction of people and technology. People problems are caused by the attitudes, beliefs, and actions of those for whom the system is designed. Markus says:

> The term *resistance* suggests that the problem is one of people. Some quirk of personality or some irrationality must be responsible for making some people oppose technology when others accept it so avidly. Perhaps it is a question of age and prior experience.... In any case, a focus on resistance finds explanations in people and personalities.

This in turn, suggests that solutions are to be found in the techniques for inducing change in people.[2]

While resistance is usually seen as a people problem from the designer's perspective, users often view the technology as the source of the problem. In this case, unfriendly user interfaces or other awkward design features, labelled "systems hassles" by Markus, are blamed for making the computer unusable. These can be corrected by improving the hardware and software, or the system's design.

Finally, Markus contends that resistance is best attributed neither to people nor technology but rather to the *interaction* of both. She explains how this interaction causes resistance:

> Systems that centralize control over data are resisted in organizations with decentralized authority structures; systems which alter the balance of power in organizations will be resisted by those who lose power, accepted by those who gain; resistance arises from the interaction of technical design features of systems with the social context in which the systems are used.[3]

While ESS research produces examples of resistance in the context of people problems or systems hassles, the most difficult to understand and manage is the resistance resulting from interaction between executives and computer technology within a given organizational setting. In this context, the ESS represents a threat to the "way things are done in this organization." The threat ranges from a relatively mild one (e.g., "I'll have to change some of my work habits.") to more severe ("I'm losing power."). Those who feel most threatened are likely to resist the system's implementation.

Threats to change the power structure can lead to resistance, but so can strong beliefs concerning appropriate and inappropriate uses of information. One difficulty with addressing organizational resistance is determining whether it is motivated by self-interest or by a genuine concern for the company's interests. "There's a fine line between honest resistance to a project one feels is misguided and selfish sabotage of a necessary innovation," says Keen. "The difference is a matter for conscience and self-scrutiny. In both cases, the response is political, whether 'clean' or 'dirty' politics."[4]

Just as it is important to make the clean/dirty distinction, it is necessary to distinguish between resisters and non-users. Markus is also clear in this regard. Speaking of the potential user whose decision not to use the system does not affect its value to the organization, she says, "Where one individual's use . . . is not critical to the operation of a system, that individual's choice not to use the system cannot be considered resistance. . . . Resistance is . . . when a person engages in behaviors that may result in the disruption or removal of a system that is interdependently used by others as well as by that person."[5]

When implementing an ESS, it is necessary to accept that some executives will choose not to use the technology for a variety of reasons. These people are not necessarily resisters in the classic sense, unless their refusal to use the system seriously hinders personal or organizational effectiveness. Yet they do present an implementation issue which must be recognized and managed effectively.

In sum, resistance is generally viewed as stemming from aspects of people or technology, or from the interaction between the two. In any case, resistance can be based solely on self-interest and concern for personal power, or it can be a perfectly legitimate response when a specific technology application is considered by a manager as inappropriate for that individual or the organization. In the companies we observed, four patterns emerged, each defining a different type of resistance. There were three groups of genuine resisters—two based on self-interest and one with legitimate concerns. A fourth group of more passive resisters was made up of Markus' "non-users." In the balance of this chapter we will examine why each group resists, and discuss the methods being used to manage each type of resistance.

Causes of Resistance

The four major groups of people who, for different reasons, resist implementation of executive support systems are:

1. Staff personnel who fear the loss of control over information used by executives.

2. Subordinate line managers who fear giving top management too much visibility into their operations.

3. Either staff or line managers who provide legitimate resistance created by one of three legitimate perspectives:
   a. "The business is doing fine, why change things?"
   b. "This system represents all costs and no benefits for my group."
   c. "Even if we send up the data they want, our executives won't have the context to understand it."

4. Executives, who for any number of reasons, do not want to use the technology themselves.

We will look at each of these sources of resistance in more detail.

1. Loss of control over information

Gathering, collating, and analyzing data are traditionally tasks of functional staff groups. These groups derive power by acting as "gatekeepers," advising senior management on what data to look at. (As we said earlier, in far too few cases has senior management proactively determined the information it needs to receive.) As a result, many staff groups, like subordinate line organizations, have come to believe that they "own" their data. Any change in this status quo is likely to lead to resistance.

The corporate controller at Stowe actively resisted development of ESS applications that would provide top management with direct access to performance data. Although he based his argument against supplying data on security concerns, it was clear to all involved with the system that it threatened to reduce his role as gatekeeper of operational data.

The CFO of a large food distributor had a long-standing relationship with the CEO that established him as the major source of operational information for the chief executive. When the CEO decided to broaden his sources of information by automating the collection of performance data, the CFO's power to determine what information the chief executive received was seriously threatened. He cooperated only grudgingly with the system's implementation and caused many delays.

In another case, the department that controlled cost data at Auto Electronics refused to share it with production managers who needed the information to cut costs. The cost department argued that what the company paid for parts was almost a trade secret, and sharing it increased the chances of leaks to the competition. Senior executives in the company believed, however, that the cost department realized sharing this valuable information would reduce the power they derived from controlling access to it.

At one telecommunications company, the executive vice president of marketing tried to install a system to monitor the progress of the dozens of marketing projects underway in his group. Traditionally, assistant vice presidents had collected this information from project managers before passing it up to the EVP. The new system, however, threatened to bypass the AVPs. Seeing a threat to their information-filtering function, the AVPs refused to take part in the implementation process. Not one responded to the developer's repeated requests for input as to what applications or data the system should contain.

In yet another situation at a consumer products company, a confrontation between ESS sponsors and the corporate controller became inevitable. The latter made it clear that his department "owned" the company's financial data, and he would decide how to present the data, including which variables could be compared side-by-side. "Our financial people are paranoid about losing control of providing information to top management," said a system developer in that company.

2. Giving top management too much visibility into operations

Subordinate line managers have traditionally controlled access to their performance information, limiting senior management access to standard weekly, monthly, or quarterly reports. ESS can change this, however, by giving executives more direct access to unfiltered operational data. This increased visibility into line operations is frequently seen as a threat to the autonomy of unit managers and is a common source of resistance.

At United Retailing, the operating sponsor said that before installing an ESS for the vice president of operations, only the regional managers knew what the real numbers were. "The VP was managing in the dark," says the sponsor. Thus, when the system was being installed, some regional managers tried to persuade developers to delay the performance data from getting to the VP until the managers saw it and prepared answers to questions they anticipated from their boss. Developers refused to give in to the pressure because they knew the operations VP would be "furious" if the information was delayed.

On a similar note, Keen reports on an ESS where the head of R&D for a major multinational company wanted to centralize coordination of geographically dispersed units. The system would have been of great value and easy to design, but once division managers learned of the executive's plans their strong reaction led him to cancel the project on short notice. For the unit managers, the ESS represented a major threat to their autonomy and provided too much visibility into their operations.[6]

At Michigan Motors, subordinates showed little interest in a system being designed for the general manager because they assumed he would not use it. Shortly after it was in place, however, the GM was looking at a back-orders report and something about transmissions-parts orders caught his eye. He called the transmissions manager in the plant and began questioning him about the numbers. During the call the GM directly challenged the figures the manager was giving him and mailed a hard copy of the graphs from his ESS to the manager with a request that he reconcile the numbers. The next day the head of the materials organization "came screaming" to the ESS project manager asking, "Who authorized you to go into our data?" From then on, developers had more difficulty getting access to data for the ESS.

ESS developers and senior management at Lockheed–Georgia agreed to a policy that executives could not access data in subsystems controlled by functional managers. ESS managers, however, found that enforcing this policy was not always easy. For example:

> Paul Frech assumed the presidency of the Lockheed–Georgia Company in June 1984, when Ormsby was promoted to group president. Frech's background was in manufacturing. By this time the manufacturing control area had developed their own

MIDS subsystem and Frech was anxious to gain access to it so he could monitor the manufacturing data. Needless to say, the manufacturing manager considered this to be his data and did not want the President or any other chief executive to be able to have free access to it. At least six times in his two years as president, Frech asked the MIDS staff to be granted access to the Manufacturing Subsystem of MIDS. Six times we had to carefully explain to him the reason for the policy and offer to update the Executive MIDS with any manufacturing information that he wanted to track on a regular basis. We also recommended that he talk with the manager of Manufacturing Control to discuss specific MIDS displays that he may wish to see.[7]

3. Legitimate resistance
Unlike the patterns of resistance above, which stem from a desire to maintain existing power relationships, there are several forms of resistance that result from different, often logical, perspectives of staff and line managers.

3a. Legitimate resistance: no need to change things. Frequently an objective of ESS is to create change in an organization. Not surprisingly, perceptions differ between executives and subordinates about the need for change. This difference sometimes appears as resistance by subordinates who do not recognize the need for a new system.

The chairman of a diversified health care company tried to encourage his executive team to improve their information system for several years and finally delegated the project to his CFO. The company, however, had been highly profitable for many years, and other top managers generally saw little need to change things. Even though the chairman recognized the long-term competitive advantages of integrating computer technology into the firm's management process, most other company executives did not. Consequently, the chairman and CFO had great difficulty generating political support for the system and development continued very slowly.

Gary Gulden of The Index Group has developed a useful way of identifying managers likely to support an ESS project and those likely to resist it. Managers' attitudes can be plotted on the matrix shown as Figure 10–1, according to factors af-

Figure 10–1
Assessing Attitudes Towards ESS

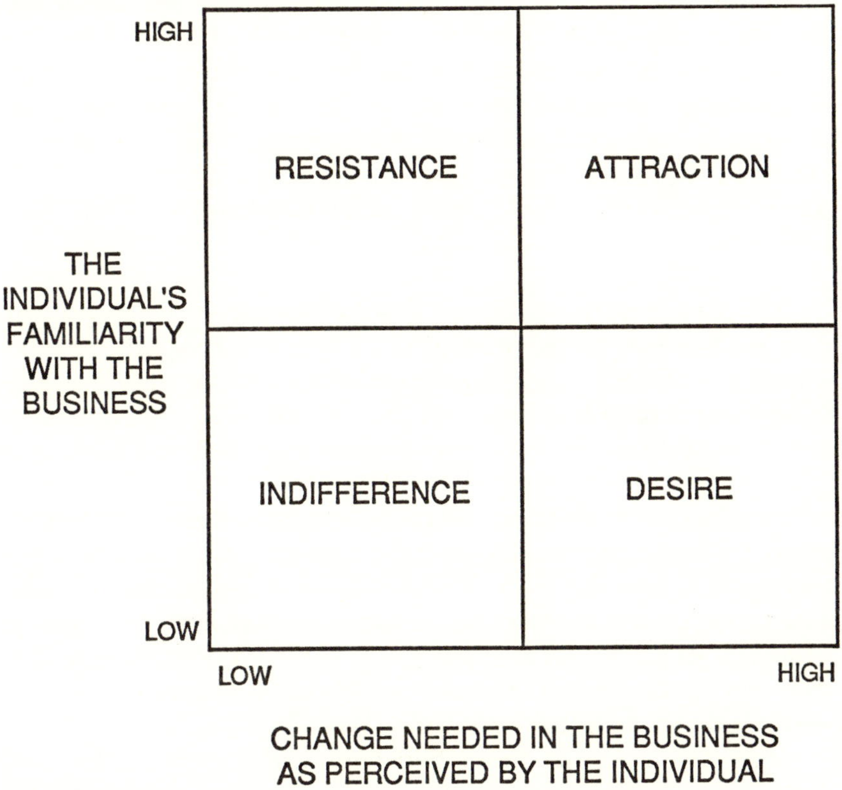

	RESISTANCE	ATTRACTION
	INDIFFERENCE	DESIRE

HIGH

THE
INDIVIDUAL'S
FAMILIARITY
WITH THE
BUSINESS

LOW

LOW   HIGH

CHANGE NEEDED IN THE BUSINESS
AS PERCEIVED BY THE INDIVIDUAL

fecting desire for or resistance to an ESS. The dimensions are the individual's degree of understanding of the business, and the amount of change in the business the manager perceives as necessary. An executive in a new job who perceives that change is needed in the business is most apt to back an ESS. On the other hand, an executive who knows his or her role thoroughly and who sees little change in the business environment is apt to strongly question and often resist as unnecessary the installation of an ESS. The other two cells in the matrix represent intermediate positions.

In the case of the health care company above, the chairman and his senior management team had years of service with a consistently profitable business. Only the chairman recognized the vastly changing business conditions. In Figure 10–1, the chairman would be plotted in the upper right cell because he was clearly "attracted" to ESS. On the other hand, his senior managers' long familiarity with the business and low perceived sense of business change put them predictably in the "resistance" quadrant, which made implementing an ESS quite difficult.

3b. Legitimate resistance: The system appears to be all costs and no benefits to subordinates. Fulfilling the data requirements of an ESS usually requires additional effort and resources from subordinate line and staff groups. The costs of supporting the new system can be an unwelcome burden to these units when they do not perceive benefits for their own sub-organization. In one high-tech company, program managers felt the need to designate an additional person to provide the information fed into the ESS. The added cost led to considerable resistance on the part of project managers. At first, they saw no benefit to the ESS for themselves or the company. Rather, they saw it as a bureaucratic move which only created additional work and expense for their units.

Similarly, at one diversified chemical company, the CFO installed an ESS to improve the corporate reporting system. The operating units, however, saw virtually no benefits in the system for themselves. Moreover, it complicated their reporting requirements significantly. The divisions complained constantly about the new system and tried to keep it from being implemented.

Several other firms we studied saw the need to identify the benefits of the system to the company as a whole to overcome honest resistance by subordinates. Diversified Electronics enhanced a reporting system to provide senior management with better information. But the system put new burdens on the operating units, who had to supply data and analysis in more restrictive formats and time frames. In the end, the CFO and corporate controller visited the divisions to explain the value of the new system to the operating units. Although some elements of resistance types 1 and 2 may have been present, the CFO's judgement that the resistance was principally legitimate appears to have been correct. The system was accepted thereafter.

3c. Legitimate resistance: Executives lack context to understand data. Subordinates often fear that top management will misinterpret raw data. They believe that the data needs to be massaged first so that it can be presented in a context that executives can understand and use effectively for decision making. For example, the general manager of Auto Electronics wanted to know about the quality of worklife in his plants, so he asked to monitor the number of grievances filed by the union. Personnel management, however, refused to supply this information. They reasoned that because they considered a significant number of the grievances to be clearly without merit, the raw numbers could be misleading. Personnel held firm to this position, and the GM never got this information for his system.

Fear of providing raw data to top management is derived from uncertainty about how it will be used. A legitimate case can be made that providing data out of context can do more harm than good. But this argument can also be a smokescreen to protect certain "fiefdoms" from uncomfortable probing by top management.

4. Executive non-users.

Yet another type of "resistance" to ESS comes from executives themselves, who decide not to use the technology because they see no value in it for them. As Markus points out, these managers should not be considered resisters if their decision not to use an ESS has little impact on the system's value for others.

Managers' reasons for choosing not to use an ESS vary. One of the most common, however, is that the system provides inadequate functions or information for the particular executive. At one firm, the vice president for technology development was given a system designed by the CFO. The VP described his reaction:

> I must admit that my hackles were up even before the system arrived. There was no way I was going to have a system someone

told me I must have. I publicly made a point of how hard it was to turn on and get the system up, and the response time was pretty awful.

Early on I made a nuisance of myself saying I don't want the "package" of information they were providing everybody. Instead, I said I wanted project updates, but the developers couldn't make the system flexible at all. They tried to give everyone the same package of capabilities, but they didn't realize that we all wanted to do something different.

Another reason executives choose not to use ESS is that the user interface does not suit them. For example, many will not use a system which demands that they type. Grady Baker, executive vice president at Georgia Power and a computer user himself, presents a widely held view: "My observation is, first of all, [executives] can't type, they don't want to learn to type and they will not learn to type. My advice to IS managers is any application they are going to come up with should have a one-keystroke implementation period."[8]

We observed a significant number of executives who do type at a reasonable level and feel quite at home with a keyboard. However, executives who do not type are unlikely to adapt to the keyboard, unless the system requires only a few keystrokes. The best way around this problem is to provide a simpler user interface. For this reason, there is a significant trend toward both mouse and touch-screen technologies by ESS designers.

In the end, some senior managers simply find an ESS too difficult to use when compared to the benefits it provides. "Systems hassles," leading to rejection of ESS, are evident in the case of one chief executive who had his workstation removed. He says:

The IS people came up and I had two 45-minute training sessions. That was adequate to get going, but getting through the security process was still a problem for me. More important, however, the data was not useful enough for me to really want to spend a lot of time getting into the system. It was often a month out of date. After awhile, I just had them take the whole thing away.

Managing Resistance

Given these four potential sources of resistance to ESS, how are developers anticipating and managing the problem? The approach depends, in large part, on the cause of the resistance. We will review each one in turn.

Overcoming staff resistance to loss of control over information. The most effective approach here uses education and persuasion to convince subordinates that, while management will access information directly, their roles will not be diminished and may actually be enhanced. This, in fact, does happen. In a number of the companies studied, key staff personnel, such as the controller, were initially hostile to the ESS. Yet, increased analytical demands on the staff sparked by the system, and the increased capability provided by the ESS to meet these demands, has more than made up for the staff's loss of "data ownership." In fact, their jobs have become more interesting.

While the power of the executive sponsor can also be used, education about the need for the system due to changing business conditions often paves the way for relatively resistance-free implementation.

At Xerox, for example, ESS project manager Ken Soha convinced senior management that he needed at least six months to do the education and persuasion necessary to gain support among corporate staff and line managers. Top management was not willing to wait this long initially, but Soha showed them examples in other firms where failure to anticipate organizational resistance led to failure of executive systems. He convinced Xerox executives that implementation without staff commitment would make long-term success more doubtful.

In Xerox, as in other firms, what followed was a process of education, negotiation, and selling of the benefits of an ESS. Negotiation is important, because often ESS designers can build increased capabilities for the staff into the system, ensure key data check points, and meet other staff needs without compromising the system's design.

ESS developers at The New England, a financial services company, recognized early on the potential problems that might arise from data ownership issues. To address the problem, developers made all of the data suppliers part of the project, consulting with them frequently and inviting them to ceremonies launching the system. "If we didn't get data owners involved, we would have been unable to deliver the system," says Gregory Ross, vice president for corporate information services. "The key point is to make sure that even though we changed how the information was presented we did not change data ownership and control. The way we handled that is we left them with control of the switch that determines when their data goes onto the system."

In each firm, the process of managing data ownership issues depends on the culture, the degree of change brought about by the system, and the level of support from the executive sponsor. At Xerox, Gillette, and The New England, for example, where loss of control over information was a significant issue, the process of managing organizational resistance was accomplished through education and negotiation. In each case, the sponsors knew the culture would support nothing else.

Overcoming subordinates' resistance to increased top management visibility into their operations.   Perhaps more important than educating staff to reduce resistance, is the problem of dealing with the fear or outright hostility toward increased scrutiny into their areas of the business by senior management. Two approaches appear to be effective. One uses the power inherent in the executive's position in the organization. The second, and certainly more desirable in most cases, is the sensitive, sometimes negotiated, use of the data and analytic capabilities newly available to top management. A Boeing executive who is an ESS user comments:

> Management resistance to change is greatly affected by the way executives . . . use or abuse the increased information. If we're on the phone all the time to our subordinates . . . because of what we've seen in the details of the data, there will be a lot of resistance to the system. If we let each manager do his job without too much "help," everything will be all right.[9]

Much of the resistance we found occurred during the early stages of ESS installation when subordinates felt uncertain of what would happen when executives gained access to more timely, detailed, and accurate data. Middle managers in several companies feared that top management would use the data as a "club." Don Palmer of Gillette offers one example:

> We found that the most effective way of eliminating political resistance was not in what you had access to but how you used the information you had available. If it was used in an "I gotcha" fashion, that would have increased the resistance dramatically. But, instead, the information was used in a fashion consistent with our culture, which tends to be laid back, and we did not make a big issue that we knew something when a new problem occurred.
>
> For example, we gave a demonstration of Pilot's Command Center software to each of the operating companies. At one of the demos a sales vice president saw a chart that projected daily sales activity for his business by product line. He said, "God, if Derwyn ever gets hold of this, my phone will be ringing off the hook." And I responded that Derwyn has had this information for over a year, and has he had any phone calls? It is how you use the information that counts. We had to develop a real sensitivity to that.

In one midwestern plastics company, the vice president, who had initially developed an ESS for monitoring sales, subtly discouraged the president from getting on the system. Data ownership was a sensitive issue in this company, and the vice president had been careful to use his access to improved data from the operating units in a way not threatening to the organization. The president had a more confrontational management style, however, and the VP feared that the chief executive would use the data abrasively, challenging the performance of managers in a way bound to create organizational resistance to the system. As a result, the vice president carefully discouraged the president from going on-line, and eventually the idea was dropped.

After studying three systems at Boeing, Turner concluded:

> Overall, as use of the system matures, experienced users become less fearful of the impacts of greater information in the hands of the executives. And, as executives (in the words of one vice

president), "behave responsibly with the information the system gives them, they don't use it as a club over the heads of their subordinates and this takes the fear of it away."

This is not to imply, however, that resistance is not an issue with executive support systems at Boeing. There were several instances . . . where executives and their subordinates expressed concerns over how the executives use their greater access to data. These concerns are much more prevalent in the less mature environments than where the systems have been in use for several years.[10]

In the end, developers often find it is much easier to build a system that does not demand new, more detailed information from subordinates. This is what creates the greatest uncertainty and, hence, most of the resistance during implementation. Palmer explains Gillette's experience with information from internal company sources:

> We dealt with the data ownership problem simply by building on the existing flows of information. We operated on the principle that if the information already came into Derwyn's office, then access to it was already approved. We did not ask for things he was not already receiving, and that relieved much of the tension between the operating units and the headquarters group. We never asked MIS to violate this and, as a result, they felt comfortable in that they were not being put in the middle. We've continued with that philosophy, and on the rare occasions when we have wanted some information he wasn't already receiving, we have gone directly to the manager of the operation to ask for it.

Palmer suggests that this policy is easy to implement because senior managers are usually overloaded with data. Simply using it effectively can have a high payoff.

> We made a conscious decision not to ask for things Derwyn was not already seeing because he was receiving so much to begin with that we didn't have to. It was a bit of packaging that made the managers more comfortable. What people didn't realize, however, was that if I have access to the telephone directory that is one thing, but if I can see the names on all the people on one street, that is something quite different. When we started showing people the system, they recognized that they had been

giving us all that information, but that we could never make anything out of it before.

In some cases, where top management is justifiably seeking increased visibility into operations, the only way to overcome resistance is by bringing direct political power to bear. Most often, this occurs where the ESS is designed to assist in a major organizational change. In these instances, executives cannot negotiate with subordinates over the system design without undermining its purpose. In writing about the use of power as a general implementation strategy, Markus states conclusions which are readily applicable to the ESS environment. She says:

> Obviously, the goals of system implementors will frequently involve making changes in the existing organizational information flows, power channels or value systems. . . . In this case, the greater the dissonance between the existing organization and the proposed system, the greater the need for implementation tactics based on power and politics.
>
> Frequently, when political implementation strategies are called for, [subordinate] participation as a tactic is strongly counterindicated, in direct contradiction to much prevailing MIS wisdom. . . . If [subordinates] are given a genuine opportunity to participate, they will try to change the proposed designs in ways which meet their needs to the exclusion of others, which can lead to the failure of managers and systems analysts to achieve their . . . objectives.[11]

For example, at United Retailing, the operations vice president was trying to stem major revenue losses in the company's 1,000-store chain. To do this, he needed more timely and better-quality performance information. Changing the existing information flows threatened regional and store managers, but the vice president could not afford to negotiate if he was to keep the company from going bankrupt.

At Banco Internacional, President Mike Jensen used his ESS to change the way the bank was managed. When he took over, Jensen found that lower-level managers often lacked knowledge of customer account status and profitability. Because the business was so volatile, Jensen wanted his organization to focus more carefully on the numbers critical for profitability.

He did this by using an ESS to monitor the numbers himself, thus forcing the rest of the company to do the same. Jensen clearly recognized his subordinates' reluctance to accept the system. He said, "It wasn't in their bones that we had to use MIS to understand our numbers. So I pushed it on them."[12] As expected, Jensen's hard-nosed approach produced significant resistance at first, but because of his strong commitment to the system, over time it was accepted and its value recognized by the organization.

Handling legitimate resistance. Education, persuasion, and the inclusion of system features useful for the resisters are the most effective approaches when subordinates are legitimately reluctant to support an ESS. To help gain acceptance of the new system at Diversified Electronics, the CFO and the corporate controller went to the divisions. The controller says:

> We didn't try to shove this system down anybody's throat. We had meetings with the divisional CFOs and explained what was happening, what the issues were, and sold them on how it would eventually help them. We pointed out that part of their frustration with the existing system was that they were getting asked a lot of dumb questions by corporate, questions that would be cleared up by a more streamlined and cleaner reporting system. Another advantage we talked about was how the system would help them become more familar with PCs, which were to be an integral part of the project. Backward MIS departments in some divisions made this an attractive feature.

In the case of an ESS designed to monitor large manufacturing programs, one program manager strongly resisted the system because his project was well behind schedule and he didn't want this fact put on-line. The operating sponsor turned this situation around by showing the manager how he could benefit from a system capability that not only indicated he was short of parts, but also helped explain why. "The key," said the sponsor, "was to build in a capability that provided information of real use to the program manager. It was finding this key application that helped to get the user to buy in."

Dealing with executive non-users. We have emphasized throughout that many senior managers, for a number of valid reasons, do not see ESS workstations as useful. The main tactic used in handling "resistance" among these potential but extremely hesitant users is to make executive automation clearly optional. Many firms, like Lincoln National, made a conscious decision that use of ESS should be a matter of personal choice.

ESS project manager Jim Tunis says, "Politics influenced the way the system was initially implemented. We did it workstation-by-workstation, only at the user's request, instead of pursuing mass departmental installations, which would have created a lot of political problems. Our strategy, however, undermined user resistance because there couldn't be any complaints about the system being forced on anybody."

This tactic is inappropriate for some executive sponsors, such as Robert Wallace, executive vice president of Phillips Petroleum Company, who want their entire management teams on-line and communicating. Wallace turned to forceful persuasion. One of Wallace's direct reports, Ben Jones, manager of planning, budgeting, and correlation, says:

> Not everyone in the management team was immediately in favor of the system. Wallace gently, but very firmly, insisted that we all use it. If he had not, I would not have fooled around with it. I had had a bad experience about three years ago with a computer system that was so difficult to work with it was not worthwhile. If Wallace had not provided strong encouragement, I still would not have a PC in my office. He did the right thing. Now, at my level, we can all see the benefits and the system is spreading downward to levels of younger managers where the resistance is less.

Wallace's persuasion was helped by the fact that Jones and other executives at Phillips, after long service in the company, were being buffeted by changes in the industry. Thus they fell in the upper right hand corner of Figure 10–1, and were at least mildly attracted to the new managerial tools. As Jones notes:

> The pressure that Boone Pickens put on this company together with industry conditions undoubtedly also helped reduce our resistance. In 1984, with Pickens' takeover attempt, we downsized rather considerably. Our total staff is down 40 percent since 1981. That provided a significant incentive to look for tools to help us do the job better with fewer staff. Everyone at my level

with whom Wallace deals certainly understood that situation only too well. We needed all available tools to keep us from "drowning."

SUMMARY

In the end, anticipating and managing the political impacts of ESS is a matter of identifying the potential sources and causes of organizational resistance, then recognizing the symptoms of opposition to the new system. This latter task is not always easy because, as we have shown, resistance to ESS development can be subtle and passive, yet still very effective. Keen summarizes the strategy of those who would undermine a system:[13]

- Lay low.

* Rely on inertia.

* Keep the project complex, hard to coordinate, and vaguely defined.

* Minimize the implementers' legitimacy and influence.

* Exploit the developer's lack of knowledge of the business.

Add to this list such overt tactics as refusing to supply data for the system, and we see plenty of ways an ESS can be undermined. Once resistance is identified, however, there are three ways to address it: ignore it, overpower it, or take a more political approach, relying on education and persuasion. Only those too powerless or unsophisticated to deal with implementation politics would choose to ignore it. Overcoming resistance solely through the use of power is extremely risky to the long-run health of the system, and it requires the right combination of business need, strong executive sponsorship, and organizational makeup to succeed.

The final way to manage organizational resistance is more participative, through education and persuasion. This requires identifying those with a stake in the ESS early on, negotiating to gain their support and generally building momentum for change. This can be a difficult and frustrating process, but often it is the only way to develop an ESS that will become an integral part of the firm's management processes.

All approaches to managing resistance have limitations, which is why the most successful developers frequently use a combination of the direct-power and participative approaches. Overpowering resisters, if carried too far, can hurt morale and make resistance more subtle. Negotiating change, on the other hand, sometimes takes too long and runs the risk of succumbing to inertia. Thus, a combination of the two approaches is often seen. Although discussing DSS, Keen anticipates the role of the executive or operating sponsor in the ESS world, saying:

> Information [systems] development must be spearheaded by a general, not coordinated by aides-de-camp. . . . The issues of negotiation seem central. To position a system one must clarify objectives, respond to resistance, adjust other components of the Leavitt Diamond (Task, Technology, People, Structure), and block off counterimplementation. The politics of data make it essential that negotiations be handled by a fixer, well-linked into senior management's decision making. Large scale change is a process of coalition-building; this cannot be done by staff analysts, who are too easily caught in the middle with no formal powers.[14]

Here, Keen argues for relying on an executive or operating sponsor to utilize either power or negotiation, or both, to manage organizational resistance. Any other approach to an ESS is bound to be less effective.

NOTES

1. M. Lynne Markus, *Systems in Organizations* (Boston, Mass.: Pitman, 1984).
2. Ibid., p. 5.
3. M. Lynne Markus, "Power, Politics and MIS Implementation," *Working Paper No. 59*, Center for Information Systems Research, Sloan School of Management, MIT, Cambridge, Mass., May 1982, p. 7.
4. Peter G. W. Keen, "Information Systems and Organizational Change," *Communications of the ACM*, vol. 24, no. 1, January 1981, p. 28. Copyright 1981, Association for Computing Machinery, Inc., reprinted by permission.
5. Markus, *Working Paper No. 59*, p. 12.

6. Peter G. W. Keen, "The On-Line CEO: How One Executive Uses MIS." Unpublished working paper, Micro Mainframe, Inc., 1983, p. 31.

7. From Lynda Applegate, "Lockheed-Georgia Company: Executive Information Systems," case 9-187-135, pp. 8-9. Boston: Harvard Business School, 1987. Reprinted by permission.

8. Avery Jenkins, "The (PC) Wit and Wisdom of GP's Grady Baker," *PC Week*, May 27, 1986, p. 46.

9. Jeffrey L. Turner, "Executive Support Systems: A Comparative Study." Master's thesis, Sloan School of Management, MIT, Cambridge, Mass., May, 1985, p. 30.

10. Ibid., p. 54–55.

11. M. Lynne Markus, "Implementation Politics: Top Management Support and User Involvement," *Working Paper No. 75*, Center for Information Systems Research, Sloan School of Management, MIT, Cambridge, Mass., September 1981, p. 29.

12. Keen, "The On-Line CEO . . . ," p. 10.

13. Keen, "Information Systems and Organizational Change, p. 30."

14. Ibid., p. 31.

CHAPTER 11

MANAGING ESS EVOLUTION
AND SPREAD

Once an ESS is in place and the initial applications are being used by one or two senior managers, the system's sponsors and designers are confronted with new problems of managing ESS evolution and spread. In this chapter, we define *evolution* as the growth of the ESS application set available to users. *Spread*, on the other hand, is the increase in number of executives and subordinates who have access to the system.

Because ESS tend to evolve and spread in erratic and unpredictable patterns, there are few hard and fast guidelines for managing this "follow-on" part of the implementation process. Generalizing about the management of ESS growth is difficult because these systems differ along a number of dimensions. The focus of the applications is the most obvious way in which they differ. For some the orientation is toward office support (e.g., Lincoln National, Beneficial); for others it is planning and control (e.g., Diversified Electronics, Lockheed–Georgia) and a few are designed primarily to support thought processes (e.g., Thermo Electron).

ESS differ along a second dimension—their orientation toward individual versus organizational support. We will discuss this in more detail below. Finally, ESS vary even within application areas, given the unique organizational environments in which they are built and the specific support needs of each executive.

Nevertheless, from our discussions with ESS developers, there appear to be five strategies commonly followed by developers to facilitate the process of managing ESS evolution and spread. These are:

1. Striving for explicitness in system goals and scope.

2. Working toward fast, flexible response to rapidly changing user demands.

3. Managing expectations.

4. Ensuring continued availability of adequate IS resources—technology, data, and staff.

5. Identifying "early adopters."

1. Striving for Explicitness in System Goals and Scope

Because ESS prototypes are often developed quickly and without much planning, there is a tendency not to articulate the system's objectives or the underlying implementation philosophy.

A useful step in this articulation process is to *create a vision* of the system. ESS development can be structured to some extent by surfacing the executive's rough, often tentative, perception of how the technology will be used and how it will affect the organization. Ken Soha, the operating sponsor at Xerox, brought this about by repeatedly asking President Paul Allaire and other senior managers to articulate their vision for the ESS. Soha kept asking, "What is it going to feel like when we have a fully functional ESS?" The answers he got helped him formulate an implementation strategy.

One important aspect of the vision is whether the system is being designed to support individual executives on a "standalone" basis, or whether it is designed for organization-wide support of major business processes. As was noted in Chapter 2, early ESS tended to be designed as personal systems to support individual executives, but the current trend is toward organizational systems whose applications are intended for the managerial team in a communication-based system with broader impact.

Of the 30 systems we studied, six were essentially designed as personal-support systems, such as those at ICL, Georgia

Power, and Northwest. Five of these six systems were judged successful by their users. Another 19 ESS were organizational in nature, such as those at Lincoln, Beneficial, and Diversified Electronics. Of these, only nine were considered clearly successful, while another six were modestly useful, and four failed to provide any real value. A third category consists of those systems which start out as personal ESS but evolve into organizational systems after the executive sponsor's initial support needs have been realized and he perceives value in extending the system. We found five ESS, including Gillette, in this category. Four are successful and the other is moderately useful.

The differences in these success rates are apparent. A system designed to be an organizational ESS faces many more hurdles than a personal system. The sheer size of the system, the usually more complex technology, the greater number of users who have to be supported (or, whose resistance must be overcome), and the increased needs for staff involvement and data access make such systems more difficult to install, evolve, and spread. If the intent of the executive sponsor is to develop an organizational system, early clarification of this purpose, and iden ⋅ tification of the scope of the management hierarchy to be served, are extremely useful. This will make many technical, personnel, and data-resource decisions, as well as decisions on necessary implementation steps, clearer and more straightforward.

One significant element of the ESS vision is the initial vertical spread of the system. The expected organizational boundaries of the system affect the hardware and software selected for the initial applications. These technology choices can affect the system's ability to spread beyond its original boundaries deeper into the organization.

Jim Tunis at Lincoln National describes his firm's approach as "a totally democratic system for both executives and secretaries. It's a system based on low-cost, high-penetration terminals with a wide range of capabilities. We're selling a service, not fancy iron." Beneficial is another example of high penetration where the executive sponsor wanted as many managers and staff personnel as possible on-line. In this case, broad-based automation is viewed as critical to improving organizational— not just executive—productivity.

This broad-based approach stands in contrast to the design philosophy at Auto Electronics, where expensive, customized workstations are the heart of a system available only to top management and privileged subordinates. Acknowledging the philosophy that underlies applications and technology choices is important because it influences how an ESS is able to grow.

Hardware choices alone, in terms of workstation cost and the response time dictated by CPU capacity, can be significant. Equally important is the design philosophy underlying the system's software. Systems aimed, for example, at supporting a few executives with interactive menus can prove inadequate when workstations are demanded by a broader set of users, some of whom desire to go directly to data elements. We return to another perspective on this point later in this chapter.

2. Working Toward Fast, Flexible Response to Rapidly Changing User Demands

ESS spread tends to be unpredictable, as evidenced by the experiences of two companies using Pilot's COMMAND CENTER software. In one of these companies, spread has come slowly and painfully. "We had hoped for progress more quickly," says one ESS manager. "But we underestimated the lack of shared enthusiasm for the system. It was more of a selling situation than we anticipated, as the operating units were more reluctant to provide information and were more sensitive to the political implications than we expected. We now realize it will take a lot longer to gain the cooperation of others in spreading the system."

A recent study of a major bank produced a very different description of ESS spread:

> The proliferation of use of the system has been rapid. Shortly after the head of the International Banking Group (IBG) began using the system, his direct reports began asking for it. The divisional manager's deputy and the divisional controller quickly began using the system. The propagation of the system then spread to parts of IBG outside of New York: offices in Asia and London began accessing the system. In the second wave of proliferation, use of the system began moving across the organization. The bank's Economics Department began clamoring for access to the Pilot data base as did the Risk Review Group. Lastly,

the system began its push upwards. The vice chairman of the bank was shown the system by the IBG division head and was notably impressed. Now there is a push to get a PC into the chairman's office.[1]

The wildfire spread of the bank system is sometimes represented at an individual level by those who unexpectedly and suddenly find new opportunities for their own ESS use. Ken Soha, ESS manager at Xerox, emphasizes that developers must be very sensitive to sudden changes in the executive's view of technology and perception of its value. He notes that both the level of interest and specific needs of top management will sometimes change quite unexpectedly, and ESS designers must be prepared to capitalize on any newfound interest.

3. Managing Expectations

Probably the most critical issue in the evolution of the ESS application set is managing user expectations. Many frustrations develop based on false executive perceptions of when a new application will be available and what it will support. Successful prototype demonstrations present a paradox. They show progress and help maintain momentum, but they often breed unrealistic expectations because they fuel an executive's imagination as to the potential and desirability of the system. The ESS manager at Michigan Motors offers a typical example. He says, "We showed our executive committee a prototype of the ESS, and the next day the general director of quality asked for the equipment. He wanted to start using it right away. It wasn't to be delivered for another six months."

The need to manage expectations is oft-stated in the information systems field. Nowhere, however, is it more important than in ESS implementation, evolution, and spread. Most senior managers have little background to enable them to understand the amount of technical, systems, and organizational effort necessary to turn an ESS design into a stable, effective, easily expandable system.

4. Ensuring Continued Availability of Adequate IS Resources—Technology, Data, and Staff

Chapter 8 identified implementation issues involving three major categories of IS resources. If these issues are not addressed appropriately in the early stages of development, they may plague sponsors and designers as ESS use grows. For example, significant constraints on ESS spread can result from early hardware and software choices. Implementers at Banco Internacional found themselves severely constrained when they tried to add more terminals to their system built on a mini-computer. The problem was even more acute because the technical limits became evident just as management demand for the system peaked.

Response time is also constrained by technology. As system use grows, developers must anticipate the impact of putting more users on-line. Few things drive managers away from the terminal faster than consistently sub-par response time, something that seems to be a common problem when new users are added to an ESS.

The problems of data management were also noted in Chapter 8. These can become a major barrier to spread if not dealt with as the ESS prototype is being developed.

Several developers insisted that the lack of adequate IS staff was by far the biggest obstacle in the evolution of ESS. Sponsors at Gillette, United Retailing, Firestone, and Michigan Motors all cited a shortage of IS staff as a barrier to ESS expansion. The operating sponsor at United Retailing, an executive assistant to the vice president of operations, described the problem this way:

> The VP was impressed with the system in January, particularly by how far it had progressed since being initiated in October, but not a lot has happened in the last two months. Nowadays the VP asks, "Can't we put the store reference file up on the system?" Or "Can't we get sales by . . . ?" He's always asking for access to new things, but there's no progress because of insufficient manpower.

As increasing user perceptions of what is possible and desirable catch up with the finite IS resources, developers often are forced to step back, plan, and make choices about resource allocations. Additional resources are often called for, and IS resource allocation can become an even more pressing problem as an ESS grows larger and more sub-projects are involved.

5. *Identifying Early Adopters*

Even with the support of an executive sponsor, it is difficult to *force* the spread of an ESS. For this reason, many developers follow the well-known but often ignored strategy of seeking out "early adopters"[2] likely to accept and experiment with the new technology. A degree of resistance is almost inevitable from many, sometimes most, potential users as ESS use spreads through an organization. But, in most segments of every organization, one can find people who visualize the positive implications of an innovation and are motivated to be the first to use it. Identifying these early adopters and working with them to demonstrate the value of ESS can be a key strategy in the effective spread of ESS.

CONCLUSION

Managing ESS evolution and spread is one of the most difficult aspects of implementation because it does not lend itself as nicely as one might like to rational planning, and there are few rules that can be applied. In each case, the interaction between the technology, its users, and the organization is unique. The vice president of IS for a large telecommunications company sums up the problems of managing ESS growth this way:

> There is a certain amount of patchiness in ESS development. Group A always seems to be ahead of Group B, or vice versa. We are always getting questions like: "How come our region hasn't gotten terminals yet?" We wait until the pressure on IS is almost unbearable. But giving in to these demands too soon is dangerous because they may get a system without the proper foundation. Managing ESS growth is a sweaty-palm exercise. It's a balance between reasonable knowledge of the technology, reasonable controls, and a "try-it-you'll-like-it" philosophy.

NOTES

1. Hans Paal Bunaes, "Anatomy of an EIS Development Tool." Master's thesis, Sloan School of Management, MIT, Cambridge, Mass., June 1987, p. 74.
2. Everett Rogers, *Diffusion of Innovation*, 3d edition (New York: Free Press, 1983), pp. 246–247.

CHAPTER 12

THE IMPACTS OF ESS

In Chapters 4 through 6 we noted that a number of executives are using computers, with some impact on their daily operating methods and the ways they carry out their many roles. But what is the impact of these systems on their organizations? The evidence is far from clear.

In fact, we are *quite* uncertain about either the short-range or ultimate impacts because the initiation of ESS in most of the sites we visited was only one of several significant changes taking place. In addition, most of the systems had been in place for such a short period of time that their impacts could not realistically be observed.

It was clear, however, that major changes were taking place in the organizations we saw. And, in many cases, executives with whom we spoke highlighted the role of the ESS in their progress toward managerial objectives of decreased staff levels, increased spans of control, role change, or organizational change.

The presence of one or more of these managerial objectives in each case is instructive. Although a few of the impacts described to us appear to have "just happened" as a result of the ESS, most of them are the result of conscious managerial efforts along several fronts. The ESS is merely a facilitator. As Robey notes, "information systems do not *cause* structural changes in organizations. Structural change may or may not accompany system implementation. When it does, the changes in structure appear as consistent companions to either rational management objectives, political strategies, or both."[1]

Decreased Staff Levels

There were two related managerial objectives that came up in company after company: reductions in staff and middle management, and increases in span of control. Both of these impacts ultimately point toward a flattening of the organizational pyramid.

In "Getting Control of Staff-Work," Drucker addresses the need to reduce staff:

> Since the 1950s at many major manufacturing companies, staff employment has grown five to ten times as fast as the number of "operating" people in production, engineering, accounting, research, sales, and customer service. The unchecked growth and excessive power of service staffs is considered by practically all our foreign critics to be a serious weakness of U.S. industry, and a major cause of its poor performance.[2]

In "Skimming Management's Midriff," Drucker highlights the equally excessive growth of middle management:

> Middle management has been exploding in the last few decades. In many companies the "middle" between the first-line supervisor and the corporate top has been growing three or four times faster than sales, even before adjustment for inflation.
>
> Middle managements today tend to be overstaffed to the point of obesity. . . . This slows the decision process to a crawl and makes the organization increasingly incapable of adapting to change.[3]

Several firms we studied implemented an ESS to help reduce staff, or at least anticipated this as an impact of the system. Xerox has 600 staff and management in its corporate headquarters in Stamford. President Paul Allaire says:

> The major objectives of our ESS were to make both top management and the staff organization more effective. Our business is becoming more complex and sophisticated, but we have said there will be no increase in staff expenses. We wanted to invest in technology rather than people and, as we took down the head count, we had to make them more effective. We're putting the tools in place to do the job we have to do without adding people. In the last three years, we've achieved a 5 percent reduction per year in total headquarters costs.

Gillette North America's controller Don Palmer anticipated a reduction in the number of "data acquirers," those in staff positions whose job is primarily to collect information. This function could now be done more efficiently by the ESS. A telecommunications company executive, however, focused on the information middlemen. "There are people in this organization whose only job is to answer questions about the budget. This technology squeezes them. Technology will have a big impact on these information providers."

On a similar note, one Boeing executive says:

> Changes in roles and hierarchies are coming in the long term. Empires will be affected. I see the elimination of some middle managers. They are not yet feeling the crunch, but it's coming. I'm willing to experiment with fewer levels of management and a greater span of control. I believe [the ESS] will eliminate managers and allow us to work with lower overhead.[4]

Other executives are not targeting staff reductions, but rather are looking to increase staff productivity and grow without adding more people. A vice president at Boeing supports this concept: "I don't think the system will reduce people, but it will give us higher capacity per person. We'll be more productive in our capacity to earn, i.e., we will generate more earnings per person."[5]

Some results are already apparent. They tend to be in organizations where ESS are tied into office automation, decision support systems, and other technology enhancements of staff as well as executives. At ICL, Mike Forrest, director of business operations, insists that the spread of information technology throughout his unit has resulted in a significant headcount reduction. He estimates that, in 1980, 20 people were doing work that is today handled by six people because of increased analytical capabilities, as well as word processing which allowed reductions in the secretarial staff from five to one.

Forrest sees benefits in these cutbacks. "Reducing head count doesn't just save you money. It makes it easier to find people with the skills you need because it's much easier to find the right skills in six people than in 20. It also reduces the people-management load and increases the amount of time I can spend on managing the issues."

While reducing staff and middle-management overhead is likely to remain an objective of many ESS projects, it takes competitive pressures or an executive with a "lean and mean" attitude toward the business to put these reductions in place. The ESS manager at the telephone company mentioned earlier found this out when he tried to eliminate a division manager's post, vacated by retirement. He felt the ESS had improved organizational performance enough to make the cutback feasible, but underestimated the interpersonal dynamics involved. He says:

> The whole situation—that is, reducing the headcount in administrative services—turned on something that had nothing to do with the system. I suggested that we eliminate the division manager's job but, because of a recent reorganization, we had a surplus division manager, and top management put him in there. Also, a district manager's job could have been split up and the responsibilities given to two other managers, but that job was also filled with a surplus district manager.

Span of Control Increased

The other organizational impact facilitated by ESS is an increased span of control for managers. Due mostly to the electronic communication capabilities of ESS, examples of increased span of control are easier to find than those of reductions in staff head count, and the effect on organizational structure is more immediate. Increasing span of control leads to fewer layers in the organizational hierarchy, something Drucker sees as essential:

> In the past thirty years levels have increased even faster than middle-management jobs. . . . Every additional level, however, increases rigidity. Each slows the decision-making process. And it is a law of information theory that every relay (that is, "level") halves the information transmitted and doubles the noise. Levels should increase much more slowly than numbers, if at all.
>
> With the age structure of the managerial population changing rapidly . . . the "ninety-day wonder" in management is about to be replaced by people with years of experience. . . . And the "span of control" can then be substantially widened as subor-

dinates will be expected to take responsibility for upward communications and for self-control. Then, as attrition creates a vacancy on one level, one abolishes the level.[6]

Drucker argues that in the last few decades an oversupply of young managers has led to an increased number of management layers which inhibits organizational effectiveness. Reducing these layers, which means increasing the span of control, is essential to increasing productivity and improving communications within the organization. Drucker, however, sees another force behind increasing spans of control. That is a move to the "information-based organization." He explains:

> The organization of the future is . . . a structure in which information serves as the axis and as the central structural support. A number of businesses . . . are busily reshaping their managerial structure around the flow of information. . . . The information-based structure is flat, with far fewer levels of management than conventional ones require. . . . But such levels of management . . . [that] remain in information-based organizations find themselves with far bigger, far more demanding, and far more responsible jobs.
>
> The information-based structure makes irrelevant the famous principle of the *span of control*, according to which the number of subordinates who can report to one superior is strictly limited, with five or six being the upper limit. Its place is being taken by a new principle—I call it *span of communications*: The number of people reporting to one boss is limited only by the subordinates' willingness to take responsibility for their own communications and relationships, upward, sideways and downward. "Control," it turns out, is the ability to obtain information. And an information system provides that in depth and with greater speed and accuracy than reporting to the boss can possibly do.[7]

CEO Ian Rolland at Lincoln National has 14 direct reports, and no executive assistant. He attributes his ability to maintain such a large span of control to the ESS, particularly its electronic mail capabilities, which allow him to keep in close touch with subordinates. Broad spans of control are the rule at Lincoln, where heavy terminal penetration makes it easier for managers to communicate. Senior Vice President David Allen says his direct reports have increased from two to seven because he can now monitor and delegate more effectively. Jim Tunis, who managed ESS implementation at Lincoln, sums up the impact of the company-wide system this way:

> The system appears to be flattening out the company's organizational structure. High-level management can assimilate more information from more subordinates electronically, so the span of control of these managers is increasing. However, first-level supervisors must have personal contact with their subordinates, so the system is not increasing their span of control.[8]

At Xerox, President Paul Allaire also sees ESS changing the organization: "In lots of companies, middle management acts as a filter for information and this causes delays. Our system allows executives to work directly with professionals and analysts without the filters, which are being eliminated. The ESS is flattening organizational structure and is increasing our span of control."

The chairman of a large manufacturing company who constantly uses his terminal says, "We have just gone through a major personnel adjustment, the object of which was to reduce layering and to correct the inevitable problem of one guy managing only two or three others. I think the availability of an ESS was an effective support for this. It makes it easier to get rid of layering, but it's not the cause."

Changing Staff Roles

A more definitive and consistent impact of ESS deals with the work responsibilities of staff analysts and executive secretaries. Not only will ESS tend to reduce, over time, the size of the staff supporting top management, but the nature of their work is already changing. In companies like Xerox and Diversified Electronics, ESS are driving the automation of performance-reporting systems, and speeding up the collection and processing of data. Diversified's controller explains the impact on his staff:

> One of the objectives of the system was to make sure our staff was doing more professional work, such as analysis, and less clerical consolidation. Under the old system, financial analysts spent about 80 percent of their time doing clerical work and 20

percent analysis. Today, those figures are about 40 percent clerical and 60 percent analysis, and by year-end it should be 20 percent clerical and 80 percent analysis. The key to this system is the time it frees up for executives and staff to do more substantive analysis of things such as potential acquisitions and operational problems.

Ken Soha at Xerox offers a related view:

In the future, the role of the staff will change from presenting information to adding value. Today, most of their time is spent packaging and presenting information to management. Tomorrow, more time will be spent analyzing and adding value to the numbers, and there will be fewer analysts doing it. Currently, at the management committee meeting, the staff provides information, but in the future executives will be getting this same information from the system before each meeting.

The role of staff analyst is changing in companies where executive support systems are taking over the tasks of consolidating and delivering information to senior management. Not only is staff productivity improving, but expectations about the added value these people provide is increasing. Analysts are doing more involved analysis in shorter times in response to more sophisticated executive requests.

Another role sometimes changed by ESS is that of the controller. Often central figures in ESS implementation because of their control over financial data bases, controllers' responsibilities are sometimes expanded significantly as is the case at Gillette North America. Controller Don Palmer explains the change:

Because of the ESS, the controller starts to get involved in the market size, market share, and productivity statistics—all sorts of things that have not been in his domain previously. You don't want to set up separate reporting arms, and the logical reporting focus is the group that's already doing reporting in the financial area. As a result, the controller becomes much more broadly involved in the business. He understands the interrelationships of different factors, and he really becomes the reporter, the measurer, the monitor of the business. With this much-improved information base, it's easy to become more actively involved with strategic planning issues. We see the same thing happening in each of the divisions. The controllers are becoming much more actively involved in strategic planning.

Changing Secretarial Roles

In several companies we studied, there was evidence that ESS had changed the roles of executive secretaries, turning them more into executive assistants. At one manufacturing company, the chairman's secretary is trained on Lotus 1-2-3 and Focus to retrieve data for her boss. One vice president at Lincoln National sees his secretary now as an administrative assistant, helping him more with budgets and maintaining data bases, and doing less traditional clerical work. This executive types most of his own memos, while electronic mail has eliminated much paperwork in the office.

Our findings are supported by previous research into the impact of information technology on secretarial work. One study by Bullen, Bennett, and Carlson reported:

> Secretaries stated that they have found the time to organize tasks and create procedures for smoothing work flow that they could not even think about before. This has been stimulated both by time saved through computer support and by access to the tools powerful enough to create these procedures. Some tasks in this category include automated distribution lists, reminder files triggered by a clock, and financial monitoring and analysis systems. Another stated advantage of the existing office automation tools is the ability of the secretaries to take on new tasks, many of which are self-initiated. Here it is not a case of doing more of the current tasks or of doing them faster, but rather of making use of entirely new functions.[9]

Organizational Change

There is an underlying sense among many executives who install ESS that these systems can be a powerful force for organizational change. The changes, however, have as yet been limited to two types:

1. A change in business focus, sometimes affecting the whole company.

2. Power shifts, altering the relative influence of functions, departments, or individuals, and often unforeseen and difficult to identify.

Let us look at examples of each. Company-wide or departmental changes in business or strategic focus are by far the most significant type of change created by ESS. They are uncommon, however, in part because such change requires an executive who envisions using this technology to create change.

When Mike Jensen became president of Banco Internacional, he found that a lot of lower-level managers worked with inadequate data. Account officers, for example, often did not know about an overdraft or major deposit, nor did they have timely knowledge of account status or profits.[10] In the highly volatile business of international banking, Jensen wanted to create a more marketing-oriented organization run by profit center managers and tightly controlled from the top. Through his ESS, the president encouraged his subordinates to become more attentive to business details. In assessing the impact of Jensen's ESS, Keen offers this perspective:

> What's interesting about this is that a CEO has been able to get a major organizational change by pushing down a business concept. This system is just a vehicle. Jensen is really implementing a marketing strategy. He's made his managers focus on information in a new way. . . . Everyone agrees that it's contributed to profits.[11]

Another example of business change created through an ESS occurred in a marketing-support unit at ICL. The group's director wanted to establish a quality improvement program in his organization. He recognized that mistakes in developing and introducing products that later needed changes to satisfy customers were expensive to the corporation. These problems ranged from major ones, such as a software error that prevented a system from running, to minor complaints from a customer who was unable to understand an entry in a manual.

The executive had his quality manager prepare a small data base that produced 50 graphic charts each month showing the different levels of incidents (from major to minor) by product line and the time it took to resolve each incident for the customer. The director says:

> I used this in reviewing my line managers each month. We would sit together and call up the charts relevant to his business and look at the progress month by month in improving our

response time and in reducing our backlog of incidents. This not only showed my managers that it was costing them money to carry out this level of maintenance, but they also saw the value of taking preventative steps to avoid these problems in the first place.

The director's quality-monitoring system had an almost immediate impact on the organization. In its first year, the average number of incidents reported by customers declined 25 percent. And, because problems were being fixed faster, the average backlog of incidents decreased by about 35 percent. The executive also recognized the impact on operating methods:

> At the same time, we saw a distinct shift in the culture. Development managers were now starting to carry out code inspections, defect analyses, and design audits much more regularly and with a greater sense of urgency than before. We were tracking their progress on these using graphic displays each month.
>
> In other words, the system was helping to build a culture of not only improving customer satisfaction after installation, but also of developers starting to take steps to improve products before they were even introduced. Over time, we gradually introduced more review processes to encourage people not only to look at things after the event, but also to look at how we were affecting our future product lines.

The reporting process used by this manager, and by others in this book, could have been developed without an ESS. However, in his view, it was a combination of the availability of the technology which focused his attention on its capabilities, and the relative ease of developing the quality monitoring system through the ESS that encouraged him to undertake this key project.

Power shifts among functional groups, departments, and individuals are another type of organizational change supported by ESS. These are difficult to assess because power, in the sense of relative influence, is so hard to measure. But in a number of cases, an ESS enhanced a department's or individual's influence so dramatically that there can be little question of the system's impact. One vice president of personnel contends his ESS strengthened the perceived importance of the personnel function in his company:

If you take a reasonably long time frame—say two and a half years, because technology doesn't change things instantly—the personnel function has become recognized as a function that actually does control, does know the underlying trends in, and does understand the manpower position in the organization. Three years ago that would have been regarded—wrongly—as the domain of the finance function. But now the personnel function has irrefutable data and trend analysis capability, and, therefore, is recognized as the authority on manpower issues in the organization. . . . No other department can take such an authoritative stance on the absolute manpower numbers and where we are going.

This personnel VP feels the detailed data provided by his system allowed his department to reclaim some functional responsibilities and respect from the finance department. The latter had gained authority in manpower decisions over the years because it had access to the most information about the organization.

In general, finance departments seem to be the biggest winners and losers in the poker game of power redistribution created by changing information flows. They either lose power, often subtly, as above, where another department gains independence through access to its own sources of functionally critical data; or the finance group gains strength by centralizing control over financial and performance information.

One of the best examples of a finance group gaining power through an ESS is at Diversified Electronics. There, the controller acknowledged that enhancing the reporting system created a data base that came to be regarded as the corporation's only source of performance data. The finance department's power was greatly increased vis-a-vis the divisions since it controlled access to this data base.

There is yet another kind of power shift created by ESS. This is the enhanced influence executives gain by monitoring individual and organizational performance through the computer. The controller at Diversified Electronics characterizes the phenomenon this way:

The system acts as sort of a "hidden hand" tightening up the control process by its very presence, even down into the organization where the system doesn't physically exist. The fact that we ask the divisions to explain variances through the ESS each month does more to control our business than anything, because that means they've got to ask the same questions of their people (e.g., "Why are margins lower? What happened to your costs this month?"). They know that the president, the CFO, or the controller is going to ask them these questions, so they'd better have the answers.

Executive support systems extend or leverage the authority and psychological presence of the senior manager using the system. Some use it to target areas on which they want subordinates to focus. Others create changes in behavior through improved access to performance data, and occasional demonstration of that knowledge.

For example, the director of ICL (U.K.) at one time accessed a data base of customer breakdowns to monitor the status of equipment reliability and customer attitudes. "The chief value I got was the organization knew I was doing it," he says. "If the people below know you are taking an interest, it affects their attitude."

An article describing the ESS developed by Alexander Giacco, former chairman and CEO of Hercules, a chemical manufacturer, concluded, "The personal computer in Giacco's office—and the information system it represents—sends a powerful message to senior managers throughout the organization. First, they'd better keep on their toes when it comes to their businesses, and second, let the boss know of any potential trouble before he discovers it himself. I'm sure there are managers who stay on top of things every day, just knowing Giacco has a computer in his office,' says one Hercules vice president."[12]

The CEO of a large food distributor says, "Just handing the numbers out [indirectly through an ESS] puts a lot of pressure on my executive group for performance in particular areas. That's why they don't want me to get access to so much detail."

A director of manufacturing concludes, "A screen on the senior guy's desk is a preemptive strike on middle management if they believe he can analyze their actions day-to-day. And because people down in the organization know I can see the information, they pay more attention to it."

One manager at Banco Internacional described how bank president Mike Jensen used his ESS: "In the beginning he was calling everyone: 'What happened with X?' We thought [expletive deleted] we had to be prepared at 8 o'clock every morning. But Mike doesn't call anymore so much because he knows we're prepared."[13]

The indirect evidence provides a strong case that an ESS can affect subordinates' behavior in a way that far transcends the system's actual capabilities. Noting this, one executive distinguishes between what the system *actually* does for him and "what I let others *believe* it does for me." Effects on perception alone, however, are probably ephemeral. In fact, a well designed ESS does provide increased information and insight into the organization. Since information is power, this leads to enhanced power. However, it is the way this power is used that most affects the organization. This varies hugely from executive to executive. Heineman at Northwest and Jensen of Banco Internacional used their systems aggressively to create changes in organizational behavior. On the other hand, Phillips at Gillette has consciously used his ESS in a way that does not threaten the autonomy of division management.

As we said at the outset, our understanding of the broader impacts of ESS on organizations is tentative. Nevertheless, there is significant evidence—much of it second-hand and inferential—that executive support systems are at least facilitating or enabling certain changes in the organization. Reduced numbers of staff and middle management, increased spans of control, changing staff roles, and the use of ESS to facilitate organizational change and enhance power are all recognizable impacts of senior management systems. They deserve further study.

NOTES

1. Daniel Robey, "Computer Information Systems and Organization Structure," *Communications of the ACM*, vol. 24, no. 10 (October 1981), p. 686.
2. From THE FRONTIERS OF MANAGEMENT: WHERE TOMORROW'S DECISIONS ARE BEING MADE TODAY by Peter F. Drucker. Copyright © 1986 by Peter F. Drucker, p. 194. Re-

printed by permission of the publisher, E.P. Dutton, a division of NAL Penguin, Inc.

3. From THE FRONTIERS OF MANAGEMENT: WHERE TO-MORROW'S DECISIONS ARE BEING MADE TODAY by Peter F. Drucker. Copyright © 1986 by Peter F. Drucker, p. 200. Reprinted by permission of the publisher, E.P. Dutton, a division of NAL Penguin, Inc.

4. Jeffrey L. Turner, "Executive Support Systems: A Comparative Study." Master's thesis, Sloan School of Management, MIT, Cambridge, Mass., May 1985, pp. 29–30.

5. Ibid., p. 40.

6. From THE FRONTIERS OF MANAGEMENT: WHERE TO-MORROW'S DECISIONS ARE BEING MADE TODAY by Peter F. Drucker. Copyright © 1986 by Peter F. Drucker, p. 201. Reprinted by permission of the publisher, E.P. Dutton, a division of NAL Penguin, Inc.

7. Ibid., p. 204

8. Ralph H. Sprague and Barbara C. McNurlin, eds. *Information Systems Management in Practice* (Englewood Cliffs, N.J.: Canning Publications, 1986), p. 415.

9. C. V. Bullen, J. L. Bennett, and E. D. Carlson, "A Case Study of Office Workstation Use," *IBM Systems Journal*, vol. 21, no. 3 (1982), p. 368.

10. Peter G.W. Keen, *"The On-Line CEO: How One Executive Uses MIS."* Unpublished working paper, Micro Mainframe, Inc., 1983, p. 9.

11. Ibid.

12. David Roman, "A Top-Down MIS Mandate," *Computer Decisons*, November 18, 1986, p. 30.

13. Keen, *"The On-Line CEO . . . ,"* p. 10.

CHAPTER 13

SOME FINAL THOUGHTS

It is difficult to end a book like this without making predictions about the future. The experience of the last few years suggests that caution is called for; the field of executive support systems is evolving so quickly that making predictions is difficult at best, and perhaps even foolish. Yet one cannot study an area in-depth without having several strong impressions. Most of these have been aired in one way or another in the preceding chapters. In this final chapter, however, we will concentrate on six impressions which should be highlighted.

First, it is evident that ESS is just emerging from the pioneering stage and must be treated in this context. ESS are where transaction processing systems were in the early 1950s, or where decision support systems were situated in the early 1970s. In both cases, the applications were still relatively new. There were no proven paths to successful implementation. Each system was a seat-of-the-pants installation. A body of knowledge had begun to evolve, yet each case seemed to break some new ground.

Given this level of uncertainty, it still takes real *faith* in the potential of ESS for an executive to lead his or her management team into this difficult applications area. The technology remains far from perfectly adapted to executive use, although it is improving rapidly. The organizational implications of ESS are not well understood. The systems are disliked, if not feared, by many subordinates and staff personnel. The most urgently needed data is most often unavailable, poorly structured, or both. And the cost/benefit of these systems is anything but clear.

When we dig beneath the surface of even the most successful systems, tales of frustrations and difficulties that had to be overcome are plentiful. At the same time, there is also a clear recognition of the benefits, however intangible, and a strong sense of the "rightness" of the systems. Derwyn Phillips of Gillette, one of the first executives to sponsor an ESS, sums up most of this by saying:

> We are clearly in the early stages in the application of information technology to the senior management role. My own efforts in this area have been made because I see the inevitability of information technology for the successful senior manager. For this reason, as well as the many tangible benefits we see in working with the system, I have been willing to go through the pain of being on the leading edge.

William Smithburg, chairman and CEO of The Quaker Oats Company, has found the development of his ESS time consuming and expensive but, in the end, a worthwhile process. He explains:

> My goal for the ESS was to create the most useful corporate data base possible for the top 30 executives in the company. It probably took us three years before what I would consider a meaningful data base existed. This clearly is a long term process, and it was a lot more expensive than I had anticipated. But now every senior executive has a PC in his office, and the system has snowballed in a very positive sense. It provides me more information than I ever had before, and I get it fast. As a result, I feel better about the decisions I have to make. I can't conceive of living without it. Once you get used to a system like this, it's just essential.

Our second strong impression of ESS is that it is just one tool in the armament of senior managers. Many executives believe it is a very significant tool, and one which is changing the way they and their organizations perform their jobs. Yet executive support systems must not be blown out of proportion. Much of the work done by senior managers will receive no— or at best, marginal—support from an ESS. Determining the character and potential of a subordinate, performing ceremonial functions, and a large number of other tasks require other approaches and tools. ESS, we suspect, will grow and be useful on a much broader scale than is seen today. But these systems are only managerial tools. As such, their effectiveness depends heavily on their users, and how they are used.

Third, executive support systems are not for everyone in the next few years. Many executives have a well-honed set of alternative tools to accomplish the same ends. For a number of reasons cited earlier in this book, some top managers are extremely reluctant to get directly involved with computers. And there is little hard evidence with which to insist that they should.

Today, each executive has a different viewpoint on the usefulness of information technology. Some who have become accustomed to the capability of an ESS find it almost unbelievable that other key executives cannot grasp its significance. Speaking about the chief financial officer of his *Fortune* 100 company, the executive sponsor of a divisional ESS system laments:

> The CFO of our corporation is a very smart man who came up through our treasury department. He had a computer workstation put on his desk last year. But after a few months he had it taken off. I asked, "Why'd you have it taken away?" He said, "Hell, I didn't need that damn computer." I asked, "Why not?" "What the hell could I get out of that thing?" he replied. Billions of dollars flow through his organization every few weeks—billions, not millions. Yet he wasn't interested in the hedge rates. He's got that delegated away. You see, it's a difference in management style.

It *is* primarily a difference in managerial style. But it is also a matter of perception of the technology, the tasks which are most important to the executive, and the degree to which the organization's culture encourages executive computer use, as well as a host of other factors. For whatever reason, there is little doubt that for the next several years many executives will not use these systems.

Fourth, office support, especially electronic mail, and planning and control systems, will continue to be the prime uses of ESS, since the ability to communicate and to exert effective control at senior levels are ongoing managerial "musts." The use of these systems, however, will vary and will depend heavily on the way each executive approaches his or her role. Some will design their ESS to support a decentralized management philosophy, while others will use theirs to make possible their involvement in operational situations. Phillips of Gillette clearly represents a relatively "hands-off" approach:

> My position in this company puts me in a facilitator role. I avoid directly interfering in my subordinates' businesses. That's very important in a decentralized company. I don't want to bother them with a lot of queries. A reporting system like ours allows one to answer many questions about performance through the system. The ESS gives me the capacity to be somewhat more sensitive more quickly to what is going on in each of our businesses. It enables me, without bothering subordinates, to see where the soft spots are with both customers and products. You do not have to inquire directly. One can manage more loosely, at arm's length, and still be relatively confident of what is going on.

Wallace of Phillips Petroleum, however, sees ESS as a way for him to become more involved in the management of the business. In this vein, he says:

> If, in the pricing area, I see things happening early in the morning, I may call the vice president of marketing and tell him that I am looking at a particular screen. In five or ten seconds, he can be up on the same screen and we can talk from that screen. We may flip through three or four charts, talk about the things that we see happening, share our thoughts, and think about the actions we should take. When I hang up we've conducted, in a few minutes, a discussion that in the past might have required a 15–20-minute get-together late in the afternoon, looking at hard copy. The probability is that we wouldn't have picked up the issue for three or four days, maybe a week. For an executive, timely data is necessary. If it is not timely, the value is no longer the same, and often it is useless.

Our fifth and perhaps strongest impression of ESS is that, while the immediate benefits are seen in office and planning and control systems, the ultimate payoff (and the real benefit for planning and control) is the enhanced understanding of the business environment these systems can provide for senior executives. In fact, it is the development of richer, more up-to-date, and more sharply defined "mental models" of their business environments that is the real—but usually unspoken—driving force behind the development of many of these systems. A clearer, sharper understanding of the business environment is the major payoff of the most successful systems we saw. It is in this area that we believe ESS ultimately will have its greatest impact. Let us again turn to Derwyn Phillips of Gillette:

> Because of the graphic approach we have taken, I now see the business differently and better. Not only can I see it in a longer time frame, but it is also possible to recognize and focus on trends, which historical, numerical data does not allow. Readily available graphics provide a different perspective. I am able to see those areas where I should be involved and, more important, those that I can leave alone.

Robert Wallace of Phillips Petroleum relates his increased understanding to action:

> With our system, I have a much more complete understanding of important parts of our business environment. Let me give you an example. We made $50 million last year on crude oil trading. We made that driving things very much from the executive level. We had managers and traders and all of the other backroom people, but the real dollars were made because senior management was staying on top of all the events we could perceive on a daily basis that were moving us towards some opportunities. And we were able, through our increased understanding, to quickly make a decision to act. The alternative is to sit in an ivory tower waiting for the guy down below to work up enough courage, and perhaps insight, to start pushing his notion of a business opportunity up the system. In that case, by the time the idea gets to the top the chance may be gone. Some of these opportunities, like last year in crude oil, were opportunities that existed in a day, or a two-day timeframe, maximum. To take advantage of these, an executive must have a very clear perception of the state of the business in key areas.

Last, but not least, it is clear to us that the spread of ESS is inevitable. Technology does change the way people work. It is a rare company of any size today that does not have all of its transaction processing systems on the computer. Increasingly, staff departments are relying on computer-based DSS, or other computer access. Thus it is logical that we should find clear advantages for senior executives in the use of workstations customized for their particular needs. Wide-spread ESS use will not happen overnight. But it is inevitable.

BIBLIOGRAPHY

Agor, Weston H. "The Logic of Intuition: How Top Executives Make Important Decisions." *Organizational Dynamics*, vol. 14, no. 3, Winter 1986, pp. 5–18.

Allison, Graham T. *Essence of Decision*. Boston, Mass.: Little Brown and Company, 1971.

Alter, Steven L. *Decision Support Systems*. Reading, Mass.: Addison-Wesley, 1980.

Anthony, Robert N. *Planning and Control Systems: A Framework for Analysis*. Boston, Mass.: Division of Research, Graduate School of Business Administration, Harvard University, 1965.

Applegate, Lynda M. "Lockheed–Georgia Company: Executive Information Systems." Case study No. 9-187-135. Boston, Mass.: Publishing Division, Harvard Business School, 1987.

Argyris, Chris. "Management Information Systems: The Challenge to Rationality and Emotionality." *Management Science*, Vol. 17, No. 6, February 1971, pp. B275–B292.

Bariff, Martin L., and Jay R. Galbraith. "Intraorganization Power Considerations for Designing Information Systems." *Accounting, Organizations and Society*, vol. 3, no. 1, 1978, pp. 15–27.

Barnard, C.I. *The Functions of the Executive*. Boston, Mass.: Harvard University Press, 1938.

Beer, Stafford. *Cybernetics and Management*. New York: John Wiley & Sons, 1959.

Bennett, John L. *Building Decision Support Systems*. Reading, Mass.: Addison-Wesley, 1983.

Bernstein, Stanley, and R.V. Ferrara. "The Patriot Electronic Information System." *Program Manager*, September-October 1983, pp. 35–38.

Bikson, Tora K.; Barbara A. Gutek; and Don A. Monkin. *Implementation of Information Technology in Office Settings: Review of Relevant Literature.* Santa Monica, Calif.: Rand Corporation, 1981.

"The Boardroom Visionary." *Business Computing & Communications.* June 1986, pp. 22–27.

Borbely, Jack. "Executive Decision Support (EDS)." *ONLINE*, July 1985, pp. 70–72.

Bowen, William. "The Puny Payoff from Office Computers." *Fortune*, vol. 113, no. 11, May 26, 1986, pp. 20–24.

Boynton, Andrew C.; Michael E. Shank; and Robert W. Zmud. "Critical Success Factor Analysis as a Methodology for MIS Planning." *MIS Quarterly*, June 1985.

Bralove, Mary. "Some Chief Executives Bypass, and Irk, Staffs in Getting Information." *The Wall Street Journal*, January 12, 1983, pp. 1, 22.

Brief, Arthur P., and H. Kirk Downey. "Cognitive and Organizational Structures: A Conceptual Analysis of Implicit Organizing Theories." *Human Relations*, vol. 36, no. 12, 1983, pp. 1065–1090.

Brookes, C.H.P. "A Framework for DSS Development." *DSS-85 Proceedings.* San Francisco, Calif., pp. 80–97.

Bullen, C.V.; J.L. Bennett; and E.D. Carlson. "A Case Study of Office Workstation Use." *IBM Systems Journal*, vol. 21, no. 3, 1982, pp. 351–369.

Bullen, Christine V., and John F. Rockart. "A Primer On Critical Success Factors." *Working Paper No. 69*, Center for Information Systems Research, Sloan School of Management, MIT, Cambridge, Mass., June 1981.

Bunaes, Hans P. "The Anatomy of an Executive Information System Development Tool." Master's thesis, Sloan School of Management, MIT, Cambridge, Mass., June 1987.

Burkan, Wayne. *Decision Support Systems in the End-User Environment.* Text of presentation at POSPP General Meeting, New Orleans, January 1986.

Carlisle, James H. "What Every CEO Should Know about Office Automation." *Chief Executive*, Winter 1982/1983, pp. 26–29, 32, 34.

Carlson, Sune. *Executive Behavior: A Study of the Work Load and the Working Methods of Managing Directors.* Stockholm: Strombergs, 1951.

Carroll, John M. "Satisfaction Conditions for Mental Models." *Contemporary Psychology*, vol. 30, no. 9, 1985, pp. 693–695.

Crawford, A.B., Jr. "Corporate Electronic Mail—A Communication-Intensive Application of Information Technology." *MIS Quarterly*, September 1982, pp. 1–13.

Crescenzi, Adam D., and J.F. Rockart. "Engaging Top Management in Information Technology." In *The Rise of Managerial Computing*, eds. John F. Rockart and Christine V. Bullen. Homewood, Ill.: Dow Jones-Irwin, 1986.

Crowston, Kevin, and Michael E. Treacy. "Assessing the Impact of Information Technology on Enterprise Level Performance." *Working Paper No. 143*, Center For Information Systems Research, Sloan School of Management, MIT, Cambridge, Mass., October 1986.

Cyert, Richard M., and James G. March. *A Behavioral Theory of the Firm*. Englewood Cliffs, N.J.: Prentice-Hall, 1963.

Daft, Richard L., and Robert H. Lengel. "Information Richness: A New Approach to Manager Information Processing and Organization Design." In *Research in Organization Behavior*, eds. B. Straw and L.L. Cummings. Greenwich, Conn.: JAI Press, 1984.

Daft, Richard L., and Robert H. Lengel. "Organizational Information Requirements, Media Richness and Structural Design." *Management Science*, vol. 32, no. 5, May 1986, pp. 554–571.

Daft, R.L., and K.E. Weick. "Toward a Model of Organizations as Interpretation Systems." *Academy of Management Review*, vol. 9 no. 2, 1984, pp. 284–295.

Davis, David. "Computers And Top Management." *Sloan Management Review*, Spring 1984, pp. 63–67.

Davis, G.B., and M. H. Olsen. *Management Information Systems: Conceptual Foundations, Structure and Development*. New York: McGraw Hill, 1985.

Davis, Leila. "Learning to Walk with a New Computer System." *International Management*, July 1983, pp. 47–50.

Dearden, John. "SMR Forum: Will the Computer Change the Job of Top Management?" *Sloan Management Review*, vol. 25, no. 1, Fall 1983, pp. 57–60.

De Long, David W., and John F. Rockart. "A Survey of Current Trends in the Use of Executive Support Systems." *Working Paper No.*

121, Center for Information Systems Research, Sloan School of Management, MIT, Cambridge, Mass., November 1984.

De Long, David W., and John F. Rockart. "Identifying the Attributes of Successful Executive Support Systems Implementation." *Working Paper No. 132*, Center for Information Systems Research, Sloan School of Management, MIT, Cambridge, Mass., January 1986.

Dick, John R. " 'Automating' Your Chairman." *The Magazine of Bank Administration*, July 1986, p. 36–38.

Dickerman, Margaret. "The Evolution and Diffusion of an Executive Support System: A Case Study." Master's thesis, Sloan School of Management, MIT, Cambridge, Mass., June 1985.

Dock, V. Thomas. "Executive Computer Use is Doomed without Five Key Properties." *Data Management*, December 1985, pp. 27–30.

Donaldson, Gordon, and Jay W. Lorsch. *Decision Making at the Top.* New York: Basic Books, 1983.

Drucker, Peter F. *The Effective Executive.* New York: E.P. Dutton, 1967.

Drucker, Peter F. "Playing in the Information-Based 'Orchestra'." *The Wall Street Journal*, June 4, 1985.

Drucker, Peter F. *The Frontiers of Management.* New York: E.P. Dutton, 1986.

Elmer-DeWitt, Philip. "The Granite State of the Art: A Computer Buff is Transforming New Hampshire." *Time*, January 27, 1986, p. 70.

El Sawy, Omar E. "Personal Information Systems for Strategic Scanning in Turbulent Environments: Can the CEO Go On-Line?" *MIS Quarterly*, March 1985, pp. 53–60.

"ESS in the Real World: A Roundtable Discussion." *Insights*, Issue 15. New York: Booz•Allen & Hamilton, 1986, pp. 9–10.

Falvey, Jack. "Real Managers Don't Use Computer Terminals." *The Wall Street Journal*, February 7, 1983, p. 22.

Fayol, H. *Administration Industrielle et Generale.* Paris: Dunod, 1950. First published in 1916.

Fersko-Weiss, Henry. "Personal Computing at the Top." *Personal Computing*, March 1985, pp. 68–79.

Fiderio, Janet. "EIS Evolution: Polaroid System Poised to Enter the CEO's Office." *Computerworld*, vol. 20, no. 43, October 27, 1986, p. 45, 51.

Friend, David. "Distilling Executive Information." *Information Center*, vol. 1 no. 8, August 1985, pp. 36–40.

Friend, David. "Executive Information Systems: Successes, Failures, Insights and Misconceptions." *DSS-86 Transactions*. Providence, R.I.: The Insitute of Management Science, 1986.

Friend, David. "100 EISs Later ... Action Items and Key Points." Unpublished paper, Pilot Executive Software, Boston, Mass. 1986.

Glavin, William F. Speech to the Society for Information Management, Miami, Fla. March 27, 1987.

Goodhue, Dale; Judith A. Quillard; and John F. Rockart. "The Management of Data: Preliminary Research Results." *Working Paper No. 140*, Center for Information Systems Research, Sloan School of Management, MIT, Cambridge, Mass., 1986.

Gottschalk, Earl C., Jr. "Executive Computing." *The Wall Street Journal*, September 16, 1985, pp. 23c, 37c.

Greiff, Barrie S., and Preston K. Munter. *Tradeoffs*. New York: Mentor, 1981.

Gunner, Holly. "Executive Information Systems: The Real Payoff Is in Improving the Link between Information and Management Processes." *DSS-86 Transactions. Providence, R.I.: The Institute of Management Sciences, 1986.*

Hardwick, James. "Information Support for Senior Executives." *DSS-86 Transactions*, Providence, R.I.: The Institute of Management Sciences, 1986.

Henderson, Bruce D. *Henderson on Corporate Strategy*. New York: Mentor, 1982.

Henderson, John C.; John F. Rockart; and John G. Sifonis. "A Planning Methodology for Integrating Management Support Systems." *Working Paper No. 116*, Center for Information Systems Research, Sloan School of Management, MIT, Cambridge, Mass., September 1984.

Hollis, Robert. "Real Executives Don't Use Computers." *Business Computer Systems*, vol. 3, no. 7, July 1984, pp. 41–42.

Horton, Thomas R. *What Works for Me*. New York: Random House, 1986.

Houdeshel, George, and Hugh J. Watson. "The Management Information and Decision Support (MIDS) System at Lockheed–Georgia." *MIS Quarterly*, vol. 10, no. 5, March 1987.

Huber, George P. "The Nature and Design of Post-Industrial Organizations." *Management Science.* vol. 30, no. 8, August 1984, pp. 928–951.

"Interview with Donald Palmer, Controller, Gillette, N.A." Boston, Mass.: Pilot Executive Software, 1986.

Isenberg, Daniel J. "How Senior Managers Think." *Harvard Business Review,* November-December, 1984, pp. 81–90.

Isenberg, Daniel J. *Managerial Thinking: An Inquiry into How Senior Managers Think.* Forthcoming book.

Jacobson, Gary, and John Hillkirk. *Xerox: American Samurai.* New York: Macmillan Publishing Co., 1986.

Jaques, Elliott. *A General Theory of Bureaucracy.* Hampshire, England: Gower Publishing Co., 1976.

Jenkins, Avery. "The (PC) Wit and Wisdom of GP's Grady Baker." *PC Week,* May 27, 1986, p. 46.

Johnson-Laird, P.N. *Mental Models.* Cambridge, Mass.: Harvard University Press, 1983.

Jones, Jack William, and Raymond McLeod, Jr. "The Structure of Executive Information Systems: An Exploratory Analysis." *Decision Sciences,* vol. 17 no. 2, Spring 1986, pp. 220–249.

Kanter, Rosabeth Moss. *Men and Women of the Corporation.* New York: Basic Books, 1977.

Katz, Michael S. "Executive Support Systems: The Unfinished Job." *Insights,* Issue 15, pp. 3–6. New York: Booz•Allen & Hamilton, 1986.

Keen, Peter G.W. " 'Interactive' Computer Systems for Managers: A Modest Proposal." *Sloan Management Review,* Fall 1976, pp. 1–17.

Keen, Peter G.W., and Michael S. Scott Morton, *Decision Support Systems: An Organizational Perspective.* Reading Mass.: Addison-Wesley, 1978.

Keen, Peter G. W., and Richard D. Hackathorn. "Decision Support Systems and Personal Computing." *Working Paper No. 47,* Center for Information Systems Research, Sloan School of Management, MIT, Cambridge, Mass., October 1979.

Keen, Peter G. W. "Decision Support Systems: A Research Perspective." *Working Paper No. 54,* Center for Information Systems Research, Sloan School of Management, MIT, Cambridge, Mass., March 1980.

Keen, Peter G. W. "Information Systems and Organizational Change." *Communications of the ACM*, vol. 24 no. 1, January 1981, pp. 24–33.

Keen, Peter G.W. "Value Analysis: Justifying Decision Support Systems." *MIS Quarterly*, vol. 5 no. 1, 1981.

Keen, Peter G. W. "The On-Line CEO: How One Executive Uses MIS." Unpublished working paper, Micro Mainframe, Inc., 1983.

Kiechel, Walter, III. "Why Executives Don't Compute." *Fortune*, November 14, 1983, pp. 241–246.

King, William R. "Editor's Comment." *MIS Quarterly*, October 1985, pp. xi–xii.

Kogan, John. "Information for Motivation: A Key to Executive Information Systems That Translate Strategy into Results for Management." *DSS-86 Transactions*, Providence, R.I.: The Institute of Management Sciences, 1986.

Kotter, John P. *The General Managers*. New York: Free Press, 1982.

Kotter, John P. "What Effective General Managers Really Do." *Harvard Business Review*, vol. 60, no. 6, November-December 1982, pp. 156–167.

Kull, David. "Matching Workstations to Executive Styles." *Computer Decisions*, October 1984, pp. 212–225.

Lecht, Charles. "Managers Won't Need Micros. . . ."*Business Computer Systems*, vol. 3, no. 9, September 1984, pp. 31–34.

Levinson, Eliot. "The Implementation of Executive Support Systems." *Working Paper No. 119*, Center for Information Systems Research, Sloan School of Management, MIT, Cambridge, Mass., October 1984.

Macbeth, Mike. "Terminal Anxiety. (What really happens when computer terminals invade the head office?)." *Canadian Business*, vol. 56 no. 5, May 1983, pp. 103–107.

March, James G. "Bounded Rationality, Ambiguity, and the Engineering of Choice." *Bell Journal of Economics*, vol. 9, Autumn 1978, pp. 587–608.

Markus, M. Lynne. "Power, Politics and MIS Implementation." *Working Paper No. 59*, Center for Information Systems Research, Sloan School of Management, MIT, Cambridge, Mass., October 1980.

Markus, M. Lynne. "Inplementation Politics: Top Management Support and User Involvement." *Working Paper No. 75*, Center for

Information Systems Research, Sloan School of Management, MIT, Cambridge, Mass., September 1981.

Markus, M. Lynne. *Systems in Organizations*. Boston: Pitman, 1984.

Mason, Richard O., and Ian F. Mitroff. *Challenging Strategic Planning Assumptions: Theory, Cases and Techniques*. New York: Wiley, 1981.

McCaskey, Michael B. *The Executive Challenge: Managing Change and Ambiguity*. Cambridge, Mass.: Ballinger Publishing Co., 1982.

McIntosh, Henry E. "The Executive Information System: A New Dimension in Effective Decision Making." *Public Utilities Fortnightly*, February 4, 1982, pp. 63–67.

McKenney, James L. "The Influence of Computer-Communications on Organizational Information Processing." Unpublished working paper, Boston, Mass., Harvard Business School, 1985.

"MDs Attack Growing Data Bombardment." *Chief Executive*, February 1984, pp. 6–9.

Merchant, Kenneth A. *Control in Business Organizations*. Marshfield, Mass.: Pitman, 1985.

Meyer, N. Dean, and Mary E. Boone. *The Information Edge*. Agincourt, Ontario: Gage Educational Publishing, 1987. Published in the U.S. and internationally (except Canada) by McGraw-Hill Book Company, New York, NY.

Mintzberg, Henry. "The Myths of MIS." *California Management Review*, vol. 15, no. 1, Fall 1972, pp. 92–97.

Mintzberg, Henry. *The Nature of Managerial Work*. New York: Harper & Row, 1973.

Mintzberg, Henry. "Manager's Job: Folklore and Fact." *Harvard Business Review*, July-August, 1975, pp. 49–61.

Mintzberg, Henry. "An Emerging Strategy of Direct Research." *Administrative Science Quarterly*, December 1979, pp. 582–589.

Mittman, Brian S., and Jeffrey H. Moore. "Senior Management Computer Use: Implications for DSS Designs and Goals." *Proceedings of DSS-84 Conference*, Institute for Decision Support Systems, April 1984, pp. 42–49.

Moore, Jeffrey H. "Senior Executive Computer Use." Unpublished working paper, Stanford Graduate School of Business, Palo Alto, Calif., 1986.

Murphy, C.J. "The Global Factory: Managing the 'New Realities' In Worldwide Manufacturing." Speech to the Society For Information Management, March 6, 1986, Scottsdale, Arizona.

Naylor, Thomas H. "Decision Support Systems or Whatever Happened to M.I.S.?" *Interfaces,* vol. 12, no. 4, August 1982, pp. 92–94.

Nulty, Peter. "How Personal Computers Change Manager's Lives." *Fortune,* September 3, 1983, pp. 38–48.

Nyce, Edward, and Richard E. Groppa. "Electronic Mail at MHT." *Management Technology,* vol. 1, no. 1, May 1983, pp. 65–72.

"Office Automation Restructures Business." *Business Week,* October 8, 1984, pp. 118–142.

Ouchi, William. "A Conceptual Framework for the Design of Organizational Control Mechanisms." *Management Science,* vol. 25, September 1979, pp. 833–848.

Perham, John. "The Computer and the Top Honcho," *Dun's Business Month,* vol. 121, no. 5, May 1983, pp. 72–73.

Phillips, Lawrence D. "Decision Support for Managers." In *The Managerial Challenge of New Office Technology,* edited by Harry J. Otway and Malcolm Peltu. London: Butterworths, 1984, pp. 80–98.

Pounds, William F. "The Process of Problem Finding." *Sloan Management Review,* Fall 1969, pp. 1–19.

Rinaldi, Damian, and Ted Jastrzembski. "Executive Information Systems: Put Strategic Data at Your CEO's Fingertips." *Computerworld,* October 27, 1987, pp. 37–50.

Rinehart, Gary D. "EIS in a Public Utility." *DSS-86 Transactions,* Providence, R.I.: The Institute of Management Science, 1986.

Robey, Daniel. "Computer Information Systems and Organization Structure." *Communications of the ACM,* vol. 24, no. 10, October 1981, pp. 679–687.

Rockart, John F. "Chief Executives Define Their Own Data Needs." *Harvard Business Review,* March-April 1979, pp. 81–93.

Rockart, John F., and Christine V. Bullen. *The Rise of Managerial Computing.* Homewood, Ill.: Dow Jones-Irwin, 1986.

Rockart, John F., and Michael E. Treacy. "Executive Information Support Systems." *Working Paper No. 65,* Center for Information Systems Research, Sloan School of Management, MIT, Cambridge, Mass., November 1980.

Rockart, John F., and Michael E. Treacy. "The CEO Goes On-Line." *Working Paper No. 67*, Center for Information Systems Research, Sloan School of Management, MIT, Cambridge, Mass., April 1981.

Rockart, John F., and Michael E. Treacy. "The CEO Goes On-Line." *Harvard Business Review*, January-February, 1982.

Roman, David. "Executives Who Love Their Personal Computers," *Computer Decisions*, January 1983, pp. 142–158, 177–178.

Roman, David. "A Top-Down MIS Mandate." *Computer Decisions*, November 18, 1986, pp. 30–32.

Salerno, Lynn M. "What Happened to the Computer Revolution?" *Harvard Business Review*, vol. 63, no. 6, November-December 1985, pp. 129–138.

Schwartz, R. Malcolm. "Executive Support Systems: Closing a Loop." *Insights*, Issue 15, pp. 1–3. New York: Booz•Allen & Hamilton, 1986.

Scott Morton, Michael S. "The State of the Art of Research in Management Support Systems." Reprinted in *The Rise of Managerial Computing*, John F. Rockart and Christine V. Bullen, eds. Homewood, Ill.: Dow Jones-Irwin, 1986, p. 325–353.

Shoor, Rita. "Executive Computing: Still a Long Way to Go." *Infosystems*, December 1985, pp. 51–52.

Simon, Herbert A. *Administrative Behavior.* New York: Macmillan Company, 1957.

Sprague, Ralph H., and Eric D. Carlson. *Building Effective Decision Support Systems.* Englewood Cliffs, N.J.: Prentice Hall, Inc., 1982.

Sprague, Ralph H., and Barbara C. McNurlin, eds. *Information Systems Management in Practice.* Englewood Cliffs, N.J.: Prentice-Hall, Inc., 1986.

Sproull, Lee, and Sara Kiesler. "Reducing Social Context Cues: Electronic Mail in Organizational Communication." *Management Science*, vol. 32, no. 11, November 1986, pp. 1492–1512.

Stanat, Ruth. "Building a Document-Dased Competitive Intelligence System." *DSS-86 Transactions*, Providence, R.I.: The Institute of Management Sciences, 1986.

Sullivan-Trainor, Michael. "Gillette Buys Its EIS, Firestone Builds." *Computerworld,* October 27, 1986, pp. 38, 42.

Sundue, Donald G. "Genrad's On-Line Executives." *DSS-86 Transactions,* Providence, R.I.: The Institute for Management Sciences, 1986.

Thompson, J.D. *Organizations in Action.* New York: McGraw-Hill, 1967.

Treacy, Michael E. "Supporting Senior Executives' Models for Planning and Control." In *The Rise of Managerial Computing,* edited by John F. Rockart and Christine V. Bullen. Homewood, Ill.: Dow Jones-Irwin, 1986, pp. 172–189.

Treacy, Michael E., and David W. De Long. "Executive Support Systems Technology and Design." Unpublished paper, October 1985.

Turban, Efraim, and Donna M. Schaeffer. "A Comparative Study of Executive Information Systems." *DSS-87 Transactions,* Providence, R.I.: The Institute of Management Sciences, 1987.

Turner, Jeffrey L. "Executive Support Systems: A Comparative Study." Master's thesis, Sloan School of Management, MIT, Cambridge, Mass., May 1985.

Viste, Gerald. "Executive Use of Interactive MIS." Speech to American Assembly of Collegiate Schools of Business, May 3, 1984, Phoenix, Ariz.

Wagner, G.R. "DSS: Dealing with Executive Assumptions in the Office of the Future." *Managerial Planning,* March-April, 1982, vol. 30, no. 5, pp. 4–10.

Weick, Karl E. *The Social Psychology of Organizing.* Reading, Mass.: Addison-Wesley, 1979.

Weick, Karl E. "Theoretical Assumptions and Research Methodology Selection." In *The Information Systems Research Challenge,* edited by F. Warren McFarlan. Boston, Mass.: Harvard Business School Press, 1984.

Weiner, Norbert. *Cybernetics: or Control and Communication in the Animal and the Machine.* Cambridge, Mass.: MIT Press, 1948.

Whiteside, David. "Computers Invade the Executive Suite." *International Management,* August 1983, vol. 38, no. 8, pp. 12–18.

Widener, W. Robert. "Computer Graphics in the Boardroom." *Management Technology,* June 1983, pp. 43–46.

Williamson, Oliver E. *Markets and Hierarchies.* New York: Free Press, 1975.

Wilson, Diane. "CEO Assumptions Concerning Information Technology." Speech to Center for Information Systems Research Summer Session, June 15, 1987, Cambridge, Mass.

Wrapp, Edward H. "Good Managers Don't Make Policy Decisions." *Harvard Business Review,* September-October 1967, pp. 91–99.

Zmud, Robert W. "Supporting Senior Executives Through Decision Support Technologies: A Review and Directions for Future Research." In *Decision Support Systems: A Decade in Perspective,* edited by E.R. McLean and H.G. Sol. Amsterdam: Elsevier Science Publishers B.V. (North-Holland), 1986, pp. 87–101.

INDEX